90p 18/-

D0540919

S

THE LONSDALE LIBRARY

Editors: THE EARL OF LONSDALE, K.G., G.C.V.O., D.L., & Mr. ERIC PARKER

*" The Lonsdale Library will do for our youngsters what
the Badminton did for us."—The Spectator.*

VOLUME VII

FOX-HUNTING. Edited by SIR CHARLES FREDERICK, BT., M.F.H.
With contributions by Cecil Aldin, M.F.H., Major M. E. Barclay, M.F.H., Earl Bathurst, M.F.H., Isaac Bell, M.F.H., Colonel M. Borwick, M.F.H., Captain Bowden Smith, Lt.-Col. Geoffry Brooke, Major Burnaby, M.F.H., Captain L. C. R. Cameron, Richard Clapham, Captain J. D. D. Evans, M.F.H., Charles McNeill, M.F.H., Major G. R. Mott, Major Guy Paget, Otho Paget, M.F.H., Eric Parker, A. P. Pollok, M.F.H., Lord George Scott, Col. A. G. Todd, C.B.E., D.S.O., Captain E. Venn, & Major V. D. S. Williams, M.F.H.
*With 4 colour plates, 18 reproductions of hunting pictures & 45 illustrations.
Edition de Luxe, limited to 360 copies signed by the author, signed frontispiece by
Lionel Edwards. Full Leather, £5 5s. n. Qr. Leather, 36s. n. Full Buckram, 25s. n.*

VOLUME VIII

WINTER SPORTS. Edited by the HON. NEVILLE LYTTON
With contributions by Captain Duff-Taylor, Lord Knebworth, Alexander Lorimer, Miss Madden, Hubert Martineau & Colonel Moore-Brabazon.
Voluminously illustrated. Qr. Leather, 25s. n. Full Buckram, 15s. n.

EARLIER VOLUMES

VOLUME I
THE WAY OF A MAN WITH A HORSE. Lt.-Col. GEOFFRY BROOKE. Edition de Luxe, 360 signed copies, signed frontispiece by Lionel Edwards. Full Leather, £5 5s. n. Qr. Leather, 31s. 6d. n. Full Buckram, 21s n.

" The whole volume teems with sound & practical advice on every branch of horsemanship."—*The Field.*

VOLUME II
TROUT FISHING FROM ALL ANGLES. ERIC TAVERNER. Edition de Luxe, 360 signed copies, with a collection of exquisitely tied flies. Full Leather, £5 5s. n. Qr. Leather, 31s. 6d n. Full Buckram, 21s. n.

" The best all-round book on brown trout fishing that has appeared in this generation." *Times Literary Supplement.*

VOLUME III
SHOOTING BY MOOR, FIELD & SHORE. ERIC PARKER & other authorities. Edition de Luxe, 360 signed copies by Eric Parker & signed etching by Winifred Austen. Full Leather, £5 5s. n. Qr. Leather, 31s. 6d. n. Full Buckram, 21s.n.

" Within its covers is the wisdom of the shooting world of to-day."—*Shooting Times.*

VOLUME IV
FINE ANGLING FOR COARSE FISH. ERIC PARKER & other authorities. With 148 illustrations. Qr. Leather, 25s. n. Full Buckram, 12s. 6d. n.

" The most complete manual on the art of coarse fishing that has ever been issued." *Doncaster Chronicle.*

VOLUME V
LAWN TENNIS. WALLIS MYERS. With 65 illustrations. Qr. Leather, 25s. n. Full Buckram, 12s. 6d. n.

" It is excellent. I only regret it was not available five years ago when I was reading all lawn tennis books to learn all I could about the game."—RENE LACOSTE.

VOLUME VI
CRICKET. A. P. F. CHAPMAN, P. G. H. FENDER, D. R. JARDINE & other authorities. With 55 illustrations. Qr. Leather, 25s. n. Full Buckram, 15s. n.

" In every case the writer is an expert in the department he is dealing with & to say that the volume must remain the standard work on cricket for years to come is to give a very faint idea of its value & its merits." *The Field.*

SEELEY, SERVICE & CO. LIMITED

THE LONSDALE LIBRARY
of Sports, Games & Pastimes

Editors

The Right Hon. The Earl of Lonsdale, K.G., G.C.V.O., D.L.

&

Mr. Eric Parker
Editor-in-chief of the " Field "

Plate 1

" THE OPEN CHRISTIANIA, FINISH OF THE TURN "

NOTE THE WEIGHT ON THE RIGHT FOOT, THE RIGHT SKI EDGED AND LEADING, THE LEFT FOLLOWING ROUND.

THE LONSDALE LIBRARY
VOLUME VIII

WINTER SPORTS

By Viscount Knebworth, Captain S. Duff-Taylor,
Lt.-Col. J. T. C. Moore-Brabazon, Hubert Martineau,
Alexander Lorimer, M. S. Madden. Edited by the
Hon. Neville Lytton   ᴖ   ᴖ   ᴖ   ᴖ   ᴖ

With sixty-seven
ILLUSTRATIONS

LONDON
Seeley, Service & Co. Ltd.
196 Shaftesbury Avenue
1930

BROMLEY
PUBLIC
LIBRARIES

AL.
C

CLASS

R 796.9

AC.
BN 524369

Printed in Great Britain

THE
LONSDALE LIBRARY

DEDICATION TO
HIS ROYAL HIGHNESS THE PRINCE OF WALES
&
EDITORS' INTRODUCTION
BY
The Rt. Hon. The Earl of Lonsdale, k.g., g.c.v.o., d.l.

IT is with a deep sense of the honour conferred on the Lonsdale Library of Sports, Games and Pastimes that the Editors have received permission to dedicate its volumes to His Royal Highness the Prince of Wales. Their first wish is to express their gratitude for being allowed to associate with the Library the name of an acknowledged leader of British Sport in the highest and best meaning of the word.

It is now a long time since a Library of volumes on Sport and Games was first put before the public. During these many years great changes have taken place, in men and in methods; how numerous and how great those changes have been, it needs no more than a glance at the text and illustrations of the older existing volumes to discover. The traditions, the customs, the guiding principles of the great sports and games doubtless remain; but as the years go on new discoveries are made, new developments follow, new methods are found to be successful. In the process of time, these demand notice and explanation.

It would not be difficult to give examples of many such changes. A few may suffice. To take the sport of shooting first, even twenty years ago almost nothing was known of the nature and causes of what was vaguely called " disease " in grouse. The knowledge which research and examination have given us of these to-day has profoundly affected methods of moor management. Again, in regard to fishing, it is only of recent years that we have been able to piece together the life history of the salmon by means of the reading of scales ; we have learned much of the powers of vision of fish ; and there have been many improvements in the manufacture of rods and tackle. To come to games. In cricket there have been alterations in the rules, fields are placed differently, modes of batting and of bowling are not what they used to be ; in golf, changes in the standards of clubs and of the ball have in turn altered standards of play ; and the lawn-tennis of modern Wimbledon is a different game from that of a past generation.

It is believed, therefore, that the Lonsdale Library should fill a gap. Its aim is to help and to instruct. It is intended in the first place for the beginner who wishes to learn all that the written word can teach him of his chosen subject, and to obtain authoritative advice on gear and in practice. But it is also hoped that the more experienced sportsman may find matter of interest in the pages of the Library, either in the bringing together of newly discovered facts or new suggestions for study, or in the comparison of other sportsmen's or players' opinions with his own. No pains have been spared to make the text and the illustrations as full and representative as possible, and if the various volumes succeed in their double appeal to the tyro and to the expert, the Library will have fulfilled the purpose of its Editors, which is, to make it complete.

Lonsdale

FOREWORD

THE great popularity of winter sports dates from the Grindelwald Conference. This was organized by Sir Henry Lunn in 1892 ; its object was to unite all the Christian churches ; as Lord Lytton once said in a witty speech : " Sir Henry Lunn is a courageous man—once he set out to convert the Pope of Rome to Protestantism." Naturally the Conference failed, but *à quelque chose malheur est bon*—Sir Henry noticed that mid-winter in the high Alps is an earthly paradise—the gloom and fog and damp are left in the valley below, while up in the eternal snows the sun is often too hot to bear and the sparkling atmosphere is more of a tonic than the finest champagne. He soon turned his organizing ability to propagating this important discovery. His remarkable son Arnold Lunn and Vivian Caulfeild became experts on the technique of ski-ing and soon surrounded themselves with a host of promising pupils. Largely owing to their efforts, English ski-runners of to-day can compete on equal terms with the continental champions.

In England, our summers are generally cold and our winters often warm and muggy—hence there is a tendency to go and sun-bathe on the shores of the Mediterranean during the summer holidays and to fly to Switzerland to find a real winter at Christmas time.

Surely it is a wonderful thing, for a moderate sum of money, to be able to indulge in a sport which exercises every muscle in the body, which requires balance and self-control and which enables you without harm to your neighbour to satisfy your love of speed and contempt of danger amid surroundings of unsurpassable loveliness.

NEVILLE LYTTON.

CONTENTS

LIST OF PLATES

B

LIST OF TEXT ILLUSTRATIONS

SKI-ING
BY VISCOUNT KNEBWORTH

CHAPTER I

THE HISTORY OF SKI-ING

SKI-ING is an International sport and its history largely the history of European countries other than England. The author of these few chapters on ski-ing would like to make it clear from the first that he is writing principally for English readers and that he intends to deal with that aspect of ski-ing which is most interesting to Englishmen. He regrets that he cannot read German or Norwegian or Swedish. For the facts contained in this chapter he is indebted to Mr. Arnold Lunn's comprehensive and admirable *History of Ski-ing*. Mr. Lunn is the only Englishman who has attained a position of International importance in the ski-ing world. His book *Alpine Ski-ing* has been translated into French and Japanese, and is, in the opinion of Marcel Kurz, the best existing work on the subject. Mr. Lunn's *History of Ski-ing* is the only book in the English language which deals with the historical as distinct from the purely technical side of ski-ing, and for taking it as the basis of this chapter I make no apology. Mr. Lunn must be content with the knowledge that if he writes the best work of its kind in the English language he must expect to be plagiarized.

Though to all intents and purposes ski-ing history begins in the latter part of the nineteenth century, the actual use of ski is of great antiquity.

Procopius, writing between A.D. 526 and 559, speaks of a race of Skrid finnars or "gliding Finns," presumably as distinct from some other Finns who did not glide. In 1574 a Zurich Professor Simler wrote a book called *De Alpibus Commentarius*, in which the following passage occurs :

"Moreover, those who wish to cross deep snow in places where there is no path make use of the following device to prevent their being swallowed up. Small and slender planks are taken, or circles of wood similar to those which are employed to construct casks. The feet are securely attached by ropes to these discs. By this means one's tracks are enlarged, one is not swallowed up and scarcely sinks into the snow. We read in Xenophon something similar. The Greeks, in fact, whilst traversing the mountains of Armenia by a snowy route, instructed by the natives, enveloped in small bags the feet of their horses, who would otherwise, treading on their unprotected hoofs, have sunk in the snow up to their bellies."

In 1689 an Austrian writer, Valvasor, published a book called *Die Ehre des Herzogtumes Krain*, which tells of the habits of the peasants in Carniola, an Austrian province. These peasants were apparently excellent ski-runners. They used short ski—about 5 feet long—and were extremely efficient both at turning in and out of the trees on a steep wooded slope and at running straight in the open, which manœuvre they performed by leaning back stiffly on their sticks. Valvasor, though he was aware that the Lapps used ski, had seen ski-ing in no other district besides Krain.

Many references to ski-ing are found in the old Scandinavian sagas, and Earl Rognvald of the Orkneys ranks it among one of his nine accomplishments. In Scandinavian mythology the goddess of ski-ing was called Ondurris.

The use of some kind of snow-shoe must obviously be of extremely ancient origin in countries which have regularly to compete with snow conditions in the winter. Mr. Crichton Somerville believes that from some primitive form of snowshoe ski, as they are known to-day, must have been evolved. Dr. Fowler, however, challenges this idea. He writes : " It is a fair canon of criticism in the evolution of primitive tools that the simplest is generally the oldest ; and nothing can be much simpler than a split lath of wood. That the ski was evolved by taking a wooden patten, covering it with hide, lengthening it and then taking away the hide, is, to put it mildly, improbable."

There is, however, all the difference in the world between attaching a split lath of wood to your feet, to prevent yourself sinking too deeply into the snow, and using that same lath of wood for the purpose of ski-ing down a mountain.

Mr. Marshall, from a study of the early Finno-Ugrian languages, suggests that ski, as distinct from snow shoes or pattens, were known to the inhabitants of Northern Asia some thousands of years before Christianity.

In Sweden ski have been used from a very early date for purposes of war. In 1200 King Serre sent out a Captain

and company of ski-runners to reconnoitre.   Gustavus Vasa
and Gustavus Adolphus both used troops on ski in winter
and early spring campaigns.

The early uses of ski were all utilitarian, and it is interesting that ski were known in Cumberland many years before
ski-ing as a sport was popularized in Scandinavia and Central
Europe.   Dr. Savage, first Vice-President of the Alpine Ski
Club, said at the first Annual Dinner of that Club :

" Some forty years ago, I began the active exercise of my profession
by being a Medical Officer to Cumberland mines, and there I had a wide
moorland district. The winters were long and there was an abundance
of snow, when I heard the old inhabitants talk of what they called ' shees,'
and I got one made. The small children soon caught the infection, and
out of the staves of sugar casks they manufactured quite handy ski."

But all these early uses of ski are veiled in mystery.   Throughout history there are occasional and scanty glimpses of an Army
reconnaissance patrol here, of an ancient peasant custom
there, of grim Earls from a saga, of North Country English
miners, employing, with what ease and familiarity we can
only guess, snow-shoes in the form of ski.   And yet ski-ing,
known probably in Northern Asia two thousand years before
the birth of Christ, only developed into a scientific sport
within the memory of living man.   Ski-ing was practised for
other than utilitarian purposes only at the end of the nineteenth century, and was not moulded, in Central Europe at
any rate, into a scientific recreation until the first decade of
the twentieth.

The pioneers were naturally the descendants of those Scandinavian Vikings who had numbered ski-ing amongst the prime
accomplishments of man.   In 1870 the Telemark peasants
paid a visit to Christiania and gave an exhibition of ski-ing.
In 1877 the Christiania Ski Club was founded, and in 1879
the first real jumping competition was held on the Huseby
Hill.   Of this memorable occasion Mr. Crichton Somerville
has given the following account :

" The Huseby slope was one which, only a few years previously, had
been described as highly dangerous and impossible to descend when snow
was fast and in good condition. The leaping competition proved most
highly interesting, though in some respects quite comical. Every man,
except the Telemarkings, carried a long, stout staff, and on that, so
they thought, their lives depended. Starting from the summit, riding

their poles, as in former times, like witches on broomsticks, checking the speed with frantic efforts, they slipped downwards to the dreaded platform or ' hop,' from which they were supposed to leap, but over which they but trickled, as it were, and landing softly beneath, finally reached the bottom somehow, thankful for their safe escape from the dreaded slide. But then came the Telemark boys, erect at starting, pliant, confident, without anything but a fir branch in their hands, swooping downwards with ever-increasing impetus, until, with a bound, they were in the air, and 76 feet of space was cleared ere, with a resounding smack, their ski touched the slippery slope beneath and they shot onwards to the plain, where suddenly they turned, stopped in a smother of snow-dust and faced the hill they had just descended ! That was a sight worth seeing, and one never to be forgotten, even if in after years such performances have been, in a way, totally eclipsed."

In the same year, 1879, the first recorded open ski race was held in Sweden. Racing on ski in Sweden was first introduced by a schoolmaster, who arranged a competition for his pupils. The race was downhill and ended on the ice of a lake. Whichever child reached a furthest point on the ice, punting with the sticks being forbidden once the lake was reached, was declared the winner. The Lapps were the supreme exponents of long-distance racing, as they had for many years used ski as a means of getting about in winter on hunting and other excursions.

In 1879 also, M. Duhamel, having seen Swedish ski at the Paris Exhibition of the previous year, began to ski at Grenoble. In 1883 W. Paulcke started to ski as a schoolboy at Davos, and in the Hartz Mountains D. Ulrichs, the chief Forest keeper, was already vaguely familiar with the art of ski-ing and was also the proud possessor of a pair of ski. In 1884 the Brocken was ascended on ski by, first of all, two Norwegians, then two Germans, and finally two Englishmen whose names are not remembered. In 1888 Colonel Napier began to ski at Davos, and in the following year a Norwegian, O. Kjelsberg, intro-duced ski-ing at Winterthur and Dr. Pilet began to ski at Colmar. Zdarsky went to Lilienfeld. In 1890 Captain Vor-weg, who had learnt in Norway, started to ski in Germany and Iselin began his adventurous career at Glarus. Mr. Knoker, an Englishman, introduced ski to Meiringen. In 1891 the Ski Club at Munich was founded, and Dr. Thoms experimented unsuccessfully in the Black Forest. Gerald Fox introduced ski-ing to Grindelwald, and a lady pupil, clinging desperately to him, said in a beseeching wail : " Put me above my feet. Put me above my feet."

In 1892 the Feldberg in the Black Forest was successfully and simultaneously ascended by two different ski parties, and the Ski Club, Todnau, founded. This Club in 1893 became the Ski Club Schwarzwald and remained for many years the spiritual home of those skiers who opposed Zdarsky and the Lilienfeld system. In the same year, 1893, Egger and Staubli began to ski at Arosa, the Ski Club Glarus was founded, the first races to be held in Central Europe took place at Muzzuschlag, the capital of the Austrian ski-ing world, and one winter's morning some more leisured Parisians gathered, a little surprised, round a ski-ing expedition in the Bois de Boulogne ! In 1893 also Iselin and his friends crossed the Pragel Pass (1,554 m.), from Glarus to the Muotatal, on ski. Dr. Naef, one of the party, had armed himself not with ski, but with snow rackets, with a view to testing the rival merits of these two means of Alpine locomotion. On the ascent Dr. Naef kept pace and no more with the ski-ers, but on the descent he was left hopelessly behind, eventually reaching the Muotatal an hour after Iselin and the others.

In 1894 Sir Arthur Conan Doyle, accompanied by the Branger Brothers, crossed the Mayenfelder Furka from Davos to Arosa, and described the experience of ski-ing as follows :

" You come to a hard ice slope at an angle of 75 degrees, and you zig-zag up it, digging the side of your ski into it and feeling that if a mosquito settles upon you, you are gone."

In 1896, under the auspices of the Ski Club Schwarzwald, W. Paulcke published a pamphlet on ski-ing which had a wide circulation, and in the same year Zdarsky's book *Lilienfelder Ski-lauf Technik* gave the fruits of his eight years' work to the world. Chamonix was first " opened " as a winter sports centre in 1898, and Arnold Lunn there put on his first pair of ski in that year. By the end of the nineteenth century, ski-ing as a sport was definitely established in Central Europe. The controversies of the twentieth century were not as to the possibility of ski-ing in Alpine country, but between the different schools of thought as to the best technique to adopt for this purpose.

In 1900, the year that the Ski Club Bern was founded, the

first German long-distance race for the championship was held,
and in the following year the first jumping competition. The
Richardson Brothers founded the Davos English Ski Club, a
competition was held between Italian soldiers, the first Swiss
race took place at Glarus and the Grindelwald Ski Club saw
the light of day. In 1903 Rickmers started to teach ski-ing
at Adleboden and Caulfeild was introduced to ski by G. Dobbs
at Château d'Oex. In 1905 the first Swiss championship,
awarded on the combined result of a long-distance race and
jump, was won, as it should have been, by Iselin, and in 1910,
an important year in the history of British ski-ing, Caulfeild
published his book *How to Ski*.

Ski-ing in Central Europe is perhaps of great antiquity,
and Valvasor's comments on the technique of the Krain
peasants certainly does not suggest that they were conscious
of any Scandinavian influence. But the art was lost or forgotten, and when ski-ing reappeared in the nineteenth century,
it appeared as a new and entirely experimental sport. It is
to Norway that ski-ing in Europe owed both its origin and, at
first, its technique. The Norwegians were in almost every case
the pioneers, and when the Norwegians did not actually come
themselves, ski were introduced by men who had learnt their
use in Scandinavian snowfields. The influence of Dr. Nansen's
description of his ski traverse of Greenland was considerable,
and Nansen himself was given a place in the ski-ing Olympus,
to which he was not really entitled.

It so happens that Norwegian ski and Norwegian technique
are not really suited to Alpine country, and in consequence
of this the difficulties with which the early pioneers in Europe
had to contend were enormous. Norwegian ski-ing developed
along purely utilitarian lines, and for covering considerable
distances of comparatively flat country on hard snow the
Norwegians used long thin ski with insecure bindings, which
are totally unmanageable in Alpine country. The bindings
used by early ski-ers in Europe were made of cane. The ski
had no toe irons, and while straight running was just possible,
any attempt at turning inevitably resulted in the foot coming
off the ski. Norwegian ski and methods, however, continued
for many years to be the criterion, and the difficulties of adopt-
ing these to European conditions may be understood by the
description which the early writers and pioneers gave of the

art of ski-ing. The first German paper devoted to ski-ing contained the following passage :

" The runners let the ski carry them where it will until the air acts as a natural break and brings them to rest."

The following passage, even more ingenuous, was quoted by Zdarsky from the *Wiener Fremdenblatt* :

" On the descent, the ski runner leans back upon his stick and shuts his eyes. Then he darts downwards straight as an arrow, and continues until he can no longer breathe. He then throws himself sideways on the snow, and waits until he regains his breath, and then once again hurls himself downwards till once more he loses his breath, and throws himself on the snow ; and so forth, till he reaches the valley."

It is to Zdarsky's credit, however, that he refused to accept unchallenged the Norwegian criterion and retired to Lilienfeld, where, with elaborate experiment and great determination, he eventually evolved a technique of his own. Rickmers, one of his most enthusiastic pupils, said that Zdarsky was a fascinating man of inventive genius, who had never allowed anyone to serve him either for love or for money. He built and ran the house in which he lived at Lilienfeld himself, and there, in an isolated seclusion, he matured and taught the Lilienfeld ski-ing technique.

The principal feature of the Lilienfeld school was the use of a long and strong single pole. The ground around Lilienfeld is steep and wooded, and Zdarsky set himself to its conquest on ski. He first of all invented a binding of the kind known later as a spring binding, which consisted of an iron sole hinging on to the ski at the toe. He concentrated on the stemming turn, and with the aid of the pole, could turn with perfect control on any slope. The ski which he used were broader and shorter than Norwegian ski, and for that reason more handy among the trees and more buoyant on soft snow. The single pole, the short ski, and the stemming turn, were the hall-marks of the Lilienfeld technique, and its great asset was that it was easily and quickly learnt by the novice. Zdarsky gave free instruction and gathered round him a great band of followers, whom he drilled like a Prussian colour-sergeant. He waged a bitter and perpetual warfare both with the Black Forest and Norwegian exponents of ski-ing. He even challenged the Norwegians to a competition on his own ground

and on his own terms, which challenge was refused. Herr
Horn, however, visited Lilienfeld on behalf of the Norwegian
Ski Association, and the following is an extract from his
description of his run with Zdarsky and his followers :

> " I had now seen enough, and ran down in the same fashion. My ski
> were more slippery, I moved faster than I really wanted to and in a very
> short time I found myself beside Zdarsky. When the rest of the party
> rejoined us, the descent through the wood was resumed. Here I felt myself
> at home. I do not know how the others came through. I suddenly found
> myself leading and saw nothing more of my companions until the evening,
> when we met again at the Schwarzen Adler."

Meanwhile, in the Black Forest, the ski-ing pioneers were
studiously adhering to what they believed to be the Norwegian
technique. Ski-ing in Norway developed principally around
Holmenkollen, and demanded of the runner not so much
downhill turns at high speed as jumping and straight running
in or out of tracks. Not to be able to turn when going at
speed over steep, difficult slopes would be a hopeless handicap
in Alpine country. But at the same time, to sit on a long pole,
or indeed to use a single pole at all for jumping or for long-
distance ski-ing would be absurd. The Norwegians, in consequence, never ski-ed with a single stick as Zdarsky did, though
sitting on the sticks has never been regarded with such scorn
in Norway as it later became in Central Europe. The Black
Forest school of ski-runners insisted that the use of the single
pole was incorrect, as the single pole was not used in Norway.
But they further developed a series of stickless downhill turns
(other than the stemming turn) which they believed to be in
the best Norwegian tradition, and which were, in point of fact,
practically unknown in Norway. At the first Olympic Games,
which included ski-ing, held at Chamonix in 1924, an American
who had ski-ed in Switzerland, asked one of the Norwegian
runners what the difference between a " telemark " and
" christiania " was. He was told that a telemark was a stop
turn made to the left and a christiania to the right !
Paulcke in Germany and Vivian Caulfeild in Switzerland,
pursuing what they believed to be the Norwegian ideal,
succeeded in evolving a technique which dispensed with the
long pole of Zdarsky and was much more suitable to Alpine
country than anything ever known in Norway.
Since that time many and various ski turns have been

invented, experimented with and discussed. There are those who advocate the christiania turn, those who worship at the shrine of the stem, and those who still reverence the comely telemark. But telemark, christiania or stem, the existence and work of Zdarsky has been justified, and a form of ski-ing suitable to steep Alpine country has been evolved, even if it is not the same form that he himself once taught.

There is still a school of ski-runners in Austria which adheres to the tenets of Zdarsky. But for the most part his faith in the use of a single pole has been discarded. The stem turn which he taught is, however, regarded in Austria as a funda-mental principle of ski-ing, and in the Arlberg there has grown up, under the presiding genius of Hannes Schneider, a school of absolutely first-class ski-runners. Schneider teaches the stem turn and the stem turn alone, which his pupils have shown to be practicable in all forms of snow and under all conditions. The Austrians adopt a low, crouching position, and some of the best Alpine runners have gone out into the world from the nurseries of St. Anton.

In Switzerland, the Swiss and the English have learnt side by side, though it was not until some years after the War that the best English runners approached even the general standard of Swiss ski-ing. In Caulfeild's book, published in 1910, he explains that " to ski like an Englishman " was a deprecatory expression used widely among the Swiss. But the reason for this is fairly obvious. The Swiss have long displayed an intelligent prejudice for living in Switzerland. The English have tended to visit that country only for a few holiday months in each year. Constant practice, therefore, enabled the Swiss to become highly proficient at a sport which, until quite recently, the English regarded as a mere holiday amusement.

It would be impossible to conclude this chapter on ski-ing history without saying some word about the tremendous strides which England has made in the past few years. England is not a country regularly accustomed to long months of snow in the winter, and, for the most part, only those who are rich enough to enjoy a holiday in a Swiss hotel have been able to try their hand at ski-ing. These were content for many years to put on ski, roll about in the snow, laugh, and return sunburnt to their office work. But the English are a competitive people, and when a new generation began to grow up, accustomed

from childhood to the use of ski, the standard of performance
was appreciably raised. In early days it was to the credit of
Englishmen that they refused to accept unchallenged either
the Norwegian or the Lilienfeld technique, but, in a long
struggle, succeeded in adapting a combination of both to
Alpine requirements. Subsequently it was the English who
first began to race downhill on ski and incidentally raised the
standard of British ski-ing thereby to an unpremeditated
height.

In 1908 a ski meet, held under the auspices of the Ski Club
of Great Britain, took place at Kitzbuhel. There was included
in the meet a " combined curving and speed race (Downhill)."
The significance of this meeting is that it was the first time
any race had been run not according to the accepted Scandinavian standard of racing—partly uphill, partly downhill and
partly along the level. The race was a purely downhill race
and as such a departure, and the first departure, from all
previously accepted ideas of competitive ski-ing.

In 1921 the first British Championship, recognized both by
the Ski Club of Great Britain and the British Ski Association,
was awarded to Leonard Dobbs on the result of a downhill
and a style competition.

In 1924, a cup presented by the British Ski Association was
raced for by Swiss and English runners. The cup was won
by a Swiss, A. Gertsch of Wengen, but an Englishman,
C. E. W. Mackintosh, was second. In the autumn of the same
year the Schweizerische Akademischer Ski Club was founded
with the object of encouraging downhill racing in the Swiss
Universities. This club was the first on the Continent to follow
the British example and award a championship on the result
of a downhill race. In January 1925, a team representing
Great Britain raced against this club and was defeated. In
December of the same year the British Universities Ski Club
was founded and, in 1926, raced against and defeated the
Schweizerische Akademischer Ski Club. It may be said that
this victory marks the first time in its history that British ski-ing
had reached a standard of international excellence.

In the above races since 1921 a slalom race was part of the
competition. A slalom race is a timed descent of about 600
to 800 feet between flags, and is designed to test a ski-runner's
ability to place turns accurately and at high speed.

Plate 2

"THE ARLBERG KANDAHAR"

TAKING A STEEP SLOPE IN A STRAIGHT RACE.

In 1929, the first international ski meet which included, as an experiment, a downhill race took place at Zakopane in Poland. The race was Hindmarsh started (see chapter on Competitive Ski-ing, Downhill). Fifty-nine competitors entered, of which the British sent a team of eight—two of whom were ladies. With two or three exceptions, the team was a representative one. An Englishman, W. Bracken, finished second and the sixth, eighth, tenth and twelfth places were also filled by British competitors. The two ladies, Miss Elliot and Miss Sale-Barker, finished thirteenth and fourteenth respectively.

In 1928, 1929 and 1930 the Arlberg Kandahar race was held at St. Anton as an open downhill competition for runners of all nations, professionals as well as amateurs. In 1928, W. Bracken was fourth in the final result, in 1929, out of 83 starters, twenty-fifth and in 1930, out of some hundred competitors, seventh. In 1928, an Englishwoman, Miss Elliot, was second in the ladies' race, in 1929, Miss Sale-Barker was first and in 1930 another Englishwoman, Miss Carroll, was second. The standard of downhill ski-ing in the Arlberg Kandahar is probably the highest anywhere in the world. All the finest downhill runners in Central Europe, the home of downhill running, compete, and the difference between victory and defeat is a question not of seconds but of fractions of seconds. In the downhill race in 1930 the first forty-seven competitors were within a minute of each other.

The Schweizerische Akademischer Ski Club, largely on the initiative of Dr. Walter Amstutz, has been a keen advocate of downhill racing and has organized a series of International University Ski meetings, in which, owing to academical studies, the English have not been able to play a very active part. In the winter of 1930, however, the second Students' Olympic Games were held at Davos in January. Great Britain entered a team and, in the combined result, was fourth. The first Englishman home in the downhill race was thirteenth, in the long-distance race twenty-fifth, in the slalom sixth and in the jumping fourth.

The above details have been included in this chapter because they are a necessary part of ski-ing history. It is in the field of competitive downhill ski-ing that the British have in recent years taken the lead. The ready response which has greeted this movement is proof that it is but the inevitable and logical

c

result of adapting the use of ski to Alpine conditions. While
the perfect master of ski technique should, perhaps, be as
proficient at ski-ing or racing over one kind of country, and
with one kind of technique, as over and with another, yet there
is room in the ski-ing, as in all other sporting worlds, for
specialists. The British need not be ashamed to take credit
for the fact that they have evolved a particular kind of ski
racing of their own, and that this innovation on previously
accepted standards has been received in International circles,
if not without disapproval, at least with " resolute resignation."
In *Der Schnee-Hase,* the official organ of the Schweizerische
Akademischer Ski Club, the following tribute appeared in 1928
from Count Hamilton, the Hon. Secretary of the International
Ski Federation :

" I have had every opportunity for watching Lapps ski-ing, both among
the mountains and in the woods. I have been filled with admiration for
their skill, but I must admit that I admired even more the skill of Dr.
Amstutz (Switzerland) and Bracken (British ski champion, 1929) whom I
saw ski-ing at Murren. I must, however, make the reservation that the
Lapps, of course, with their loose ski and primitive equipment, reach the
limit of what is possible much sooner than those who are provided with
the best possible material. . . .

" The incredible skill which I admired at Murren awakened a great
interest in downhill racing. Certainly we could do worse than introduce
these races into Sweden without, of course, altering or superseding our own
types of racing. Mid-Europe originally took its ski-ing from the North.
It has made the best possible use of the gift. It has developed ski-ing and
has added something more, characteristics which we in turn must take over.
This exchange of experience between North and South is one of the pleasant-
est of the developments of International ski-ing.

" Downhill races and slalom races, once they assume a definite form,
will undoubtedly prove of the greatest possible importance in the develop-
ment of our sport."

At the International Congress held at Oslo in 1930 downhill and slalom racing were officially accorded international
recognition.

Amongst the ski-ing fraternity the world over there must
inevitably be controversies of a kind. There are those who
enjoy and put their whole faith in the delights of touring,
whether it be over the high ground or the low. There are also
those who prefer the more competitive delights of racing,
whether it be long-distance racing or downhill racing. Finally,
there are the jumpers. All these variations of the same sport

require a different technique and a different standard of proficiency, for which reason controversy of a kind is the inevitable and perhaps delightful companion of the ski-ing world. But the whole art and conception of ski-ing is still in its infancy. Scientists declare that in the life of the world (taken as seventy-five years) the whole history of man on earth represents only a period of three days. But in those three terrific days of man's existence there is much food for thought. If the infant hours of ski-ing are so small as to be scarcely calculable, yet they have already given much pleasurable enjoyment to one generation and may still be the delight of generations to come.

CHAPTER II

HOW TO SKI

THE essence of good ski-ing is abandon. This is true of ski-ing simply *qua* ski-ing. The man who uses ski in the High Alps, or who finds himself benighted on some unfrequented Pass, would, of course, be a fool if he concentrated on acquiring an atmosphere of abandon. But in such circumstances a man would not be thinking primarily of how to be a first-class ski-er. He would be thinking of his own personal safety and not of ski technique. But he who has time to practise the pure art of ski-ing should concentrate from the beginning on abandon. Spring, lightness, careless self-confidence, an easy, comfortable rhythmical movement—these things are fundamental in ski-ing. I cannot do better than quote at the very beginning of this chapter from Mr. d'Egville's book *Modern Ski-ing* :

" Refuse to believe that your skis are permanently and irretrievably glued to the snow. Assure yourself that you can lift one or other of them when you want to. Try it. Do it. Bend down. Stand up. Keep loose, free and easy. Whistle."

That is the essence of ski-ing. For the rest, the glory of the sport is that it is an individual one, which each can adapt to his own methods and liking.

The Englishman who visits the Alps, or indeed any part of the world, blessed in winter with a consistency and texture of snow almost unknown in the British Isles, can get a great deal of fun out of ski-ing in less than a week. On the other hand, he may ski for years and never acquire sufficient knowledge or efficiency to call himself a master of the art. In this respect, and in this respect only, ski-ing is like golf. Golf, which to my mind is a game only to be played by those who can no longer play anything else, presents an infinity of possibilities. The scratch player who plays faultless round after faultless round, finds that every stroke he plays is a new one and that his game is never quite as perfect as he could wish.

The twenty-four handicap player, chasing his ball from gorse-bush to bunker, and from bunker to long grass, obviously finds all the variety he requires. It is so with ski-ing. There is variety enough for all. For the expert who has attained the heights by prolonged practice and familiarity, perhaps from childhood ; for the beginner, who rolls from snowdrift to snowdrift and bounces from bump to bump. Like golf, ski-ing can be indulged in by all and sundry. Unlike golf, it requires some-thing of strength and courage, vitality and physical fitness. But no one, until he has tried, has any idea of how brave he is.

The sport of ski-ing is little more than progressing, be it uphill, downhill, or along the level, with unnatural and in-ordinately long pieces of wood attached to your feet. Yet it is the greatest sport in the world. And herein lies a funda-mental truth. The most important thing which the beginner, and indeed even the more experienced ski-runner must con-centrate on, is the sensation of feeling at home on his ski. To some this may seem the final goal reached after months, perhaps years, of application. To others it may seem an obvious and rudimentary idea. But to progress with six feet of wood attached to either foot is not a natural means of locomotion, and until it is accepted as such, the point of ski-ing is not at all understood. I lay stress on this point because it is a common sight to see men and women struggling desper-ately, not so much with their ski as with the natural dislike which they feel for them. To conquer a prejudice may be a noble endeavour, but it is not always a pleasing one. The excuse, and the only excuse, for ski-ing is that it is a pleasure. If it is to be pain, then play golf.

Nursery Slopes.

Where two or three are gathered together in the name of ski-ing, and it is to a place where there are even more than two or three that the beginner will at first migrate, there are always certain slopes, known as Nursery slopes. These are near at hand and are intended primarily to make it easy for the beginner to undergo his first initiation into the mystery. A fair rule is—avoid Nursery slopes like poison. Nursery slopes are generally crowded. The snow on Nursery slopes is always trodden hard and pitted like a battlefield—to which such slopes often bear a great resemblance—with large holes. A man who can ski with certainty and control on Nursery slopes can ski almost anywhere. To the beginner they certainly do everything, which snow, his fellow-man, and nature can do, to breed that early and fatal loathing for his ski so detrimental to subsequent progress.

Try and find an easy slope—it need not be long—and may often be tucked away at the back of some hotel or cow-shed or shop, where the snow is comparatively untracked and the gradient is gentle. This is the kind of place in which to get familiar with the use of ski.

Downhill.

To the Englishman the chief joy in ski-ing will be found, to begin with at any rate, in sliding downhill. The first time he tries to do this, his feet will slide away in front of him and he will sit down in the snow, more deliberately even than the tired business man drops into his Club arm-chair. A primary rule, therefore, is to lean forward. Those who fall forward need not be ashamed. They have fallen—which is a fault—but the fault was in the right direction. Those who fall backwards have also been at fault, but their fault was in the wrong direction. Nothing but practice, and practice on an easy slope far from the madding crowd, can teach a man how to slide downhill on ski with confidence. It is a preliminary exercise which he may easily master in a single morning.

Turning.

But since ski-ing is only a form of locomotion, it demands of those who practise it more than just sliding down a gentle slope. The beginner will find this immediately he has descended his first slope for the first time. He will have to turn round. For this purpose the kick turn is the easiest, and the kick turn should be mastered from the very beginning. It is generally taught after the military manner, in three separate motions (see Plates 3–5) :

1. Raise the right leg and rest the heel of the right ski on the snow beside the point of the left ski. In doing this a severe strain is put upon the balance, and to counteract this strain and to prevent himself from falling over, the ski-runner has two sticks. Use your sticks to keep your balance.

2. Allow the point of the right ski to fall outwards and backwards, keeping its heel down, until the whole ski is resting on the snow, parallel with the left but pointing in exactly the opposite direction.

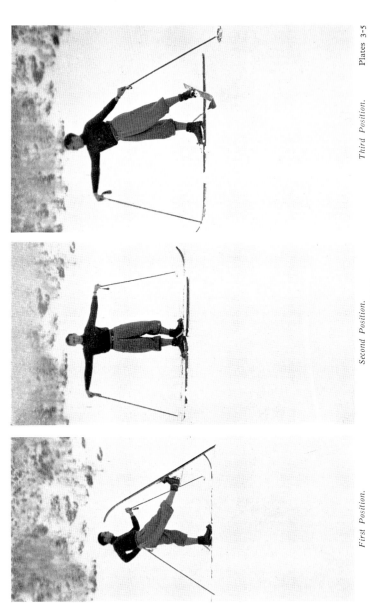

First Position.   *Second Position.*   *Third Position.*   Plates 3-5

THE KICK TURN

IN PRACTICE THE SECOND POSITION IS NEVER HELD, THE LAST TWO MOVEMENTS BEING MADE AS ONE. NOTE THE USE OF THE STICKS TO AID THE BALANCE.

3. Pull the left ski round into position beside the right. In this last move
the difficulty is to prevent the point of the ski from sticking in the snow.
To do this push down with the left heel and press upwards with the toe,
using the same muscles as when you grip your knees into the saddle on
horseback.

The turn above described has been to the right. It is
obvious that by first raising the left, instead of the right ski,
it can equally be made to the left. In practice, the first two
movements are always made as one. It sounds complicated,
but it will be found comparatively easy. It is fundamental.

Uphill.

Having turned, the beginner will now have to climb to the
top of the slope he has just slid down. In climbing there are
three things to remember. The first is—stamp your ski into
the snow. In most forms of progress on ski, the movement is
a sliding movement. In climbing, and in climbing alone,
the secret is to stamp. The second is—use your sticks. It is
a common enough thing to see ski-runners who use their sticks
as an usher in church uses the wand he carries, more as a
graceful ornament than as a practical weapon. Don't hold
your sticks half-way down the shaft between thumb and fore-
finger. Catch hold of them at the top and put your weight
on them. Push with them. The third and most important
thing of all is—don't try to climb too steeply. I remember once
seeing two boxers who had put on ski for the first time, at the
foot of a small, rather steep sugar-loaf hill. They were strong
men and the hill was a little hill. They squared their shoulders,
set their jaws, and the light of battle shone in their eyes. They
meant to kill that hill, and they started to walk straight up
it with a suggestion about them that quite soon it would be
flattened out altogether. But the hill is still there, and the
boxers would be still there too, if at the end of half an hour
they had not accepted the advice of an insignificant little
man, that they should climb round it, instead of over it. They
went up as a spiral staircase, and in five minutes stood on the
top. Climbing steeply is a question of balance and experience,
but the finest ski-runner in the world cannot walk straight up
a steep slope. The secret in climbing is to conserve your energy,
and if you slip back one step for every two you take forward,
you waste it.

In a day or two the beginner can have become sufficiently acquainted with his ski to climb and descend the easy slope which he has selected without falling about and without absolutely hating the ski on his feet. Then he may venture into the hills. When he does this, he should remember that the best ski track down any slope is a straight line following the contour of the hill. The best line on ski from a given place to another given place is a straight line. Straight running is the essence of good ski-ing, but straight running means fast running, and the beginner will at first find speed an alarming factor among the hills. He will find that practically no slope is so gradual or so unobstructed that he can run straight down it without a fall. Falling is a poor joke, precious little fun and bad ski-ing. Don't accept a fall as inevitable. Make up your mind from the beginning that you will not fall. When a slope is too steep to run straight down, descend it in a series of zigzags. Run across the face of the slope, turn your ski a little uphill to stop yourself. Do a kick turn and run back in the opposite direction. Running across the face of a hill is called " traversing." Keep your feet fairly wide apart, your weight all on the lower of your two ski, and the higher, un-weighted, ski slightly in advance of the other. To stop, put your weight on the heel of the lower foot and force the heel of the ski downhill. The points of your ski will then be leading you up instead of down the hill, and inevitably you will come to a standstill. Lean forward. This manœuvre can be carried out indefinitely and is more deserving of merit than its alternative, which is to point the ski straight down the slope, say a brief prayer and sit down. But, of course, it is not ski-ing. This much can be said. The beginner who wants to enjoy himself out ski-ing will get the maximum of pleasure if he can negotiate no matter what country without falling. More than this. He will be gaining confidence and not wasting his strength. He will learn much quicker than his companion, who on all occasions emulates the spirit of the light cavalry charge at Balaclava and falls on his face with no matter what measure of applause for his courage.

Running downhill on ski consists in being able to descend any slope, not only without falling but also *without stopping*. In order to do this it is necessary to master some form of down-hill turn which obviates the necessity of coming to a standstill

THE STEM TURN

Top.
START OF STEM TURN FROM A LEFT TRAVERSE. NOTE WEIGHT STILL ON RIGHT FOOT, HANDS LOW
AND FEET WIDE APART.

Bottom.
HALF WAY THROUGH THE STEM TURN. NOTE THE WEIGHT CHANGED ON TO THE LEFT FOOT, THE
SHOULDERS SWUNG TO THE RIGHT.

each time direction has to be changed. There are several different methods of turning on ski. Around their rival merits there rages an endless controversy carried on by the expert students of ski technique. No one can do better than read one or more of the books written on the subject by Mr. Arnold Lunn, Mr. Vivian Caulfeild, Mr. d'Egville, or one of the Continental writers. In this literature the whole subject is thoroughly discussed and analysed and the case for one turn or another made plain to the uninitiated. But the beginner need not trouble his head with controversy, and it is indeed not the object of this chapter to discriminate between the advantages of the stem turn and the open christiania, the lifted-stem and the telemark.

The Stem Turn.

The most useful turn is undoubtedly the stem turn, and it is also the easiest to learn. The stemming position is acquired by leaving the points of the ski close together, and at the same time forcing the heels as far away from each other as possible. The ski are edged and the effect of the movement is to make the ski-runner knock-kneed, a position which is as useful in ski-ing as it is hideous and useless in all other sports. The knees should be bent, the hands held low and the body leaning well forward from the waist. The tendency of this position is to force the ski, toes together, as nearly as possible at right angles to the direction in which they are travelling. The effect is, of course, a break. Having once acquired this position, which is unnatural at first, and feels, to the properly made man, extremely uncomfortable, the business of turning is easy. To turn to the right, put the whole weight of your body, still keeping this position, on the left leg. To turn to the left, weight the right leg. Once this manœuvre has been mastered on the slope of easy gradient, practice alone will make it equally easy to perform on a slope of, say, 35 degrees. The stem turn is equivalent to an inside edge on skates. The weight is on the lower of the two legs, and the ski edged inwards. In time the ski-er will learn to forget all about the other leg as a skater forgets the leg he is not skating on. The stem turn then becomes a turn made on one leg, using the inside edge of the ski as a skater uses the inside edge of his skate (see Plates 6–7).

The Jump Turn.

Though the stem turn is the most useful, I venture to put the jump turn first in the order of importance. The jump turn consists quite simply in changing direction by jumping round, and except in very sticky and crusty snow it is little used. Its importance is that it gives the ski-runner that all-important thing, a sense of spring. Far too many English runners cling tenaciously to the snow, and are at once mystified and alarmed when they are divorced from it. It is the hall-mark of the good ski-runner that he seems to come down the hill-side jumping from hummock to hummock like a mountain goat. Resilience is the most important thing in ski-ing. A stiff and set position is both ugly and inefficient. The object of the springs on a motor-car is to absorb the inequalities of the road in such a way that the body of the car moves always along the same plane. In the same way the ski-runner should use everything below his waist, and his knees in particular, to absorb the inequalities of the ground over which he travels. But there is this difference—a motor-car is a machine, and as such derives no personal satisfaction from leaving the ground. The ski-runner is human and there is no greater sense of pleasure than that which comes from jumping into the air over every small hillock which presents itself. The jump turn teaches resilience, gives to the ski-runner a sense of lightness and of spring. For that reason it is very important.

To do a jump turn to the left, run across the face of the hill with your left foot the lower of the two. Crouch down as low as you comfortably can. Reach forward with your left hand almost as far as the point of your ski and put the point of your stick into the snow in front of you and about twelve inches below you. Jump round the stick. Though it is better to practise this manœuvre on a gentle slope, it is actually easier to do it on a steep slope. The secret is to jump well out from the hill and not to bother too much about the turn. The movement of the shoulders will bring your ski round automatically. But jump big, and turn your head to look back in the direction from which you have come (see Plate 8).

The Telemark.

The most beautiful of all the turns is the telemark, but it is of use in soft snow only. In the telemark one foot is advanced

Plate 8

THE JUMP TURN

NOTE THAT THE KNEES ARE DRAWN WELL UP.

half a ski length in front of the other, the knees are bent and
the front ski leads the other round in a turn which can be as
gradual or as sharp as the runner chooses (see Plate 9).

The telemark may be done with the weight either on the
leading or on the hindmost foot. The easiest way to learn
it is with the weight on the back foot. To do a telemark to
the right, push the right ski back, keeping your weight on the
toe of the right foot until your right boot and the heel of
your left ski are level. Edge the left ski and force the heel out
until it points across the toe of the right ski at an angle of about
30 degrees. This position you must hold at all costs. The
left leg stiff, the weight of the body on the toe of the right foot,
and the left ski held out against the line of advance at an angle
of about 30 degrees. Keep your eye fixed on the tip of your
right ski and you will gradually come round. Don't try to
force it. At the last moment you may throw your weight
forward on to the left foot.

The Christiania.

The christiania is perhaps the most widely used of all turns
and is certainly the most difficult to learn. The stem turn is
the application to ski of the principle of the inside edge on
skates. The christiania is the application of the principle of
the outside edge. To do a christiania to the right, bend the
knees, and leaning well over the right foot, push out the point
of the right ski. Put your weight on the right foot. Don't
be in a hurry to come round, but as you begin to do so, turn
the right ski on to its outside edge. Keep the left ski flat, but
force the heel outwards and bend the knee inwards, so that
the ski comes round parallel to the right. On hard snow this
turn is often started with a jerk of the shoulders (see Plate 1).

An easy way to distinguish the difference between one ski-ing
turn and another is to forget about the foot which is not doing
the work. Thus in turns in which the weight of the body is
on the right foot, which is consequently doing the work, a turn
made to the left is an inside edge—a stem turn ; one made to
the right is an outside edge—a christiania turn. The telemark,
which is really only a variation of the stem turn, differs from
it in that for a telemark one foot leads well in front of the other,
for a stem the two feet remain side by side.

There are other and variations of all these turns, such as the stem-christiania and the lifted stem. But they need not find a place in a chapter of this kind. One turn follows fairly automatically after another. The beginner should take the earliest opportunity, however, of mastering some kind of turn, not so much because his ski-ing will be better, but because he will thus derive much more pleasure from it.

How to Learn.

To recapitulate for a moment what has so far been said, the way to learn quickly how to ski, with the object of filling a short holiday with a good deal of pleasure, is in three separate parts. First of all, find an easy slope of gentle gradient where there are not, if possible, twelve thousand people beside yourself doing the same thing. On this slope get accustomed to your ski. Make friends with them. Walk about on them ; climb up the slope and slide down it ; get into the way of using your sticks to best advantage ; push with them on the flat, lean your weight on them going uphill ; learn thoroughly the kick turn so that you can do it almost without thinking.

In the second place, get out into the hills. Walk quietly uphill. Save your energy. There is no hurry. Come down at your own pace. Avoid a fall like the plague. If the slope is steep, slide backwards and forwards across it. Make use of the kick turn. Bend at the knees and get the feel of the ground. Don't be stiff and don't try too much at first. A day without a fall gives much more satisfaction than a day spent recklessly on your head in the snow.

Finally, set yourself to learn one of the turns. Go back to the old slope where you first put your ski on and practise. When you are out running, do it whenever you can. The difference between being able to do downhill turns and having to stop and do a kick turn every time you want to change direction is the difference between running and walking on foot.

Straight Running.

There are certain things in ski-ing which are often neglected at the start, which are sometimes never put right, and which make all the difference between proficiency and mere performance. The most important of these has already been mentioned, and is to do with a sense of lightness and spring. For ordinary straight running various positions are advocated. For ordinary straight running there should, of course, be no single position but rather a hundred different ones. A man walking across country does not progress with the same un-changing measured stride when he walks along a road, up a hill, over a ditch, through a gate, along a railway line, across a bog, down a rocky decline, through gorse, rushes or heather. He suits his style of walking—unconsciously perhaps—to the ground over which he is travelling. If you were to say to a man, " The right way of walking is with the back straight, a pace of three feet, chest forward and hands swinging regularly at sides," and then send him over Exmoor, he would either disregard your instructions or else never reach the other side of the moor. It is equally true of ski-ing. Certain principles obtain in climbing a hill or in sliding down it, but every ski-runner must adjust his movements to suit the country he moves over. For this reason spring is an all-important factor. A runner moving stiffly in a set position and at a high speed comes to a small hummock. If he does not adapt himself quickly to the sudden rise, he shoots into the air and probably falls on the back of his head. Another moving loosely, with knees bent, will pass over the hummock, the lower part of his body absorbing the shock, without even knowing it. A third may notice the hummock and rise at it as a horse rises at a fence, but, being prepared, land on the far side perfectly safely.

In running downhill, the lower you are to the ground the lower is your centre of gravity, and the greater your resistance to any upset of balance. On the other hand, to crouch for any length of time is tiring. Again, the strain on your balance in ski-ing is greater longitudinally than latitudinally. A sudden change in gradient is much more likely to upset a man's balance than anything else. The inclination to fall over sideways on a bicycle is not great. It is admittedly greater in ski-ing, but it is not half so strong as the inclination to fall forwards or backwards. It is a good rule, therefore, to run with one ski a little in front of the other, so as to be ready to counteract any change in speed resulting from a sudden dip or sudden rise in the ground. It is far prettier to run with both feet together, and on soft snow, where the latitudinal strain on the balance is small and it is easier for a drift of heavy snow to wrench the ski apart, this is probably the best position. On hard

snow a number of good runners run with their feet apart, and
the early prejudice against this habit is, to all intents and
purposes, dead.   At the same time, I have noticed that nearly
all runners who have done any jumping keep their feet together
both on hard and on soft snow.   There is no doubt that this
is far prettier to look at, and I believe that once a runner has
got used to it, it is infinitely the better method.   The difference
is, of course, the difference between the tricycle and the bicycle.
For speed, elegance and control, the bicycle has the tricycle
beat every time (see Plates 10 and 11).

The Position of the Sticks.

It is, on the whole, more æsthetic to keep your hands low
and your sticks either trailing behind or sticking out at right
angles to your body.   Avoid the apparently irresistible tendency
to ski with one hand in front of each eye and the sticks pointed
forwards, and so held that a stumble will drive them through
your head.   This position, which seems a great favourite, is
dangerous.   But that does not matter.   It is extremely ugly,
however, and that is very important.

General Hints.

I have laid stress in this chapter on the virtue of not falling.
Falling is bad ski-ing.   A fall, in spite of the copy which it still
provides for the Press, is not a good joke but a blemish to what
might otherwise have been a good performance.   One thing,
however, is even worse than falling, and that is to walk downhill.   The principal object of ski-ing is to slide, and the
principal point of a hill—from the ski-runner's point of view
—is that it affords an excellent opportunity for sliding.   If you
want to walk down a hill, there are snow rackets, which,
attached to the feet, prevent you sinking into the snow.   There
are also paths.   But it is no uncommon thing to see people
either so timid or else so bent on not falling that they will
side-step down a steep slope, taking the greatest possible care
to see that they do not slide.   To fall may be bad ski-ing,
but to walk downhill is not ski-ing at all.   Words fail to describe
the horror with which the merest beginner will look upon a
fellow who, sooner than take any risk, meticulously side-steps
down the face of a snow slope.   Yet it is a fairly common sight.

In ski-ing it is assumed that a man running downhill knows

what he is doing and is in control of his ski. If, therefore, in
the process of descent, he runs into another ski-er, the fault is
his. This assumption is made not because it is true (too often
a man running downhill is anything but in control of his ski),
but because it ought to be true. Men and women often drive
motor-cars when they could not safely be put in charge even
of a perambulator. But the law and the public assume that
someone driving a car is in control of it simply because they
ought to be. It does not follow that everyone who skis ought,
from the day when he first puts them on, to be able perfectly
to control them. But it does follow that as long as a man is
not sure of himself, he has no business to be doing anything
which may interfere with other people. A good tip to the
beginner is : Don't, with a careless laugh, point your ski downhill and cry in a loud voice to all and sundry to beware of
your coming. This is bad form, which is perhaps not very
important, but it also tells the world that you know nothing
about ski-ing, a piece of information which most ski-ing
aspirants are anxious to withhold from the public.

As a man becomes more and more at home on his ski, as
he learns more and more to control them, as he is able to move
all the time at an ever-increasing speed and with an equal sense
of security, as the whole vast range of snow-covered mountains
opens up before him as a playground, so the joy of ski-ing
increases. There is no exercise, no pleasure, no sport to
compare with it. Beside it, all the medicines, tonics, cures,
exercises, cold baths, masseurs and doctors in the world are a
poor company. The joy of running fast down a steep slope,
over virgin snow, with your heart in your mouth and the
knowledge that at last you are really ski-ing has to be felt to
be believed. There is nothing else like it. Who has ski-ed
over the snow mountains in winter, awaits with impatience
the death of even the most brilliant of summers. He counts
the days until he can get away again to the clean mountain
air, the sunshine, the snow and his ski.

Field Jumping.

The subsequent chapters on ski-ing deal with it as a
specialized sport in one way or another, but now that the
beginner is no longer a beginner, there is a special delight which
he should become acquainted with, in the form of what is called

" field jumping." Field jumping means jumping over natural obstacles in the daily round, as compared with jumping on a specially prepared jump. It is a side of ski-ing which tends too much to be neglected and which certainly contains as much quiet amusement as anything else. If you drive over an arched bridge in a motor-car, and do it too fast, the back wheels rise off the ground. If you ski over a small bump it will lift you into the air. If you crouch down before you reach the bump and spring into the air so as to synchronize your spring with the natural lift which the bump gives you, you will find it a most agreeable sensation. A straight jump made in this way, which enables you when landing to continue your course, is generally known as a " gelandersprung." If, on the other hand, you turn in mid-air and land at right angles to the course which you were travelling (a glorified jump turn), this is called a " quersprung." Neither can be done very fast, as the landing is probably rather flat, and the jar at a high speed would therefore be considerable. But a little jumping of this kind, included in the day's run, is the greatest possible fun and is enormously beneficial to your ski-ing. If there is no natural bump, one can be manufactured with the sticks. Put your sticks—and you want long ones for this—into the snow well in front of you and jump through them, pushing yourself up on your arms in doing so (see Plate 12). The same technique will enable you, with good judgment, and a little practice, to jump over small fences, sunken paths, ditches, fallen trees, and so forth. It is possible that this may be a useful as well as an amusing accomplishment. Whenever you are practising this kind of jumping, pull your knees—when in the air—well up into your chest and push downwards with your heels, so as to keep up the points of your ski. Try and land in telemark position (i.e. with one foot half a ski's length in front of the other, and both knees bent at right angles). This is far and away the best position for taking the jar which must be felt after a drop of any size at all.

Sticks are generally too little used by the ordinary English ski-er. They are invaluable for field jumping of the kind described above. They are indispensable in climbing and will enable the man who understands how to use them properly to climb a good deal steeper than his fellow. Along the level, though this to the Scandinavian is one of the most important

Plate 9

"THE TELEMARK TURN"

HERE THE WEIGHT IS FORWARD ON THE RIGHT FOOT. THE KNEES ARE WELL BENT AND THE RIGHT SKI LEADS THE LEFT ROUND

parts of ski-ing, there is scarcely an Englishman who understands the right use of his sticks. Their function is much greater than that of the walking-stick in ordinary life. They should be used systematically to push with, so that the whole movement is as far away as possible from ordinary walking, and as near as possible to that of continuous sliding. But of this later.

This chapter has dealt with the kind of ski-ing which is practised in Central Europe, for it is to Central Europe mostly that the Englishman goes when he wants to ski. There the mountains are high and the greatest pleasure to be found in their descent. When an Englishman talks of ski-ing, he is thinking only of running downhill. The country lends itself to this criterion and a long descent over Alpine country, through woods and down very steep slopes, is not only a grand experience but a tiring one. The Norwegian criterion is a different one. His country is more undulating, and a day in the hills is spent as much in crossing over frozen lakes and climbing up easy gradients as in anything else. The Norwegian thinks of the descent only as a means of resting himself for the real business of ski-ing. He judges a man a skilled or bad ski-er in proportion to his ability to move quickly along the level and uphill. In these things, argues the Norwegian, lies the real test of ski-ing. Anyone can slide down a hill more or less, but only a good man can run uphill quickly or make a fast speed along the flat. To which Central Europe, remembering not the Scandinavian hills but the Alps, replies : Anyone can go up hills or along the flat, more or less, but it takes a good man to come down quickly over changing snow conditions and steep wooded slopes.

D

CHAPTER III

TOURING AND MOUNTAINEERING ON SKI

THERE are three different kinds of ski-ing which may be classified as mountaineering on ski, touring on ski, and competitive ski-ing. Mountaineering on ski, since definition is necessary, may be said to begin with the summer snow-line. The point of mountaineering on ski is that it takes the runner up on to the glaciers and among the high peaks. The use of ski in this case is largely utilitarian. The object of the expedition is to reach some peak, and ski are used as a necessary means to attain that object rather than the object made an excuse for ski-ing. In ski-touring, although the objective may be some lower peak or pass, the tour is only an excuse for ski-ing. The use of ski is here much less utilitarian. Competitive ski-ing, such as jumping and racing, is entirely a sport, and ski are used for no utilitarian purpose at all. Touring on ski is the more common of the three kinds, and it is of this kind that the Englishman usually speaks when he talks generally about ski-ing.

The way in which a ski-er enjoys his holiday is by getting out into the hills on his ski. If he goes a comparatively short way, he calls it a " run." If he goes farther afield, and perhaps spends the night in some hut, he calls it a tour. For practical purposes all ski-ing is either a ski-run or a ski-tour, and the difference between the two is perhaps not great enough to merit distinction.

A tour on ski must inevitably vary with the geography of the country. It may be over undulating country, across a high pass, or to the summit of some accessible peak. A ski-tour in Central Europe probably belongs to one of the two latter categories. A long, steady climb up the mountain-side, the top at last reached, the whole snow-covered world glistening in the sunshine, the ravenous appetite and its welcome satisfaction—finally, and best of all, the run down

STRAIGHT-RUNNING POSITIONS

TELEMARK POSITION; WEIGHT ALL FORWARD ON WELL ADVANCED
RIGHT FOOT. NOTE IN BOTH SKI TOGETHER, HANDS LOW.

THE CROUCH, WEIGHT SLIGHTLY BACK AND ON HEELS; ONE FOOT
VERY SLIGHTLY ADVANCED.

through swishing powder snow in the afternoon. Distance is never calculated in the Alps ; the length of a day is reckoned in the number of feet ascended, and a four-hour climb may well provide no more than half an hour's descent. But that half-hour has been worth a century of expectation and a year of steady ascent.

It is unwise to ski alone, except in country over which there will be people passing pretty regularly. A sprained ankle or a broken ski is a hard affliction to bear in solitude and often a grave difficulty to surmount without help. Man is for the most part a social animal and the majority of people, curiously perhaps, prefer the company of their friends to the silent, if more æsthetic, companionship of the snow-hills. Three or four is the best number for a run. More than four makes progress slow, on the same principle that men marching in single-file take longer to cover a piece of ground than men in columns of four. It is obvious that if three people ski together their speed is not the sum total of their best, but the sum total of their worst ski-ing ability. One good ski-er does not increase the speed of a party. One bad ski-er greatly diminishes it. As in all human endeavour which is undertaken in a social or gregarious spirit, the pace is the pace of the slowest.

Climbing.

The first part of the day will probably be spent in climbing. For a long climb, or for people not thoroughly accustomed to the use of their ski, sealskins are a great assistance. These are fastened to the sole of the ski, and while the grain of the skin allows the ski to move forward, it equally holds them from slipping back. The essence of climbing is a steady consistent pace, for it is all important to conserve your energy for the more amusing and second half of the day, the run down. There is skill in choosing the best line for an uphill track. The leader should climb, if he is leading across untracked snow, a little less steeply than he actually can. A ski track is always faster than new snow, and those following in the leader's tracks tend to slip back where he was able comfortably to stamp his ski into the new snow. Otherwise, climb as steeply as possible. But only " as possible," for there is nothing more exhausting than climbing just too steeply and slipping back, if only a quarter of an inch, at each step. The uphill track should

follow the contour of the hill.   If a gully is crossed, the climber
should not run down into the bottom of it and then climb out
the other side, but keep high all the time, and instead of losing,
rather gain height by its intervention.   If you have to zigzag
backwards and forwards up the face of a hill, make each zig
(or is it zag ?) as long as possible.   Turn as seldom as possible.

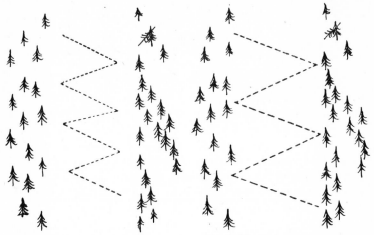

FIG. I.—A BAD TRACK.   FIG. II.—A GOOD TRACK.

This is not only less tiring but quicker.   On the climb it is
a good plan to rest at regular intervals and give the stragglers
time to get their breath and catch up.   Use your sticks all the
time to push with.   Lean on them and help your legs with
your arms.

The Descent.

So much for the ascent.   Going down, it is a more difficult
but equally important rule, to keep together.   On the ascent
people will get left behind, but rarely out of sight.   Going
down the speed is so much faster and the height lost—lost so
quickly that people are often left much more hopelessly and
helplessly behind.   Nothing is more tiring than to have to
climb back five hundred feet, perhaps, to help someone who
has lost his ski, or got held up for one reason or another.
Going down, it is even more important to rest and collect forces
at regular intervals, and above all to give the slow ones time to
get their breath.   There is nothing more exhausting or dis-

Plate 12

" A GELANDERSPRUNG THROUGH THE STICKS"

THE KNEES ARE WELL UP AND THE WEIGHT WELL FORWARD, BUT THE LEFT SKI SHOULD BE PARALLEL
WITH THE RIGHT.

heartening when you are the one who has been left behind and have at last, by superhuman effort, caught up with the rest of the party, to see all the others move on directly you reach them.

The longer the length of the tour, or the farther you are from home, the more important it is to conserve your strength and the less, therefore, the number of risks a runner must be prepared to take. In the high mountains a grave error may entail a heavy penalty and a careless fall at a dangerous moment might mean a broken leg. A broken leg might mean a night without shelter, and a night without shelter might mean a halo. Consequently the margin of error is small and the need for safety pre-eminent. On a long tour the penalties may not be so severe, but may equally be extremely unpleasant. On an ordinary run the margin of error is greater, because the penalty is perhaps no more than considerable discomfort. Racing, one can afford to take risks. But it stands to reason that for running downhill on ski a good rule is not to take overwhelming risks, for the simple reason that if your friends have to carry you home, their day is spoilt.

I have laid stress upon the importance of keeping together, and for this reason more fun will be got out of a day's ski-ing if the ski-runners are more or less of equal standards of excellence.

Four men once started to climb up a valley by an unfrequented route. Within two hundred feet of the start, one declared that he was exhausted, and so the others, since they must return by the same route, told him to sit down and rest. On the way down in the evening they saw no sign of their companion, but since they had left him only a couple of hundred feet above a railway station, they naturally assumed that he had found his own way home. But when they themselves reached home they found that nothing had been heard of him. A search party, armed with lanterns, brandy and first-aid appliances, was consequently organized and the morning's climb repeated in the dark of the night. When the search party reached the place where the man had been left, they examined the snow and found tracks leading off into a wood. In the wood was a cow-shed and in the cow-shed was the missing man, curled up in some hay, contentedly asleep. The wrath of the search party, deprived of the comfortable enjoyment of its dinner, would have been great, had the object

of their search not explained that, though his rest had been
comfortable and pleasant, he had been frequently attacked by
chamois ! The idea of some infuriated chamois attacking a
man in a cow-shed two hundred feet above a railway station
so played upon the imagination of the search party that its
anger was turned to laughter. But the moral of this story
is that even with a wise philosophy and a scintillating imagination, you can nevertheless be a great nuisance to your fellow-
men if you wander alone over the hills in winter.

Snow-Craft.

Snow-craft plays an important part in touring over unfrequented country. Hills which in the summer may be
grazing ground for cattle, can be dangerous in winter, and,
under certain conditions, there is no reason why the snow
even on nursery slopes should not avalanche. But snow-craft
is a thing which must be learnt by practice and experience,
and, even then, is largely a fifth sense. There are, however,
certain principles which may be briefly enumerated.

After a fall of new snow, south slopes (i.e. slopes facing south
and those exposed to the midday sun) are more dangerous
than north slopes. The warmth of the sun tends to loosen
the snow and start avalanches. Once the avalanche has come
down, or the snow been exposed to midday sun and nightly
frost for a few days and so become crusted, south slopes are
comparatively safe. North slopes, on which the snow lies
loosely and remains cold all day, are dangerous for a longer
period of time than south slopes. They do not crust over,
though, never being exposed to the sun, they lack the same
incentive to avalanche. The most frequent avalanches are on
south slopes. The heaviest and most deadly on north. All
steep slopes (though particularly south) are dangerous in a
high temperature, or when a Föhn wind is blowing.

Convex slopes are more dangerous than concave. On
convex slopes there is nothing to support the weight of the
snow, which is consequently more liable to slip away when
disturbed.

Avalanches.

Danger of avalanches is generally encountered on the ascent
when ski-ing. It is often necessary to traverse across the face

of a steep slope, and it is the consistent cutting effect of a ski track which loosens the snow. If a slope looks dangerous and there is no way of avoiding it altogether, it is safer to take off your ski and cross it on foot. In this way the snow is only perforated, at frequent intervals perhaps, but *at intervals*, and the same effect is not produced as by the prolonged and continuous cutting action of ski.

The advice usually given to ski-runners, if at any time they should find themselves inevitably caught in an avalanche, is to get their ski off, if they can. Ski get twisted about and become quite uncontrollable once the runner has been swept off his feet, and the chances of his wrenching a knee out of joint or breaking a leg are minimized if he is able to get his ski off in time. The principal danger of being buried in an avalanche is that you are difficult to find once it has come to a standstill, and while assistance is coming you may be suffocated. A second rule, therefore, is keep your hands above your head and wave them about, in the hopes of preventing the snow covering you altogether. This advice can hardly be called fundamental to any ski-ing expedition, but it is knowledge which all may be well advised to have at their command in case of need.

Sometimes a steep slope is encountered on the descent, and if this slope looks dangerous it is safer to run straight down it than to descend in a series of turns. There is the famous story of Caulfeild arriving with two other runners at the top of the Blumenlücke, having approached it from the Wasnegg side. Caulfeild observed that the slope looked dangerous, and that it would be safer to take it straight—an observation to which he lent greater force by appearing the next instant no longer beside his companions but in the valley below. This performance has never been repeated, and indeed the two men who were with him, in an endeavour to follow his example, so crashed and fell about the slope that had Caulfeild's fear been well grounded, nothing could have prevented a monumental avalanche.

Touring.

Ski-touring is more greatly favoured in the east of Switzerland, where a high premium is put upon snow-craft and the qualities requisite to lead an expedition into the mountains.

The Grisons and Engadine have taken this form of ski-ing to
their heart and praised beyond all other pleasures the joy of
a day well spent touring in the Alps.   But the east is not alone
in its choice and there are few Englishmen who have ski-ed
and who do not endorse this opinion.   There is the pleasure
of anticipation.   The evening spent in deciding on the expedition for the morrow, in making sure that ski and bindings are
in good trim, in settling upon necessary requirements, lunch,
an extra sweater, a camera, and other things.   There is,
further, the hardened and altogether maddening sinner who
makes a fetish of this anticipatory preparation and holds himself responsible for the outfit of all who are to ski with him
on the morrow.   He looks keenly and forbiddingly at you.
" Have you got a rucksack ? " he asks.   " What are you taking
in it ?   Have you got skins ?   Have you waxed your ski ?
It will be a long day.   Are you sure you are up to it ? "
and finally, " Eight-thirty to-morrow morning.   Remember.
Don't be late."

Far more amusing, if less efficient, is his extreme opposite,
the man who strolls down half an hour late in the morning
to a cold and angry group waiting his arrival.   He has not
ordered lunch, he can't find his ski, he hasn't got any gloves,
he lent his rucksuck to someone and doesn't know where it
is, he never wears skins, there is no hurry—and so on.

There is a great joy in the climb.   The heat and the effort
and the little extra bit of height, which at each stage makes
the whole world look different.   Familiar mountains change
their shape.   Giants become pigmies and distant peaks,
scarcely seen in the valley, suddenly rear themselves up into
immensity.   Ground which has looked steep from below seems
to flatten itself out at your feet.   The sun shines, and even as
you are wondering about it all, you have climbed a little
higher and the whole scene has changed again.   And then
just as you are beginning to feel tired, just as you have come
to accept the changed face of the landscape, just as you have
grown used to seeing unimagined distances, there is the knowledge that you are within reach of the top.   In all climbing,
whether on foot or on ski, the knowledge, the " awareness "
of the top, comes long before the top is reached, generally
before it is even in sight.   But there comes in every climb a
moment when, having thought about nothing in particular or

a great many things indeed, you become suddenly aware of
the top. You know that it exists, that it is somewhere near.
You begin to think, and to think seriously, of reaching it, and
that thought carries you upward like a stick of dynamite.
Ridge after ridge, terrace after terrace, proves as you reach it
not to be the top after all, but your ardour is only increased
and your determination doubled.

I remember one day going out alone late in the morning.
My object was to mess about on the lower slopes practising turns
and the like. The country was new to me, and I had not
been out half an hour before, suddenly, the fever was upon
me. I began to climb. "I will go up to that little knoll
above me," I said ; but once there, a new snowfield presented
itself and I added, "Well, as far as that tree." I reached the
tree, but by now I had begun to realize that all attempt to
limit my ascent was useless. Beyond the tree, an inviting
glade led upwards through the woods, and above the woods
an open snowfield stretched upwards to the skyline. Beyond
that skyline the mountain rose above me tier upon tier and
terrace after terrace into the clear blue of the heavens. Up I
went, knowing that no power on earth could hold me back
from my fixed determination to reach the top. In two hours
I stood on the edge of the last terrace and only then realized
that it was late in the afternoon and that I wanted luncheon.
The hunger which men feel when they have been days without
food, or with only an insufficient supply, may be one thing,
but the hunger which a man feels who is but an hour late for
the accustomed meal is another. I remember poking with
my sticks in the snow in the hopes of finding a piece of chocolate
left there by the last people who had climbed that hill. But
with an abandon too common among those who have eaten
in comfort, they had left nothing but orange peel. It took me
a very short time to come down that mountain, and indeed
I enjoyed the descent very little. I doubt if anyone has ever
felt the fever which drives one irresistibly upwards as I felt
it that morning. Those who have suffered from it will know,
however, that it cannot be resisted.

There is no greater feeling of exhilaration than that which
comes to the ski-runner when at last he reaches the end of
his climb. Indeed, in touring, the lure of the mountains, the
desire to reach the summit, is so blended with the joy of actual

ski-ing that often the run down is of only secondary importance.
Ski-runners who have spent nearly all their time touring are
rarely such accomplished downhill runners as those who have
stayed on the lower ground and contented themselves more
with racing and competition. There is too much of the
mountaineer in them and they find so great a pleasure in
reaching upwards into the hills that they turn down often with
heavy hearts and do not get the pleasure out of the actual ski-
running that their less imaginative, if more skilled, friends in
the valley below them understand. There is more of the
adventurer in the mountaineer than in the man who is always
touring on ski, and there is more of the same spirit in the latter
than there is in the man who is always racing. It is the
difference between the sportsman and the games player, the
man whose heart is in the wild places and the man who
glories in competition. It is the difference between the big-
game hunter and the football player, between the man who
rides to hounds and the man who hits the polo ball. Both
have their place in ski-ing.

An expedition on ski often necessitates a night in some
mountain hut, generally a welcome change to the rigours of
civilization. Most Alpine huts are luxurious and well
appointed enough, but there is the fire to be lit, snow melted
for water, food to be cooked and frozen clothing to thaw. In
one hut the chimney of the stove smoked with such violence
that it was almost impossible to stay in the hut. We asked
the guide if nothing could be done about it, but he explained
that so the chimney had been for many years, and so, as far
as he could see, it would be for ever. We then bound an old
piece of sacking round the pipe and thereafter no smoke came
into the room at all. The guide's shrug of the shoulders was
the most expressive thing I have ever seen. " You can do
that if you want to," it said, " but one day the chimney will
smoke again. What does it matter ? Are you so frail that
you cannot bear a little good wood smoke in your eyes ? "
Such is the philosophy of the hillman. The hut undoubtedly adds an element of adventure to a tour on ski, and
if you have slept sufficiently poorly, the dawn amidst snow
mountains is a sight never to be forgotten.

Ski-touring on a grand scale, or on a small scale, is indeed
the whole essence of ski-ing. Some may make the ski an excuse

for a tour, others the tour an excuse for ski-ing. It makes little difference. Out among the hills the two become strangely blended, and as a sport ski-ing has the supreme advantage of being enjoyed in absolutely ideal surroundings and under absolutely perfect conditions. The combination of sun and snow and the clear dry mountain air is perfection. In some parts of Europe conditions are not as good as in Switzerland, and intense cold and wind are frequent. In Switzerland there is rarely any wind, and the sun, even in January, is hot enough to make the lightest of garments at times too cumbersome. Some Oxford undergraduates, having raced up the Männlichen, once ski-ed, out of sight of the hut, a little way down the face which overlooks Wengen. Here, since the sun was shining, the climb had been hot and they were young, they took off their clothes and proceeded to jump about in the snow naked, except for boots and skis, as their mothers had borne them. Far below in the village of Wengen a lady novelist was having her attention directed by the good Swiss to some imaginary chamois which they declared could be seen through a telescope. It was not chamois, however, that the lady saw, but what she fervently believed to be the incarnate spirits of the mountains. To see the gnomes and the gobelins is an experience which fortune rarely accords to the eyes of lady novelists.

Not the least pleasant part of a day spent among the mountains is often the return with dark to some village in the valley below. There are three things which belong to the inns of Swiss villages, and which are better—under certain circumstances—than all other things. They are, all three of them, drinks. One is called beer, the other grog, and the third gluvein. The draught beer of Central Europe has a world reputation which needs no enlarging upon. But it tastes its best when the thirst which is born of dry mountain air is upon you, and it comes foaming up the pipe ice cold from the cellars below. Grog is a drink, no doubt acceptable at sea and elsewhere, but grog never had the taste it has when the weariness, the good physical fatigue of a long day spent strongly, fills your body. Gluvein is a speciality of the country. It is like mull claret but made of a lighter, coarser wine, sweet and flavoured strongly with cinnamon. This, too, has a taste and a welcome of its own when drunk by the stove of some mountain inn, piping hot and in atmosphere where wet clothes become

fortunately superfluous. There are some who think that
Switzerland's chief claim to fame is that the mountain air
gives you a thirst which, try as you will, you cannot acquire
in less happier climes. But he who has not gloried in the long
climb, reached the summit with a cheer of welcome, plunged
downward and known the " quick stir of wonder " as the
snow rushes past his ski, and sat tired and contented with beer,
grog or gluvein in the inn in the valley, has scarcely lived.

Sometimes this final pleasure must be renounced. Often
there are trains to catch back to hotels, or sometimes to less
pleasing duties in towns out in the plains. Often, too, there is
short time in which to catch them and no time to spend in
welcome refreshment. The mountain trains are slow, cunning
things that creep with determination over snow-bound passes
and through winding tunnels. Mountain railways are generally
a wonder of engineering triumph, but Englishmen accustomed
to the rush of expresses, to concrete platforms built up three
feet from the ground, treat them with an ill-disguised scorn.
Those in charge of mountain trains are no more pleased to
see their children treated with disdain than would be those
in charge of the " Flying Scotsman." Any attempt to pursue
the departed train and board it, though frequently made, is
received by the officials with well-merited protest. Perhaps
another joy, not wholly divorced from touring on ski, is the
excitement of catching a train, for which you are definitely
just too late.

Mountaineering.

These are some of the joys of ski-ing and the beginner, when
he has left his first easy slope, been for the first gentle run,
mastered the technique which enables him to turn accurately
and at speed, will find a great joy in long tours over hills in
winter. But if he has in him something of the mountain spirit,
he will not be content with this. He will not be content until
he has been up with his ski on to the glaciers and among the
high peaks. He will not be content until he has traversed the
Oberland by the high level route, until he has taken ski up
Mont Blanc. Mountaineering on ski, which is only the
realization of ordinary ski-touring, must find a place in this
chapter.

Mountaineering on ski really dates from W. Paulcke's classic

STUNT JUMPING WITH THE STICKS

THIS ACCOMPLISHMENT IS SOMETIMES USEFUL IN NEGOTIATING A FENCE OR OTHER OBSTACLE.

traverse of the Oberland by the Grimsel, Oberaarjoch, Grün-
hornlucke and Belalp in January, 1897. In the intervening
years since that date practically every peak in Central Europe
has been ascended on ski, though, of course, for the final climb
up to the summit over rock or ice ski have often had to be
abandoned. Among the names of the pioneers of mountain
ski-ing, those of Paulcke, Marcel Kurz, Bilgeri, Roget, Dalloz
and Arnold Lunn should be remembered.

In early days the use of ski was much mistrusted by the old
mountaineers, and in the first traverse of the Oberland some
of Paulcke's party climbed on snow rackets, trailing their ski
behind them, an experiment which their leader, a more
experienced ski-runner, viewed with quiet amusement. It was
believed that to ski roped together was practically impossible,
and the men who had climbed on their feet for many years
were disconcerted by the feel of ski and thought of them rather
as an encumbrance than as an aid to mountaineering. (This
sensation has since been the experience of many who have put
on ski for the first time, even if they had not previously been
accustomed to climbing about among snow mountains on
their feet.) Man is by nature conservative, and having done
a thing in a certain way all his life, he resents the implication
that it can be better done in any other way. The old school
of winter mountaineering on foot died hard. But in time it
was realized that the use of ski, so far from hindering mountain
climbing, was of the greatest help, and further that those parts
of a climb which had been long, dull and wearisome, were
given a new aspect and a new pleasure when undertaken on
ski. A long trudge up a snow-covered glacier is a slow and
dreary performance on snow-shoes. The same descent is no
better. On ski the climb became quicker and less tiring, the
descent an undreamt-of delight. Once ski had been effectively
used in the high mountains there was no doubt, in spite of
conservative and human prejudice, that they had come to
stay. English readers should remember that in days when
ski mountaineering was still mistrusted an Englishman, Arnold
Lunn, was one of the most enthusiastic pioneers. Mr. Lunn
has a magnificent mountaineering record and his book *Alpine
Ski-ing* is still the best work on that subject in any language.

In the early days the ski mountaineers stuck religiously to
the well-known summer routes, which often provided poor

ski-ing and were, in point of fact, not even the best lines of
approach for winter mountaineering. The introduction of ski
laid bare a whole new range of possibilities, and ground which
had hitherto been little explored became not only accessible
but actually desirable to the ski-runner.

Among Englishmen the formation of the Alpine Ski Club
—of which Sir Martin Conway was the first President—gave
a fillip to this new sport. The A.S.C. demands of its members
not only ability in the use of ski, but experience of conditions
in the high Alps as well.

Though for mountaineering the use of ski is more utilitarian
than in any other branch of the sport, it is not unusual for
ski-ing mountaineers to go out of their way, even in high
country, to find ground which, though of little value from the
purely mountaineering point of view, yet provides excellent
ski-ing. There must, however, be always a greater margin
of safety allowed when ski are used under these conditions.
Some of the best mountain guides are not, from a purely ski-ing
point of view, first-class runners. They lack dash and show no
great inclination to run at high speeds. They do not take
advantage of the ground and jump like mountain goats from
one hillock to another. There is no abandon, little grace and
less finish to their ski-ing. But the reason for this is obvious.
They have taught themselves to be safe. When life is at stake,
polish, abandon and gracefulness are comparatively unimport-
ant things. It is rare to see a mountain guide fall down when
he is on ski. The mountaineering technique is essentially a
safety-first technique. Strong steady running, deliberate turns
which can be accurately placed and executed at the slowest
of speeds, great strength, since, in the mountains, heavy packs
must be carried. He is a wise man who keeps a reserve of
energy in case of anything going wrong. The mountaineering
ski technique is rugged and powerful, steady, determined and
sure. The stem turn is the favourite with mountaineers, since
it can be forced round most surely at any pace. For straight
running, an upright position, since it is less tiring, and always
the determination not to run out of control or risk a fall.

Mountaineering on ski is probably the finest form of sport
which ski make possible, but it definitely does not produce the
most magnificent of ski-runners. It is the steam tug against
the speedboat, the trawler against the yacht. You can play

Plate 15

"THE SCHILTGRAT, MÜRREN"

about with the speedboat, drift about, go where you will in
the yacht, but the tug and the trawler must be made of sterner
stuff. They have a work to do and much hangs upon their
ability to do it. They must not fail. Theirs is a grave business.

Six men once set out on a ski-ing expedition among the
high Alps. It was a little expedition, as these things go, and
its object was not mountaineering but ski-ing. One of them
was a guide, another was Andrew Irvine, who died with
Mallory on the last and perhaps successful assault on Mount
Everest. A third was a good ski-er with much mountaineering experience. But the other three, though they were
good ski-runners, had never been up on the high ground before.
The conditions were good and there was plenty of snow. The
party were not roped, but the three were advised to follow the
guide as he knew the way between the more dangerous
crevasses. But the three had not the mountaineering spirit.
They were yachts, not trawlers. They were essentially ski-
runners and the mere proximity of a crevasse cramped their
style vastly. Religiously they followed that guide, scarcely
deviating an inch from his track, for though they understood
the ski-ing game—they were alarmed by unknown dangers
amidst the glaciers. It was an amusing situation because there
was actually no danger at all, but it gave a splendid illustration
of the difference between the two temperaments and the two
kinds of technique necessary in ski-running proper and in
mountaineering on ski.

They spent the night in the Egon von Steiger hut and Irvine
burnt the seat out of his trousers by hanging them too near the
stove to dry. In the morning the weather was bad and so they
decided to ski straight down the Lötschenthal and to attempt
no sort of climb at all. Three of them were disappointed,
three were delighted. Probably no party of ski-runners has
ever come down the Lötschenthal so fast before or since. The
pace was fairly steady to begin with, as the idea that at all
costs the guide's tracks must be followed still obtained. But
no sooner was the moraine in sight than the three began to
realize that they were getting on to ground which they understood. After the glacier was left behind, the tour developed
into a kind of race, and since all were good ski-runners and the
need for safety was now no more, the pace was fast. The
highest village in the valley, and therefore the first reached

coming from the lücke or pass, is called Blätten. The name,
carelessly pronounced in the English tongue, seemed inviting.
The time was about ten in the morning. The inn was on the
left of the path running through the middle of the village.
In the inn was the principal ski-runner of the valley. " Where
have you come from ? " he asked the three, as almost simultaneously they burst through the door. " From the Lötchenlücke," was the answer. " When did you start ? " " About
half an hour ago." " It is not possible."

Then followed an argument. The inhabitant of Blätten
explained that all his life had he lived in the valley, that in
all its length there was no one so skilled with ski as himself;
that no one knew the country as he, and that in half an hour
it was not possible to descend from the Lötchenlücke. The
three, on the other hand, denied all knowledge of the country,
of the valley, of the village, and of its inhabitants. Possible or
not, they argued, it was but half an hour since they had left
the Egon von Steiger hut and good riddance to it !

There are two ways of settling such a dispute at ten o'clock
in the morning. One is to fight, but the three were in no mood
for fighting. The other is with song, and so they called for the
entzien which is the spirit of the Lötschenthal. Song gave
place to carnival, and the inhabitants of Blätten gathered to
take part in the festival. They called for more entzien and
they called for more song. The guide arrived, a little out of
breath but grinning from ear to ear. He was hailed with a
great shout of welcome, and, since no one may drink entzien
alone, there was much filling of glasses. About an hour later
all was right with the world. The ski-runners had established
their claim not only in their own minds but in the minds of the
people of Blätten, that on ski there was no one to touch them.
The inhabitants of Blätten, on the other hand, had proved once
and for all time that there lived no other men so skilled in
song. But then came a great shattering of illusions. The party
put on ski, amidst the acclamations of the assembled people,
to continue their journey downward. The snow which lay
on the path through the village seemed yellow. It had moreover a strange way of rising up and striking whoever passed
over it savagely in the face. And so the inhabitants of Blätten
saw disappear into the distance not the champion ski-runners
of half an hour before, but a handful of novices who bumped

THE START OF THE LANGLAUF IN THE BRITISH CHAMPIONSHIP MEETING

THE WINNER, H. R. SPENCE.

Plate 16

about and swayed and crashed to the ground like the dead branches of trees on a windy day. But the inhabitants of Blätten preferred not to see but to sing.

This is not a story of mountaineering on ski, nor does it illustrate any point in that greatest of all branches of ski-ing. It shows only that there are mountaineering temperaments and ski-ing temperaments, and that the two are different sports which call for different qualities and strive after different ideals. As it did not follow in the beginning that the mountaineer was a ski-runner, so it does not follow that the ski-runner is a mountaineer. But it speaks no harm of either.

To me the most fascinating of all mountaineering stories, though it has little to do with ski-ing, is of a well-known Wengen guide. He was on a glacier with his greatest friend. They were roped and in crossing a crevasse the snow-bridge gave way and the friend fell into the crevasse. The guide was able to hold him on the rope, but was not strong enough to pull him up. For half an hour he lay on his face in the snow, while his friend was suspended on the rope in the middle of the crevasse. At the end of this time the man in the crevasse observed that they were getting no further and that there was nothing to be gained by both of them being frozen to death. " Cut the rope," he said, " I may not fall far and you may be able to get help. But if the worst comes to the worst, at least one of us will be saved." The guide cut the rope, but it had frozen so hard into the snow and ice at the edge of the crevasse that it held ! He was able to go back to the hut for help and he rescued the friend, who, though cold, was none the worse for the accident.

In all forms of ski-ing in Central Europe, the same principles obtain. When there is a difference it is one of degree. On the low ground grace, style and dash count for much ; on the high ground steadiness, endurance and reliability. But the joy of ski-ing lies principally in speed. It is fun to run steadily under control, but it is far greater to run fast under control, and perhaps the most thrilling of all sensations is to run so fast that you are just out of control, but in the knowledge that if the gods are good and you do not lose your head you will hold it and not fall.

If you want to get really well, if you want really to enjoy yourself, if you want the finest holiday in the world, you will

E

find it on ski, touring over the hills in winter. So much for the uninitiated. To those who have once tasted the wine there is only one final word to be said. When winter comes round again and you begin to think of the hills, remember, if you can, all that you felt when you came home the previous year. Don't forget, in the urgency of other important business, that for you there is only one thing in the world which is really important, only one thing which fills you with a great happiness. Don't forget—and it is easy to do so—how much you love ski-ing.

CHAPTER IV

COMPETITIVE SKI-ING

SPEED has had a charm for man since that first monumental discovery of the wheel, and probably for long before that. Men have raced on their feet, in chariots, on horseback, in motor-cars, ships and aeroplanes. But speed is, of course, purely relative. The tortoise, perhaps, thinks the hare runs quickly, the owner of a trotting pony would not attempt to compete with a motor-car, the train is still faster for practical purposes than the motor-car, and beside the speed at which the Schneider Trophy is won, the train is a slow machine. But what about light? Three hundred and fifty miles an hour seems fast enough for man, a police magistrate invariably condemns thirty miles an hour as excessive; light travels at 186,000 miles per second.

There seems to be a certain factor which qualifies man's interest in speed, and that is the degree to which he is part of the movement himself. For instance, it is more exciting to ride a horse at, say, thirty miles an hour than to travel in an express train at seventy. Man gets a greater sense of speed from running at twenty miles an hour—if he can—than from driving a car at thirty miles an hour. The nearer the ground you are, the more you come personally in contact with the movement, the greater sense of speed and the greater excitement you feel.

Running fast on ski, a man moves at about thirty miles an hour. Over a jump of ordinary size, the average speed is round about fifty. Timed over a prepared course in the *kilomètre lancé* at St. Moritz in 1930, G. Lantschner of Innsbruck did over sixty-six miles per hour. It is obvious, therefore, that for speed alone ski racing makes a great appeal to some innate quality in man.

Further, man is competitive—some more than others—but most with just that quality of personal vanity which delights in being able to do something a little better than another man.

Some mention of the appeal which ski-ing has to make both to the highly competitive, games-playing man and to the less competitive sport-loving man, has already been made. Most people rather resent a too competitive atmosphere, and it seems that the qualities which give a man an affection for sports rather than games are definitely less civilized, and, for that reason, infinitely more noble. After all, any fool can run about on a field and kick a football, but much more of human worth is called into play when it comes to finding and destroying the wild elephant in his native jungle. Any fool can race his friends along the level or down a hill on ski, but only the wise man can conquer the glaciers and the ice falls of the high mountains. It is difficult to say exactly where the line can be drawn, or where the finest qualities in both kinds of endeavour are called into play. In the writer's opinion, pig-sticking, of all sports, games or pastimes, may be said most perfectly to combine the truest form of sport with a good taste of competitive spirit. The wild pig is in many ways the finest of all animals, and to kill him with cold steel is an infinitely more exciting and exacting performance than anything which can be accomplished over the sights of a rifle. At the same time, you are generally riding after a pig in competition not only with the animal but with two or more fellow-men. For the same reason, races on ski seem to improve as they require of the runner an eye for country, a certain snow-craft, and a cool, calculating judgment ; and to deteriorate as they become mere mechanical exercises depending for success upon good training, expert technique and machine-like consistency.

Racing, in no matter what form, is largely artificial. A race-course is a specially constructed ground, the competitive instinct is almost invariably controlled and ordered by rules of one kind and another, and except for the race between tea-clippers homeward bound, there is no kind of speed competition which can be said to be entirely natural. But at the same time, the basis of racing is a natural basis, and races are organized so as to approach as nearly as possible to natural conditions. The fences in a point-to-point course are built so as to be as nearly like real fences as possible. Motor-car races are run along roads in conditions approaching as nearly as possible to ordinary touring conditions. Running races on foot, it is true, are unnatural and represent only in the smallest degree conditions which obtain in the open country. But then, racing on foot is probably the oldest of all kinds of racing, is consequently the most civilized, and for that reason the most artificial. The greatest form of competitive ski-ing is ski jumping, and it is also the most artificial. Nothing in ski jumping approaches the ordinary circumstances of ski-ing, and it is practised on a specially prepared hill and on an artificially constructed jump, neither of which can be used for any other purpose.

There are five kinds of competitive ski-ing—long-distance and endurance racing, downhill racing, slalom, jumping and ski joring.

I. LONG-DISTANCE AND ENDURANCE RACING

The oldest methods of racing on ski are the long-distance race (langlauf) and the endurance race (dauerlauf). Ski were first used in Scandinavia and were used for utilitarian purposes, that is to say, they were used to get about the country in winter. The postman used them, the woodcutter used them, the farmer and the hunter used them. The country in Scandinavia is not like Alpine country. It is hilly, but not so mountainous as Central Europe. Getting about on ski in the winter means sliding over the snow, now along the level, now uphill, now downhill. The first kind of ski race naturally owed its origin to the practice of the postman and the woodcutter. It was a race across country including ascent, descent and running along the flat. In early days the Lapps were the most experienced at this kind of sport. Their country was entirely flat and they used long ski and long sticks with which they pushed themselves along. They had no bindings other than a mere toe strap, and there is the famous story of the Lapp who entered for one of the first races. This race included among many kilometres of flat country the ascent and descent of a small hill. When he came to this hill the Lapp took off his ski and carried them up it and down the other side. Arrived at the finish of the race, an easy winner, he complained : " What do you call this ? It isn't ski-ing, it is bloody mountaineering ! "

Though the Holmenkolern meet is perhaps the best known, the greatest Scandinavian race of the present day is the Vasa Trophy held in Sweden over a course of about ninety-four kilometres. This course represents the route by which Gustavus Vasa escaped from Sweden in 1521.

For international purposes, there are two quite different kinds of race, the long-distance race, which in Central Europe is known as langlauf, and the endurance race which is known as dauerlauf. A langlauf is anything from 15 to 18 kilometres in length and a dauerlauf is from 50 kilometres upwards. To-day these races are run along a flagged track much as an ordinary foot race is run, each competitor following in the track of the man in front of him. No one is allowed to go more than ten metres to one side of the red flags which indicate the course. When one competitor wishes to pass another, he calls out and the one in front has to step out of the track and allow the one behind to go by him. These races are all run on a timing principle, the competitors starting at half-minute or minute intervals. They demand of those who take part in them great physical fitness and an untiring and accurate technique. They also necessitate a thorough knowledge of snow texture and waxing, combined with a gift of prophecy which enables a man to tell at, say, nine o'clock in the morning exactly what the weather will be like at midday.

The technique required for this kind of racing is nothing like so exacting as the technique required for downhill racing, the training on the other hand is much more so. A technical committee of experts sitting to decide upon the strain put upon the human frame by various sports, decided that by far the most arduous was ski racing, second to which came rowing. A steady rhythmical movement is as necessary to successful langlauf and dauerlauf as it is to running over any considerable distance, to rowing, or to any other protracted effort. There are, of course, innumerable different ways of progressing on ski, but for purposes of langlauf and dauerlauf there are certain movements which are generally accepted as the best.

For moving along the level or on a gentle gradient, either uphill or downhill, the accepted method is to advance in three steps at a time and to push with the sticks at every third step. Thus—(starting with the left foot), left, right, put the sticks in, throw the weight of the body forward on to the sticks and the left foot, and kick off with the right. Push. Again, right, left, sticks in, weight forward on to right foot ; kick off with left. Push. The effort is thus made on alternate feet, the rhythm

Plate 17

THE OLD STYLE

SEPP MUEHLBAUER JUMPING IN THE OLYMPIC GAMES AT ST. MORITZ, 1928.

—if it is possible to express such things in words—being *one* . . .
two—THREE ; *one* . . . *two*—THREE.

The kick with the rear foot is most important, but is only
effective if the weight of the body is thrown well forward and
brought down on to the front foot simultaneously with being
thrown on to the sticks. The sticks should be swung forward
and stuck into the snow in the course of the second step. They
should be on either side and as near to the two ski as possible.
The hands should be touching just in front of the face and
should meet again behind the back at the end of the push.
It is important to push not only with the arms but with the
whole weight of the body as well. Lean against the sticks as
a rower leans against his oars.

The ordinary method of climbing and sometimes, indeed, of
going along the flat, is simply to slide one ski in front of the
other in the usual movement of walking, pushing on the left
foot with the right stick and on the right with the left. This
is the most common way of moving on ski, and the most
elementary. It is the natural way in which the beginner will
walk when ski are first strapped to his feet. But there is a
considerable difference between the trained langlaufer running
uphill and the beginner waddling down the street, even though
each employ the same system of progression. There are two
things above all others to remember in this step. The first is
to lean right forward, so far forward that you are literally falling
on your sticks, and the second is the use of your sticks. These
should be pulled up from behind *across the body* and so stuck
into the snow that the first part of the ensuing push will be not
directly to the rear but slightly to one side. For example,
your right stick is trailing behind you. You bring it up
simultaneously with your left leg. Bring your right hand
across your chest until it is level with your left shoulder, then
put the stick into the snow. When you put your weight on
to the stick, it is evident that you must push your hand across
from the left side of your body to the right before you can
begin to push directly backward. By this means the best
possible use is made of the sticks and the utmost possible force
put into each push. It is important to remember in this
ordinary walking movement that each step should be as long
as possible, particularly when going uphill. For a short sprint,
however, little short running steps are very effective, but they

require very sound wax and cannot even then be kept up for any length of time.

There is a third step which is not often seen, but which consists in pushing with the right stick, not on the left leg, but on the right and vice versa. The rhythm and balance of this step is extremely difficult to master and is very tiring in practice, but, making use of it, a ski-er can get up a great swing and, for a little, move at a considerable pace.

The secret in a race is to vary the method of progress. The same step indefinitely repeated is monotonous and tiring. Let the rhythm be steady while it lasts, but let it also be varied. Push sometimes at every third, sometimes at every second, and sometimes at every fourth step.

Half the battle, both in the long-distance and in the endurance race, is the question of wax, and to examine this question in detail would necessitate a lengthy and technical treatise for which there is no room within these covers. The science of wax is a science unto itself and one which is only mastered with patience and application. The principle is a simple one. When weight is put on the ski vertically and at right angles from above, the wax must be such that the surface of the ski grips the snow. On the other hand, when weight is put on the ski at an angle, the surface of the ski must slide on the snow. Thus, going uphill, when the ski is not slid so much as stamped or held into the snow, the surface sticks. Sliding downhill it will run easily.

This result is further assisted by the shape of the ski, which is arched in the centre. The principle of waxing is to cover the toe, heel and groove of the ski with a running wax of sorts, the arch under the footplate with a climbing wax. Thus the weight of the body being taken under ordinary circumstances principally upon the toe and the heel of the ski, the ski will slide unless special weight is put upon its centre. This centre can easily be stamped or forced into the snow when climbing or when seeking a grip with which to push off when on the level. Under these circumstances the climbing wax will grip the snow. When ski have been skilfully waxed for a langlauf, the tendency is for them not to start sliding easily, but once they are started to move very fast and smoothly.

The art of waxing consists in knowing exactly what quality,

texture and amount of wax to put on what part of the ski to
suit what kind of weather conditions and snow temperature.
It is one thing to know the right combination of waxes which
will stick and slide best on, say, a warm muggy day ; it is
another thing to know that the day is definitely going to remain
warm and muggy ; it is yet another thing to know exactly
the right amount of wax to put on, and still another to know
how to put it on. These things are just a part of the science
of waxing.

Finally, some word should perhaps be said about sticks.
These should be light and strong. Cane is the best material.
Male bamboo is too heavy and female bamboo not sufficiently
strong. They should be well balanced—that is to say, they
should be easy to hold out at right angles to the body—and
in this position should put a minimum of strain on the wrist.
On the flat, long sticks are a great help, but for going uphill
they are only an encumbrance and can be most awfully tiring.
The best all-round length for an ordinary langlauf is such that
when the sticks are stuck in the snow they will reach not quite
up to the arm-pits.

Long-distance and endurance races are magnificent tests of
stamina and condition. They are races lasting from one to
seven hours and they require of those who compete in them a
perfect stick and ski technique as well as great physical strength.
But to those who have done their ski-ing in the Alps there
is something a little incongruous about these races. With the
exception of the Engadine valley, the Alpine country in Central
Europe does not lend itself to the same utilitarian use of ski
as do the snowfields of Scandinavia, and it is interesting to note
the growing popularity in Central Europe, at any rate, of
downhill and slalom racing, both of which are far more natural
to the geographical and snow conditions of Austria, Germany
and Switzerland.

II. SKI JUMPING

The most thrilling and perhaps the finest form of competitive ski-ing is ski jumping. For those who have never
seen a ski jump, let it be said at the beginning of this
chapter, that it is not a high jump, nor, as it is understood in England, a long jump. True, the distance jumped
is measured, as in a long jump, from the take-off to the

point of landing, but a considerable drop in height is also involved.

Perhaps to describe ski jumping to someone who has never seen it, the easiest thing would be to say that it resembles a competition in which the competitors are required to jump off the roof of a house and see who could jump *out* the farthest (the jumps to be measured from the edge of the roof to the point of landing). This is not an entirely fair comparison, but it approximates nearer to the truth than to say that ski jumping is like either the high or long jumping familiar to Stamford Bridge.

Those who have seen ski jumping or even a ski jump will realize that the sport is no mean one.

Fig. III is a sectional plan of the Olympiaschanze at St. Moritz, the jump over which the competition in the Olympic Games of 1928 was jumped, and which is believed to be as perfect a jump as it is possible to build.

The first thing that will be noticed is that the gradient does not appear to be very steep. This plan is a striking proof of certain facts which are not generally known and which are hard to believe about gradients. You may sometimes read graphic descriptions of slopes of fifty degrees steepness. You may often see slopes which appear to be not inaccurately describable as precipices, or you may have seen a ski track down a slope which you would scarcely have thought it possible to descend on ski at all. The facts are strangely disillusioning.

Forty-five degrees is probably the steepest slope on which snow will lie. Thirty-five degrees is a very steep slope indeed, and thirty degrees is the steepest slope which the average ski-er cares to take straight without a good deal of forethought and preparation.

The steepest part of the Olympiaschanze, it will be seen, is thirty-six degrees, and, though in profile, this slope does not look like the precipice it appears in real life, it represents, nevertheless, a very fair degree of steepness.

There are three other things which should be noticed about the plan, as they apply to the construction of all ski jumps.

The " inrun " (that is the slope of the hill above and previous to the platform) may start as steeply as possible but should flatten out gradually as the platform is reached so that the jumper is unaware of the change in gradient. A

Plate 18

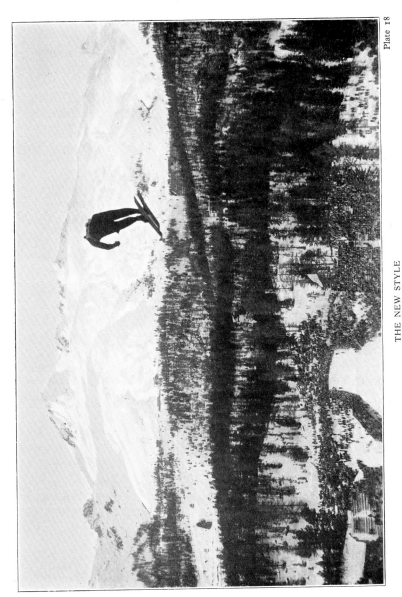

THE NEW STYLE

BRUNO TROJANI ALSO IN THE OLYMPIC GAMES, 1928.

BROMLEY PUBLIC LIBRARIES

slope which drops down steeply to the platform and flattens
out suddenly throws the jumper into the air, unsteadying
him at a moment when
he should be perfectly
balanced.

The platform itself
must be level laterally.
A platform which slopes
away either to the right
or to the left throws
the jumper into the air
crooked. It should be
level longitudinally also
or sloping a little down
the hill. It should not
slope upwards like the
platforms on many
small practice jumps,
as the jumper would
then be thrown far too
much into the air. The
height of the platform
is also important as
upon it depends largely
the length of the jump.
The height of the plat-
form on the Olympia-
schanze is about nine
feet.

A higher platform
would be dangerous as
the jumper would be
thrown out so far that
he might land on the
flat and sustain very
serious injury.

Finally, the slope of
the hill below the take-
off should be noticed.
This must not fall sud-
denly away below the

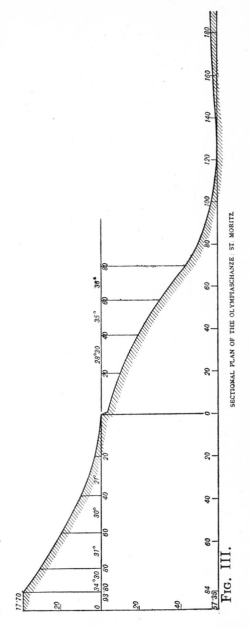

SECTIONAL PLAN OF THE OLYMPIASCHANZE, ST MORITZ

Fig. III.

platform as the jumper will then have a considerable vertical drop before he hits the ground again.

The slope of the hill should aim at following as nearly as possible the parabola described by the jumper's flight. Again, as the longer possible distances are reached, so the slope must steepen. On the Olympiaschanze, it will be seen, that a man jumping about twenty metres would land on a slope of about twenty-eight degrees, while a man jumping sixty metres would land on a slope of about thirty-five or six degrees. If a man, after jumping some forty yards and losing some fifty feet of height were to land, travelling at a speed of some fifty to seventy miles an hour, on fairly flat ground, he would break every bone in his body. It is the steepness of the slope which saves him by taking the force of the jar and thus alleviating the pressure on his legs. So much for the hill. Now for its use !

The length of a jump depends in a large degree, of course, upon the length and steepness of the inrun and the height of the platform. But given a fixed length of inrun (in competitions this is fixed, if not by the judges, then by mutual consent of the competitors), the length depends upon (*a*) timing and energy of take-off, (*b*) steadiness in the air.

A jump is no good if the jumper falls, and so its excellence must also depend upon sureness of landing. These three points (take-off, position in the air and landing) are the three things principally looked for by the judges in marking for style.

There are two quite different styles of jumping involving different technique and slightly different principles. They may be described as the old and the new style.

The old style is to approach the jump crouching right down on the back of the ski and, synchronizing the movement exactly with the edge of the platform, to straighten the body. The impetus due to the slope of the hill is a forward impetus. The effort made by the jumper is practically a vertical effort. The combination of the two decides the length of the jump. In the air, there are certain things which are characteristic of the old style. The body is very rigid and almost perpendicular, the ski are wedged tight together (and point upwards), the jumper is well on his toes and his hands are waving in a forward circular motion. (See Plate 17.) In order to land on a slope of not less than thirty degrees the jumper must get much farther forward than he was in the air after taking off. This forward lean is known as *vorlage*, and is acquired, in the old style, by the movement of the arms.

At the last moment the jumper forces the points of his ski down parallel with the slope and lands with one foot advanced and the body thrown forward with the head almost between the knees.

The old style was developed on the jumping hills of the old type. These had a high platform, a short inrun and a comparatively flat landing.

Effort in the " satz " (the technical term for the movement of taking off) and not speed was the main factor in getting length, and the landing was too flat for a great deal of *vorlage* to be necessary.

In the new style the crouch, approaching the platform, is not so low and the weight of the body instead of being on the heels is well forward and partly on the toes. The spring when the platform is reached, is a forward rather than an upward spring and the effort of the hill and the effort of the jumper are thus made in more or less the same direction. In other words, the jumper by his effort emphasizes the natural impetus of the hill, throwing himself forward into space rather than springing upwards.

In the air there are certain things which are characteristic of the new style. The body is much farther forward than in the old style and instead of being straight is often bent at the waist.

In extreme cases the top half of the body is sometimes parallel with the ski. The arms do not have to be waved strongly to acquire *vorlage*. The most expert jumpers in the new style keep their arms quite still, pointing over the heels of their ski. Those who must wave their arms to assist lateral balance, wave them very much more slowly than in the old style. The ski instead of being pointed upwards are allowed roughly to follow the contours of the hill.

They are not wedged together so tightly as in the old style, some jumpers keeping them deliberately apart so as to be able to look down in between them at the landing. The heels are kept well down on the ski. (See Plate 18.) The landing position is the same, and jumpers advance one ski so as to land in telemark position if possible, but failing which, drop naturally into a crouch with both ski side by side.

The effect of the new style is tantamount to a forward dive into space. Speed rather than effort is the factor which gives length. The body is so far forward in the air that on a small jump with a comparatively flat landing it might be impossible to hold the position without falling forward on hitting the ground. But experience has shown that on big jumps this position is safer and more productive of great length than the old.

The great secret in jumping, no matter in what style, is the perfect timing of the take-off, from which, broadly speaking, the rest follows naturally. A weak or a badly-timed satz, besides making the jumper unsteady, receives no style marks from the judges. The jumper may spring too soon or too late. He may spring crooked, to the right or to the left, or he may take off more strongly with one foot than with the other, making it impossible for him to keep his ski level and under control. In any case, unless he takes off perfectly he will be unable to concentrate on steadiness, for he will have to make frantic efforts to recover himself in the air.

Jumping competitions are judged upon a combination of length and style. The jump must be a standing one. Its length is recorded, and marks are given by two or three different judges upon the style of the performer. This system is based upon the belief that steadiness, style and beauty are as important as length. There are some who think, however, that length is all that matters and that to give marks for style in ski jumping is as foolish as to give marks for style in a downhill race or a langlauf or even an ordinary long jump on foot.

A somersault jump, perhaps the most daring feat in any sport, has been done in America by John Carleton. It is not on record whether this has been done intentionally by anyone else or not. In competitions there are often unintentional somersaults, due mainly to an error in taking off. The most sensational of these is that of J. Carlsen, a Norwegian. In 1928 he was trying on the Berninaschanze in Switzerland for the world's record and the wind got over his ski-points and turned him completely over in the air. He landed at the seventy-three-metre mark on his head which made a hole in the snow two feet deep. Miraculously enough he recovered and was able to jump again the following season.

Ski jumping is a magnificent sport and requires far more

courage and nerve than any other form of ski-ing, probably than any other form of sport. For those who have never stood at the top of a big jump it may be interesting to know that from the top nothing is visible beyond the take-off except the valley below. The landing and the slope of the hill between the platform and the valley are out of sight altogether. To be asked to go over a big jump amounts to an invitation to throw yourself over Beachy Head and to do so at very considerable speed. The average speed of a jumper over a jump is well over fifty miles an hour. Jumping is the finest possible training for ski-ing of all other kinds, and no one can call himself an accomplished ski-er until he has done a certain amount of jumping.

Five years after the War there were few Englishmen who had even been over a big jump. Jumping was looked upon with a kind of speechless awe. In the students' Olympic games at Davos in 1930 the British team was first in the first round of the jumping competition. In the final result an Englishman, John Dick of Oxford University, was fourth.

CHAPTER V

COMPETITIVE SKI-ING (*continued*)

III. DOWNHILL RACING

THE long-distance race grew up from the utilitarian use of ski in Scandinavia and, in the same way, the downhill race grew up from the practice of ski touring in Switzerland, Germany and Austria. It was inevitable that men, turning their ski downhill after a long climb and tasting the exquisite excitement of speed, should automatically find a certain satisfaction of their competitive appetite in seeing who would get to the bottom first. Downhill racing, like long-distance and endurance racing, is the result of competition in the ordinary circumstances of ski-ing.

Racing of all kinds as practised to-day is, of course, artificial. It does not follow that it is any the worse for that. The hundred and fifty yards' hurdles could not by the wildest stretch of the imagination be described as a race over a series of natural obstacles, but it is no less excellent a race in that it lacks such a description. But since races, and indeed all civilized sports, are artificial, certain rules are permissible which would not perhaps pertain to the ordinary circumstances of life. For instance, stick-riding is not allowed in downhill racing. Ski-ing, as first taught in Central Europe, depended very largely, if not entirely, upon the use of a single stick. Against this practice an uncompromising attack was launched by a later school of ski-ers. Subsequently, and when the bitterness of controversy was passed, it was admitted that under certain circumstances stick-riding for utilitarian purposes was desirable. For instance, those who ski a great deal amongst the high peaks often have recourse to their sticks, and what is of service in times of emergency cannot be altogether rotten. The objection to stick-riding is that it is bad fun, that it produces not the brave, accomplished ski-runner, but the timid, safety-first type, and that it is not æsthetic. On the low ground the ski-runner can afford to study style, and for racing

Plate 19

"THE START OF A DOWNHILL RACE"

THE COMPETITORS HAVE STARTED SIMULTANEOUSLY FROM THE TOP OF THE RISE ON THE LEFT OF THE PHOTO. NOTE THE DIFFERENT STYLES THOUGH ALL RUN WITH FEET APART.

in particular, courage and skill are necessary. Therefore, in a perfectly arbitrary manner, stick-riding is against the rules in nearly all downhill races. The rule is arbitrary in the same way that holding your opponent's arms is an arbitrary rule in boxing, and the disallowment of tripping is an arbitrary rule in football. The former is a better fight without holding. The latter a better game without tripping. Ski-ing is a better sport without stick-riding.

There are three recognized ways of starting a downhill race on ski. It may be started, like the Derby, all competitors lined up abreast, all starting on the word " Go," and the first through the winning-posts acclaimed the winner. Or it may be started, as long-distance races are started, at intervals. Competitors are given numbers, and started at intervals of, say, 15, 20 or 60 seconds. The time is taken when each passes the winning-post, and the result of the race calculated by comparison between the starter's figures and the figures of the man recording the times at the winning-post. The advantages of the first method are obvious. It is simple and there can be no dispute about the result. Competing in such a race, the ski-runner has the advantage of knowing exactly where he is. On the other hand, in the confusion and crush of the start, it is possible that an excellent, if not too strong, competitor may be almost trodden underfoot and certainly jockeyed out of an advantageous position.

The advantage of the second method is that it gives scope to the unhindered, individual ability of each competitor, who can run down the course at whatever pace he likes and need fear no tiresome intervention from his fellow-competitors. The disadvantages of this method are that, from the runner's point of view, it is not so exciting, as he cannot tell until the figures are worked out whether he is first or last. Secondly, that it needs a good deal more organization in the way of accurate time-keeping, synchronization of watches and mathematical calculation. And thirdly, that though it may be an admirable form of competition and a fine test of ski-ing technique and quality, it is not in any real sense of the word a race.

There is a third method, which is a compromise between the first two. This method is known as the " Hindmarsh start," and necessitates a race being run in two parts, the first of which should be a good deal shorter than the second. For

F

the first part of the race the competitors are started at intervals, and their time for the descent accurately worked out. The second part is started on the handicap basis of the first part. Thus, if a competitor, A, took six seconds longer over the first part than a competitor B, he would start, in the second half of the race, six seconds after B. Before the start of the second part each competitor is told what his handicap is—it may be six seconds, sixteen or sixty. The starter then starts the scratch man and counts out the seconds thereafter from his stop-watch. Each competitor starts as the handicap is called out. For instance, B in the above case would start when the starter called out " six." The first man through the winning-posts is the winner.

The Hindmarsh start obviates some of the objections to the first method, by which all competitors start together. Its disadvantage is that it necessitates a race being run in two parts.

There are three ways of starting a downhill race, but there is only one way of running in it. Ski as fast and as straight as you possibly can. (See Plate 20.)

There are, however, two schools, each with a theory as to the best method of putting this fundamental truth into practice. Dr. Walter Amstutz, a very well-known Swiss runner, is credited with the epigram : " When you ski, race ; when you race, ski." This theory is put into practice by W. R. Bracken, who, if he will forgive me for saying so, is a first-class ski-er who happens to have learnt to race. The gist of Amstutz's saying and of Bracken's ski-ing is that technique is the all-important thing. In a race, don't fall : don't lose your head : don't blind hopelessly down a precipice : don't attempt the impossible. Do these things in practice if you like, but in a race ski at your fastest safety speed and avoid risks where the odds are heavily weighted against you. Bracken and Amstutz are both teachers of this school and have both put its doctrines continuously and successfully into practice. Indeed, in racing against each other it has generally been found that if one makes the mistake of falling the other wins, and vice versa.

The other school maintains that in a race there is only one thing to do, and that is to race. The principal advocate and exponent of this doctrine is C. E. W. Mackintosh, who, if he will forgive my saying so, is a natural racer who happens to

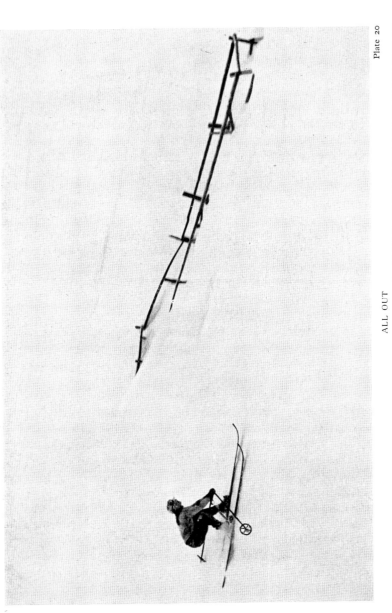

Plate 20

ALL OUT

THIS IS A PERFECT STRAIGHT-RACING POSITION.   A REASONABLE CROUCH, WEIGHT ON THE HEELS, ONE SKI ADVANCED, FEET SLIGHTLY APART, HANDS
LOW AND FORWARD.

have learnt to ski. The gist of its tenets is—certainly don't
fall, if you can help it, but don't avoid speed for fear of a fall ;
don't lose your head if you can help it, but probably you will
not be able to avoid it ; blind down every precipice, not hopelessly, but with hopeful determination ; not only attempt but
also achieve the impossible.

When the best exponents of these two doctrines meet there
is very little to choose between them. They both run every
slope straight and they none of them look like falling. What
the one calls his racing speed the other calls his highest safety
speed, but if one must pronounce between the two (and in
this book it is, after all, my duty to write down what I believe
to be the best advice) the dice would seem to be slightly
weighted in favour of the Mackintosh school.

Assume the impossible precipice. A precipice is impossible
not because it is steep but because there is no run out to it.
The exponents of the one school will take it at their fastest
safety speed, probably putting in two or three turns. The
exponents of the other school will take it straight and fall at
the bottom. If they do this and only fall at the bottom, and
fall well and get up quickly, they will on the whole defeat the
exponents of the first school. But here comes the rub. Most
of the people who take the precipice straight will do so as a
forlorn but desperate hope, and they will not really expect to
stand. Consequently they will fall *before the bottom* and be
hopelessly beaten by the exponent of the other school. There
are not many people who have the nerve and the speed sense
to hold a very fast slope straight in the course of a very fast
race, and fall only when and where they mean to. And yet
there is nothing to upset a ski-er in speed alone, and though it
may be necessary to fall at the end of the run, there should
be no reason for falling before. Practice, however, has shown
that most people under such circumstances *do* fall, fall too soon
and fall out of control. While the tenets of the Bracken school
are probably the best to adopt at the start of a racing career,
and will probably give more successful results to the ski-er
until he has reached a certain pitch of excellence, there seems
little doubt that in open competition the second theory is the
better, and its principles on the whole the more sound. After
all, and with all due apologies to Dr. Amstutz, the best way
to race is to race. The shortest way down any slope is the

straightest, and, given a good speed sense, any slope can be
held at least to the bottom.

It is a surprising fact, but people racing, all out, gloriously
out of control, oblivious to all that is going on around them,
have a remarkable way of standing on the impossible slope,
holding the incredible turn and bringing off the altogether
spectacular and unbelievable piece of ski-running.

But among ordinary folk, there is not the least doubt that
the fast, steady runner always beats the courageous but inexperienced man who hurls himself without hesitation over
the fiercest precipices and takes the most indescribable of falls.
The essence of downhill racing is that each individual must
work out his own maximum speed, accommodating himself
to the ground over which he travels, choosing his best line
and taking what risks he thinks worth while.

So much for downhill racing. The prize goes to the fastest
runner, and the fastest runner is generally the best runner.
Downhill racing, like all racing, is an artificial sport, but it is
a very fair test of a man's ski-ing ability in general and of his
Alpine technique in particular. Also, it is tremendous fun.

IV. THE SLALOM

A slalom race is shorter in distance than an ordinary downhill race, and is designed to test not so much a runner's speed
across country as his ability to turn quickly among obstacles.
It is a far more artificial form of competition than a straight
race, and it requires no snow-craft, no eye for country, though
a considerable amount of judgment. Suppose an ordinary
run on ski to be a descent of some five thousand feet, four of
which were over comparatively open country, and one of which
was through trees. A straight race would test a ski-runner's
speed and ability in descending such a course. It would prove
that he was fast over open country, safe among the trees, and
could combine running equally over the four and over the
one thousand feet with substantial success. The slalom is
designed to test his speed and ability through the trees alone.
It is, so to speak, a section of the straight race, a small but all-
important part of an ordinary day's ski-ing in Alpine country.

A slalom course may be anything from three to fifteen
hundred feet in length (" in length," of course, means in
vertical descent) and the place of trees or other natural objects

Plate 21

NEAR THE END OF A DOWNHILL RACE

MANŒUVRING FOR THE GAP IN A FENCE.

will be taken by flags. It is, if you like, a short downhill race
with a proportionately vast number of controls. But its value
as a test of ski-ing, and indeed its interest as a sport, entirely
depends upon the setting of the course. That indeed is the
only objection to slalom racing, that as it is highly artificial,
it requires someone with knowledge of the art to make it
effective. It is perfectly easy to stick flags into a snow slope
in such a way that competitors must turn between them and
may have difficulty in so doing. But it is a matter of some
artistic attainment so to stick the flags that they present a series
of obstacles very like natural obstacles in a wood, and thus
provide a good test of ski-running. (See Plate 22.)

In slalom races the flags are arranged in pairs, and both the
competitor's feet must pass over a straight line drawn between
the two flags. Each competitor runs down the course in turn
and is timed in so doing. He must pass through each pair of
flags, and if he omits one, he will be disqualified. There are
penalties (i.e. the addition of so many seconds to his time) for
such a fault, as going through a pair of flags with only one foot,
etc. The full rules of slalom racing may be found in the British
Racing Rules, published by the Ski Club of Great Britain.
The man who runs down the course in the shortest aggregate
time is the winner.

In slalom racing it is essentially technique that counts.
Here the Bracken-Amstutz school comes into its own. It
never pays to try and do a slalom course in record time.
Often have I heard people about to start down a slalom say,
" I don't care what happens. I'm going to have a crack at it."
Never have I seen anyone, having so spoken, do anything but
an absolutely rotten time. Canny is the secret of slalom. It
is the saved fractions of a second that count and not the whole
minutes attempted to be saved. Exact judgment of angle and
of pace, the minimum amount of turn and the least possible
check to speed, weight of the body, effort when effort would
appear to be needless—these are the things that count in a
slalom. An error in a straight race may be remedied.
An error in a slalom is irremediable. (See Plate 23.)

Since the setting of a slalom course is of such vital importance,
it may not be out of place in this connection to give a few
illustrations of possible variations.

The object of a slalom is to imitate as nearly as possible

natural wood running conditions, and to test a ski-runner's proficiency under such conditions. To each of the figures illustrating the various arrangement of flags for a slalom course I have added a supplementary figure showing the kind of natural conditions which the arrangement is designed to test. Thus Fig. III is what in slalom language is called a Straight Flush. Fig. IIIa is an example of a wood glade, such as may often be met on tour, and of ability to negotiate which the Straight Flush is a fair test. The gradient of the slope, in each case, may be assumed at between 25° and 30°.

Fig. IV is an example of how not to set a slalom. In it the flags are arranged symmetrically and require of the ski-runner easy, symmetrical turns. The flags in Fig. IV bear not the slightest resemblance to any kind of natural obstacles at all.

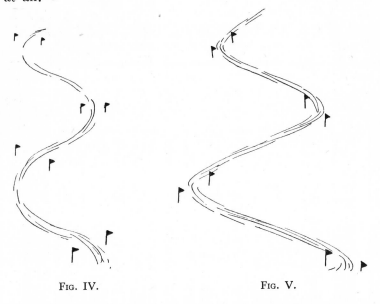

FIG. IV.   FIG. V.

Fig. V is simply to illustrate what are known as blind flags. These are so arranged that instead of being, as in Fig. IV, at right angles to the course along which the competitor is travelling, they are parallel to it and therefore " blind " to him.

Fig. VI is a Straight Flush. It is designed to test a runner's ability to do sharp, short radius turns from a steep, direct descent, sometimes known as the " drop and check principle."

The line alpha shows the course along which a first-class competitor will travel. The line beta shows a second-class

FIG. VI.   FIG. VII.

course. Fig. VII represents a glade between trees, and here

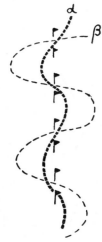

again the quickest way down is shown by the line alpha ; a safer, but less skilled, route by the line beta. It will be seen that the Straight Flush exactly tests the kind of running required for negotiating such a glade as that shown in Fig. VII.

Fig. VIII is a Short Flush. It is obvious that this arrangement tests a runner's ability to take the shortest possible line through thick trees. Running through real trees, most people would probably swing out much farther to the right or to the left, following the course beta. But the line alpha represents the shortest and quickest route.

Fig. IX is a Hairpin Bend. The lines

FIG. VIII.   alpha and beta show clearly the difference

between the course taken by a first- and second-class runner.
The line alpha necessitates only one turn on the part of the
runner, the line beta three.   The flags X and Y are necessary
to prevent a runner from taking the line gamma, and so avoiding the object of the whole arrangement.   Fig. X, again,
shows the kind of natural wood running which will require of
the ski-runner exactly that kind of turn which is tested by
the Hairpin Bend.

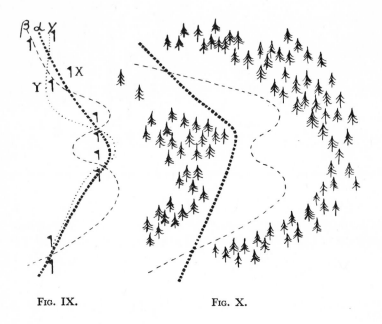

FIG. IX.   FIG. X.

Fig. XI is a Corridor and Fig. XIII a Stem Glade.   The
difference between the two is that the Stem Glade is shorter
and the turn at the bottom sharper.   The Corridor may be
taken straight with a sharp turn at the bottom which will carry
the runner out between the flags X and Y.   In Fig. XII it
will be seen that the Glade through the wood has a run-out,
though not a straight run-out.   It would be possible to run
the Glade straight, turn sharply at the bottom, and continue
down the second Glade shown as G II.   To the Glade in
Fig. XIV there is no run-out except the path.   The Glade is
steep and narrow.   It is not possible to do turns down it, as
there is not room to turn.   The only way to negotiate this kind

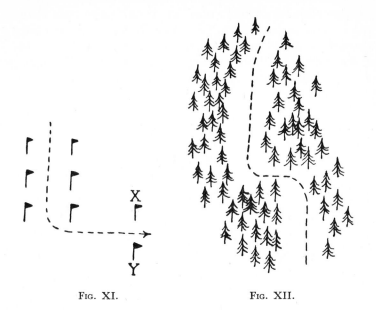

FIG. XI.   FIG. XII.

of country is by descending in a straightforward stemming
position. The Stem Glade in Fig. XIII tests this kind of

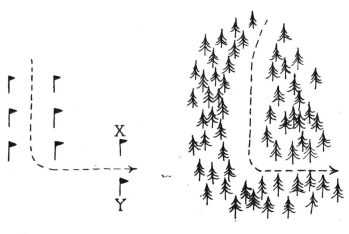

FIG. XIII.   FIG. XIV.

running. The flags X and Y must be placed well to the right of the last pair of flags in the Glade and on nearly the same level. A runner who runs the Glade straight in real life would crash into the trees. A runner who runs it straight in the slalom will overshoot the flags X and Y and have to climb back. This will cost him a great deal of time, and in a first-class slalom invariably destroy his chances of winning.

These are only a few of the possible arrangements of flags in a slalom race. They must, of course, be combined to make a good and difficult course. But these few illustrations will serve to show that the business of setting a slalom needs thought, and that just to stick a lot of flags at random into a slope and require the competitors to turn between them is not to test their ski-running ability at all.

v. SKI JORING

In a companion volume to this, Colonel Geoffrey Brooke has admirably explained that mysterious thing—the way of man with a horse. Ski joring should perhaps have found a place in that volume rather than in this. It is one thing to ride a horse and another to drive a horse, but riding a horse necessitates being on its back, and driving a horse presupposes that you are seated or standing in some vehicle which the horse is drawing. Neither of these things is true of ski joring. Again, if it is difficult to ride a horse seated firmly with a leg on each side of his back, if there is an art in driving a horse even when perched firmly upon some cart or carriage, there must be a still greater skill than either of these in controlling the same animal without either direct contact or purchase of any kind against a concrete vehicle. Ski joring consists in driving behind a horse on ski, and necessitates the mastery of such skill as this perform-ance must inevitably demand.

If a certain technique connected with the equine sciences is necessary, no description of it will be found here. This chapter is concerned not with the horse or the method of controlling it but with the man on ski behind it.

" Tailing " behind a sleigh, a motor or even an aeroplane is becoming common enough. It demands of the ski-er who indulges in it no more than a good sense of balance, an ability to break at will and the good sense to let go of his rope when

all else fails (or, in the case of the aeroplane, when the machine
actually leaves the ground).

Ski joring proper is a competitive sport, and consists in racing
on ski behind horses. (See Plate 24.)

The speed attained in this kind of race is naturally considerable, and the difficulty of controlling the horse no doubt great.

The ski-er holds on to a bar from which traces run to the
horse's collar. In the other hand he holds the reins. To
control the horse he must be able to check against the direction
in which he is travelling, and for this the most useful method is
to stem. When speed has been greatly decreased the stem
may be turned into a christiania and the horse stopped.

Races are run round a marked course and are won by the
skill with which the corners are turned and the horse controlled, much as in an ordinary race on horseback. Ski joring
requires considerable nerve, but once a certain standard of
ski-ing ability is attained relapses more into a question of horse
sense than ski sense, and for that reason cannot find any further
place in these chapters.

Other Ski Racing

Team races are also run on ski, the conditions varying with
each kind of race. Sometimes the race is between teams, all
members of which must pass the winning-post before the team
can score. Sometimes the race is a relay race.

There are also no-fall races, in which a single fall (or it may
be two or three falls) disqualifies a competitor. And finally
there are races which combine the points of long-distance
and of downhill racing.

There is one obvious difficulty in the way of the latter kind
of race. A short piece of uphill work may take the fastest
competitor ten minutes and the slowest twenty. A piece of
downhill running, double the height, may take the fastest
competitor one minute and the slowest three. Suppose one
man to be the fastest downhill and the slowest up, it is obvious
that he will gain two minutes on the descent and lose ten on
the ascent, finishing second (if there are only two in the race)
by eight minutes. This is purely a hypothetical case, but it
is obvious that whenever an effort is made to combine downhill
and long-distance technique, the advantage is all with the
long-distance specialist.

Races which include downhill, uphill and level ground have
sometimes been run on the following lines : A certain fast
average time is arbitrarily decided upon for a particular bit
of uphill climbing. For instance, there may be, in the course
of the race, an ascent of 1,000 feet. Fifty minutes is the time
decided upon by the judges that each competitor is allowed
for this section of the course. Any competitor who covered
the 1,000 feet of climbing in less than fifty minutes would gain
nothing. Any who took longer than fifty minutes would be
penalized to the extent of his extra time. The advantage of
this method is that it enables uphill and level ground to be
included in a downhill race without putting a disproportionate
premium on long-distance technique.

The disadvantage of the method is that it requires a good
deal of organization.

There are many other kinds of races held on ski, such as
obstacle races, roped races, etc. All these are but variations
of the same principles.

Some mention of the part played by the British in the world
of downhill racing has already been made in the chapter on the
history of ski-ing, but it would not be possible to conclude this
chapter without referring to the Kandahar Ski Club whose
home is at Murren. There are ski clubs founded and run by
Englishmen all over Europe and in many other parts of the
world as well. These clubs have the object of bringing together
those interested in ski-ing, and they are all affiliated to the
central organization, the Ski Club of Great Britain. There
are, further, the British Langlauf Club and the British Ski
Jumping Club, instituted comparatively recently to encourage
those respective branches of competitive ski-ing. But the
Kandahar Club, which has devoted its whole time to the
business of racing, alone enjoys an international reputation.

It was formed to encourage ski racing and, though it boasts
one cup for langlauf, its activities have been all in the field of
downhill and slalom racing. Membership of the club necessitates a fairly high standard of ski-running, and races are held
under its auspices throughout the winter, races of all kinds
and for all grades of proficiency, from the Scaramanga Cup
which is a roped race, to the Inferno Challenge Trophy which
is the longest downhill race in existence. There may be some
—there are probably many—who do not hold with the joys of

Plate 22

THE BEGINNING OF A SLALOM

A COMPETITOR IS NEGOTIATING THE FIRST PAIR OF FLAGS HAVING JUST STARTED FROM THE TOP OF
THE RIDGE.   THE THREE MEN WATCHING GIVE SOME IDEA OF THE SLOPE OF THE HILL.

racing on ski, those who prefer the pleasures of mountaineering and touring. But this much will be admitted by all—that the effect of racing on ski and the influence of the Kandahar Club has raised, in a few years, the standard of British ski-running to a height which would not previously have been believed.

Steadiness is perhaps the hall-mark of good decent ski-ing. On tour and particularly in the mountains, steadiness is absolutely essential. But the essence of really first-class ski-ing is speed and abandon, and where many may attain a good sound standard of steadiness, these things are the prerogative of a few. The contribution which downhill racing has made to ski-ing, and to English ski-ing in particular, is that it has taught people to ski with dash, courage and self-confidence. A whole lifetime of touring on ski might never produce a runner who was literally a joy to watch, whereas a week's racing will sometimes improve a man's ski-ing out of all recognition. There is no finer school in which to learn how to ski than the racing school, even for those who, at heart, prefer less competitive forms of sport in general and ski-ing in particular.

The racing fraternity is a growing one in Central Europe. It breeds fine ski-ing and fosters the best possible international relations. That, if any were needed, is its justification.

CHAPTER VI

EQUIPMENT

Clothes.

TO give some hints on equipment is the best that this
chapter can hope to do. There is no such thing as a
standard equipment for ski-ing, although every retail
shop in every town in Europe may assure its customers to the
contrary. But, sartorially speaking, ski-ing gives to those who
practise it an opportunity which appeals enormously to both
sexes. For women, ski-ing is an opportunity for wearing their
very newest and most fashionably designed clothes. For men,
it affords the equal opportunity of wearing their very oldest
and most disreputable clothes. That is a virtue which every
sport may not claim. If I was asked to give my advice as to
what clothes were the most suitable to ski in, I should say to
a woman: " Go to any shop you fancy. Choose what you think
the most artistic and what you are told is the latest design in
ski-ing suits."—(I have never yet met a woman who did not
think the latest also the most artistic fashion)—" Buy it, wear
it, rejoice in it. Throw it away, and next year repeat the
process." To a man I should say, " Go to your cupboards
and drawers. Seek out your favourite and oldest clothes,
which you are not allowed to wear at home. Take them with
you. Wear them. Rejoice in them. Bring them home, and
next year repeat the process." But judging from the appearance of the men and women whom I have seen ski-ing, this
advice is, I think, superfluous.

There are, however, certain accepted standards in clothes
to which I suppose tribute should be paid in a chapter of this
kind. For instance, wool is considered a bad medium to place
in contact with snow. A girl once indulged her sartorial
appetite by buying a ski-ing suit manufactured in the most
exquisite taste from a great quantity of yellow wool. The price
which she paid for this æsthetic outburst (quite apart from the
price she paid to its creators) was to overhear, as she finally

Plate 23

C. E. W. MACKINTOSH IN THE ARLBERG KANDAHAR SLALOM

THE IMPRESSION OF POWER, ENERGY AND SPEED CREATED BY THIS PHOTO NEED NO EMPHASIS.

reached the bottom of some hill, the remark, " Mais ce n'est pas une femme. C'est une boule de neige." There is no doubt that snow does tend to cling desperately to wool, but at the same time a large number of very experienced ski-ers always wear a sweater for the practice of their favourite art. A sweater is warm and comfortable and no better garment has yet been invented in which to practise any sport. But the limit below which a covering of wool should perhaps not be allowed to extend is the waist. To cover the nether limbs, trousers are generally accepted as the most suitable form of clothing. Some people like to have something tight round the knees and prefer riding-breeches. But for riding-breeches or trousers the material should be a smooth one, though here again the advice is perhaps superfluous, as there are few trousers or riding-breeches which I have ever seen made of wool. For women, trousers made baggy round the ankles are to my mind more artistic, and for men trousers which taper as they get longer and fit tight round the ankle. For both, dark blue is the best colour. But these things are matters of personal taste, and from the point of view of ski-ing there is nothing to choose between them.

Gloves.

Gloves are considered an important part of the ski-er's outfit and by none more important than by those who make them. The arctic design with no fingers is the type most favoured and these are certainly the warmest. On the other hand, it is extremely difficult to do anything useful with your hands if you wear gloves with no fingers. It is sometimes quite warm in Switzerland and a great many people do not wear gloves at all. But without gloves, a fall on crusted or hard snow is very apt to cut your hands, and owing to the high altitudes and the consequent thinness of the air, cuts take a long time to heal up. To those who suffer from a poor circulation and whose hands tend to feel the cold very readily, a spare pair of gloves is a good thing to carry in a rucksack.

The Rucksack.

People who intend to do much touring should certainly provide themselves with a rucksack. The most comprehensive variety is that which is built up on a metal frame and of which the weight is supported not only by shoulder-straps but also by a belt round the waist. I would advise anyone who is likely to need a rucksack to wait until they have had some experience and seen what they want, and then to buy it on the spot. For any extended or prolonged tour the following things are recommended in Mr. d'Egville's *Modern Ski-ing* as worthy of a place in the rucksack :

1. A spare tip. A ski, the point of which gets broken, is a most unmanageable impediment. There are many ingenious and useful contrivances for attaching to the point of a broken ski.

2. Wax. Ski wax, which is rubbed on to the surface of the ski, is absolutely necessary for snow which is warm or exceptionally heavy. This prevents the ski from sticking.

3. A scraper. The object of a scraper is, curiously enough, to scrape snow which has stuck to it from the bottom of your ski.

4. Copper wire for mending broken bindings.

5. A spare binding.

6. A pair of dry warm gloves.

7. Brandy.

8. Good supply of chocolate. Chocolate is the most sustaining of all foods and, if you were to get snowed up, perhaps the greatest need is for saccharine matter of some kind.

9. Dark spectacles. The glare of bright sun on the unrelieved whiteness of the snow is often unbearable.

10. A crêpe bandage, strapping plaster and morphia tablets in case of accidents.

11. A knife.

12. A compass.

To which I would add :

13. A map.

14. A spare sweater.

Ski.

The business of choosing ski is not an easy one and to differentiate between good and less good ski is a question of technical knowledge.

Ski must, of course, vary in accordance with the different uses to which they are to be put. For instance, langlauf ski should be narrow and light, downhill-racing ski broad and heavy. But certain things are fairly common to all kind of ski and should be borne in mind when you are thinking of

buying. Ski should have plenty of give in them. They should
not be too stiff and unyielding. The running surface should
be as smooth as possible and the grain of the wood, like the
grain of a cricket bat, straight and even. The best place to
feel the roughness or smoothness of the grain is on the bend
where the ski begin to turn up in front. The wood is sometimes a little rough here and if the grain is not first-rate the
surface, instead of being smooth to the touch, will be felt to
be lumpy and coarse. The points should turn up the same
amount. Lean the ski against a wall, so that their heels are
exactly together. You will then be able to see whether the
amount of turn-up is the same for each ski or not.

For langlauf a special thin ski is made in Norway, very light
and fast. Birch wood is not as good as hickory. Langlauf
ski should have plenty of spring, that is, arch, in the centre
of the ski. This prevents lateral movement and generally
holds the snow better. Also ski with lots of spring are more
easily waxed for long-distance racing.

For downhill racing ski should be broad and as heavy as the
owner can wear them without losing control. The more spring
they have the better will they hold the snow for straight
running, but the harder will they be for turning. For slalom,
ski should have practically no spring and be a little shorter than
for straight running. *Very* short ski are not easier to turn in
proportion to their shortness, and something of steadiness is
definitely lost.

Broad ski are tiring to climb in, and therefore not perhaps
the best for long tours. On the other hand, they are far the
best for running downhill. The tourer must decide whether
he will climb in greater comfort and use lighter, narrower ski,
or concentrate on the downhill part of his expedition and
bear with heavy ski on the climb. For ordinary purposes the
length of ski should be such that standing upright the owner
can just touch the top of them with his fingers. For slalom,
slightly shorter, and for downhill racing, a little longer ski are
advisable.

Bindings.

There are various ways of attaching ski to the feet. These
are known as bindings. To describe every known kind of
binding would take an infinitely long time and help no one in

particular. The toe of the boot only is attached to the ski. The heel should have plenty of longitudinal but no latitudinal play. There are four principles which underlie the better-known types of binding. They are :

1. The spring binding. This has an artificial sole which hinges on to the ski and is attached to the sole of the boot by some system of straps.

2. The Huitfeld binding. This consists of a toe iron which goes through the wood of the ski, and a strap which fastens round the heel of the boot. This strap also passes through the wood of the ski.

3. The Alpina binding. The toe iron in this binding, instead of passing through the wood, is clamped on to the top of the ski. The strap which passes round the heel of the boot is fastened to the toe iron.

4. The BB binding and its fellows. The principle of this binding is quite different. The toe iron may be either Huit-feld, Alpina, or any other kind. A hook is fastened permanently to the toe of the boot. A clip is fastened to the ski in front of the toe iron. This clip fixes on to and holds fast to the hook on the toe of the boot.

All these principles have something in their favour and something against them. The spring binding is generally out of use now. The advantage of the Huitfeld principle is that greater control is obtained by having the iron passing through the ski. The disadvantage is that the ski is weakened by being pierced. The Alpina principle is intended to avoid this defect. The toe iron is more easily adjustable than with the Huitfeld and is more comfortable too, but something is undoubtedly lost in control. The BB principle is simple and effective. It is less inclined to come off than any other binding. But it is not strong enough in itself to ensure perfect control, and it is as well to have a strap of some sort round the heel of the boot in addition. These principles can be variously combined, and indeed some combination of them all is probably the most effective. It is best for whatever strap passes round the heel of the boot to pass also through the wood of the ski. The heel of the boot is thus kept down and greater control results. For downhill and slalom racing, at least two good bindings are advisable. A ski which comes off is bound to lose a competitor the race.

SKI-JORING

A RACE ON THE LAKE AT ST. MORITZ.

Plate 24

The lapthong binding, perhaps, deserves some mention. It consists of a single raw-hide thong passing through the wood of the ski, and being fastened round the boot in a manner at once fascinating and highly technical. It takes ages to put on, but is said to be both safe (because it stretches in the event of a nasty fall) and secure once it is fixed.

Amstutz springs are an immense help in downhill running and especially for doing gelandesprungs and quersprungs. They are attached round the ankle by a strap and fastened on to the ski behind the footplate. They keep the heel of the boot down without making it rigid and they assist control quite unbelievably. Once you have got used to them it is almost impossible to ski without them.

One rule is common to all bindings. There must be absolutely no lateral movement of any kind once the boot has been attached to the ski. People differ as to the amount of longitudinal movement, but they are agreed that it is impossible to ski if you can move your boot at all without moving your ski too. A good rule is—" Have as much longitudinal movement as possible, but no lateral movement."

Sticks.

Various views are held as to the correct length of sticks. For a langlauf in which there is any amount of climbing, these should come up to just below the arm-pits. For ordinary downhill running and for touring the best length is about shoulder high, though many people have them shorter. Sticks must be well balanced and must " come up " easily in the same sense that a cricket bat or a tennis racket " comes up." Sticks that are heavy at the bottom are extremely tiring to the hands and wrists.

Boots.

It is essential to have a large pair of boots to ski in. There are many patterns of ski boots possessing various advantages and disadvantages, but there is little to choose between them. Whatever they are like, they must be large enough to wear an extra pair of thick socks under, as well as hose, or half hose (see any advertisement for stockings or socks). I have only known one man who skied in ordinary boots, but he was in every way exceptional, and, had he skied with bare feet, he

would have been a joy to watch.   His is not an example to be
followed.

Wax.

When a Foehn wind is blowing, or when the snow is thawing
for any other reason, the running surface of ski tend to stick
instead of slide smoothly.   Similarly, it is generally fairly warm
when new snow is falling, and after or during a heavy fall the
snow is sticky, with the same result.   In order to make your
ski slide properly under these conditions, it is necessary to rub
wax on them.   Wax may be rubbed in with the hand or with
a cork.   Alternatively, it may be ironed in with a hot iron.
There is considerable art in waxing ski and in knowing exactly
what kind of wax is required by exactly what texture and
consistency of snow.   But this is an art for the technical expert
and the racer in particular.

Generally speaking, the important thing in new snow is to
concentrate on getting an absolutely smooth surface, polished
like glass.   For wet warm snow which is thawing, the quantity
of wax is probably more important than the surface.   Paraffin
wax which is white and soft like a candle is very widely used,
because it can easily be rubbed on and that when the surface
of the ski is still wet.   But, by the same token, paraffin wax
can easily be rubbed off by the snow, and always is !   It is
useful in wet warm snow, and indeed on all occasions gives a
feeling of confidence, even if it does not materially increase
the speed of the ski.

For practical purposes, the best thing to do is to take your
ski, when conditions necessitate their being waxed, to the
ski shop and pay fifty centimes for having the wax put on for
you.   This is the method adopted by many, if not all, the
best downhill runners.

First Aid.

In conclusion I would say to those who are wondering what
they should take with them, in the way of First Aid outfits, etc.,
that the need for these is no greater in ski-ing than on a walking
tour, a motor journey, or a day's shooting.   I have found
iodine, cold cream and sticking plaster useful in Switzerland,
but I have also found them very useful in England, Scotland
and elsewhere.   The best medical advice I have ever known,

from a ski-ing point of view, was frequently given me by one of the finest ski-ers I have ever seen, John Carleton. Carleton was a great jumper, and he took peculiar pleasure in jumping farther than anyone else, though he more often than not failed to stand on landing. He would approach the jump with a set purpose, and he rose at it as a tiger at its kill. He would land some ten metres farther down the slope than anyone else, with so terrific a crash that often as not he sprained an ankle or wrenched a knee. On these occasions he would remark slowly, " Oh, Hell ! ", take off his ski and at once climb up to the very highest point of the hill again. I once wrenched my knee so painfully that the next day I could only walk with the utmost difficulty and disgust. Carleton said, " Oh, Hell ! " and took me to the top of the highest hill he could find. I ski-ed all day and in the evening my knee was as sound as the other one. I commend Carleton as a medical adviser to all who venture afield on ski. But failing Carleton, and if you are in doubt, consult a doctor.

To end a dissertation on ski-ing with the word " doctor " is about as pointful as to end a description of a rugger match with the word " operation." But this is a chapter on equipment and in such a chapter all contingencies should be allowed for. If you like to carry a doctor in your rucksack, well, you will be on the safe side.

S K I - I N G   E X E R C I S E S

The muscles used in ski-ing are quite different from the muscles used in the practice of any other sport. Excellent condition for running is not necessarily excellent condition for ski-ing except in so far as wind is concerned. Some people like to prepare themselves for unaccustomed exercise by Swedish and other exercises, though it is very doubtful if much advantage is derived thereby. In his book *Modern Ski-ing*, Mr. d'Egville 'suggests a series of exercises together with illustrations which people who believe in such things might be well advised to study.

The principal muscle exercised in ski-ing, and not otherwise generally used, runs down the front of the leg just outside the shin bone. This muscle is used for raising the point of the ski by pushing down with the heel and against the toe strap with the top of the toe. In running downhill it is continually in use for the preservation of longitudinal balance. The following exercises are suggested to prepare it for the more arduous business of ski-ing.

I. Stand upright on the heels, the left foot slightly advanced. Keeping the heel on the ground try and touch your left knee with the top of your left toe, and then rest the foot flat on the ground again. Repeat this about a hundred times with each foot.

II. If you have your ski at home, get them out and sit down on a chair in a normal position with your toes in the toe straps and the heel of the ski underneath the chair on which you are sitting. Have a table or the back of another chair about a foot off the points of the ski. Then, keeping your heel down on the footplate of the ski, raise its point and touch the top of the table (or the back of the chair). Bring the ski back into place and repeat the movement with the other foot. Do this about twenty times with each foot.

The same muscle is exercised by hanging by your feet from a trapeze or from wall bars, if gymnastic apparatus is available. It is also exercised in riding astride when you force your toe up to tighten the thigh and leg muscles to grip into the saddle.

The stomach muscles are also used in ski-ing and can be exercised in the usual ways.

III. Lie on your back, hands on hips. Raise your feet slowly off the ground and without bending the knees touch the ground at the back of your head. Then bring them slowly forward again to within about three inches of the ground. Do this really slowly three times if you can.

IV. Lie on your back, hands on hips, and raise both feet about three inches off the ground. Without bending the knees raise first one leg and then the other till it is at right angles to your prostrate body. Do this about twenty times, never letting your feet touch the ground.

There are other and innumerable exercises for developing the stomach muscles and they are all useful to the ski-er.

Further exercises for developing the leg muscles are as follows.

V. Stand facing a chair and put one foot on the chair. Raise yourself on that foot until you are standing upright on the chair with your weight still on the one leg. Then lower yourself again. Repeat this about twenty to thirty times on each leg.

VI. Choose a time when the Tube stations are comparatively empty and go up the downwards moving staircase and down the upwards staircase about half a dozen or a hundred times. This is the best exercise of all, but the difficulties in the way of practising it are considerable !

The following very excellent exercise for the arm muscles used in pushing with the sticks is suggested by Mr. d'Egville.

VII. Get a pair of ski sticks (ordinary sticks will do, but they should be longer than the conventional walking stick). Stand about three feet from a wall and place the points of the sticks in the angle made by the wall and the floor. Stand with your back to the wall and let yourself down on the sticks till your head touches the wall. Then push up again with your arms.

If anyone wishes seriously to prepare themselves for a winter's ski-ing the writer's advice is to give up smoking and alcohol of all sorts at the beginning of November and take the maximum amount of every conceivable form of exercise until the time for departure. Specially recommended are rugger, swimming, riding and, above all, hill walking. But is life long enough ?

SKATING

BY CAPTAIN DUFF TAYLOR

CHAPTER VII

HISTORY OF SKATING

JUST as roast pork is mythically reported to have been discovered through the burning down of a Chinese house, so doubtless the joy of swift ice transport would be discovered by one of our rude forefathers stepping on a piece of bone on the ice and shooting some yards at lightning speed before sitting down violently. For, most epoch-making discoveries are accident.

To state the exact date when skates were first used is impossible, but bone runners have been discovered in England and many Continental countries, which definitely proves that skating as a method of getting from place to place was in full swing as early as the eighth century, and there is no reason why the art may not be of much earlier origin. These skates were manufactured from the shank bones of various animals and fastened to the feet by means of thongs. It would be impossible to get an edge on a bone implement which would cut into ice, so the primitive skater had to provide himself with a staff somewhat similar to the modern ski stick to aid him in his progression over the frozen lakes and rivers. Skating at its birth thus had a slight tinge of ski-running.

We have to pass over several centuries before there is any document which mentions the art. The chronicle of Fitz-Stephen, an old manuscript of the twelfth century, is the earliest written evidence of skating in England. Practically all the earlier books on skating give quotations from these chronicles, but I make no apology for re-quoting, as the books which I speak of are so out of date that few, if any, of the modern skaters will have heard of them, much less read them.

" When the great fenne or moore (which watereth the walles of the citie on the North side) is frozen, many young men play upon the yce, some striding as wide as they may doe slide swiftly —some tye bones to their feete, and under their heels and

105

shoving themselves by a little picked staffe, doe slide as swiftly
as a birde flieth in the air or an arrow out of a cross-bow.
Sometimes two runne together with poles, and hitting one the
other eyther one or both doe fall not without hurt. Some
break their armes, some their legs, but youth desirous of glorie,
in this sort exerciseth itselfe against the time of war."

In this quaintly worded record of the earlier days of skating
it will be seen that another stage has been reached. No longer
is skating merely a means of transport, but it has now developed
into a sport. Somewhat rough and ready according to our
modern ideas, but none the less exciting. To use an old
cliché, if in the days of the Duke of Wellington it was said
that battles were won on the playing fields of Eton, in earlier
days it might have quite as easily been said that they were
won on the frozen waters when skaters first conceived the idea
of skating as a sport.

Another two centuries have to be skipped before a picture
depicting skating can be found. A woodcut dated 1498 is
probably the earliest. This shows the Holy Virgin Liedway
who was born in 1380 taking a very bad toss, from the effects
of which she suffered all her life and caused her to enter a
religious society and spend the remainder of her days in restful
contemplation instead of rude and rough sport. Some two
centuries later we find skating coming into such prominence
that our old friend Pepys mentions it in his *Diary*. Skating
has now advanced yet another step. No longer is it a rough
sport to be indulged in by the youthful apprentice, it has now
become an art in which the nobility are taking an interest.
The gentler sex are also beginning to take it up.

Pepys' reference to skating is :

" 1st December, 1662. . . . Over the parke (where I first
in my life, it being a great frost, did see people sliding with
their skeates, which is a very pretty art. . . . 15th December,
1662, to the Duke, and followed him into the parke where
though the ice was broken and dangerous yet he would go slide
upon his scates, which I did not like, but he slides very well."

There are two things that make this quotation interesting.
(1) It is probably the first mention of blade skating in this

country, and (2) Pepys uses the word ART. Skating is no
longer a mere sport, it has now risen to the pitch where grace
and elegance are acknowledged.

The great frost of 1683–4, when the Thames was frozen over
and fairs were held upon the ice, gave a great boom to skating
in this country. Skating became more than ever a favourite
pastime of all classes. Its popularity was such that even
ballads were composed about it. There is one old ballad which
is interesting from the fact that it gives the idea of skating
being used by an individual as a means of amusing the public.
In other words, exhibition skating has now been thought of.

> " The Rotterdam Dutchman with fleet cutting scates
> To pleasure the crowd, shows his tricks and his feats
> Who like a rope dancer (for his sharp steeles)
> His brains and activity lies in his heels."

In the days of Louis XVI skating was a fashionable pastime
in France. One of the French ambassadors to the Netherlands
makes the following comment on it in a despatch to his
King :

> " 'Twas a very extraordinary thing to see the Princess of
> Orange with very short petticoats, and these tucked up half-
> way to her waist, and with iron pattens on her feet learning to
> slide some time on one foot some time on another."

The reason of this quotation is that here is found yet another
advance. A lady and one of the highest rank has discovered
that in order to skate a special costume is necessary. Long
cumbersome skirts are an impediment, and although she lived
in the days when to show an ankle was to raise a blush she had
the temerity to tuck her skirts half-way up to her waist in order
that she might have the necessary freedom of action, which
is so important when skating.

Up to this time there has been no attempt at any kind of
organization. Skating has become popular and fashionable,
but it has no governing body. To Scotland belongs the honour
of founding the first skating club. The Edinburgh Skating
Club, which exists at the present day, is the oldest skating club
in the world. The Club is in possession of minute books dating
1784, but it is of much older origin than this. There is a

tradition that meetings of the Club were suspended in 1643 owing to the disturbed state of the country.

Duddingstone Loch, which lies just outside Edinburgh, and which in these times is a great rendezvous of skaters in a hard winter, was an old meeting-place of the Club. One of the old tests for membership was to be able to skate a complete circle on either foot and jump over first one, then two, then three hats. No mean feat when one thinks of the style of hat which was in vogue during that period.

It is seen that although it is difficult to say definitely which country produced the first pair of skates, there is no doubt that skating as an organized art had its origin in Scotland, and though we may not have headed the lists of World Champions during the last few years, we at least have the honour of founding this graceful and fascinating pastime.

The day of the old bone skate is now long past. It is, however, not until about 1869 that an entirely metal skate which screwed on to the boot was evolved.

In these early days there was no definite school of skating. The English style had not been invented and the International style had not even been thought of.

Several books were written in the early part of the nineteenth century. These books deal mostly with edges and the simple three turn, or heart figure as it was called. One books gives the following rather amusing advice to those beginning to learn an edge :

" When practising the outside edge the right-hand pocket of the skater's jacket should be weighted with shot and a bag of shot or weighty article should be carried in the right hand. These weights to be transferred to the left side when the left outside edge is being attempted."

Gradually a style of skating, which is known as the English school, was developed and perfected. This type of skating is still practised by a number of skaters, although the International school has by far the greater following. It was not until 1864–5 that there was any attempt to challenge the English school. During this year Jackson Haynes came to Europe and gave various exhibitions. His idea of skating was to carry out graceful movements on the ice and make the unemployed leg and arms play a prominent part in skating. In other words, to change skating from a stiff ceremonial drill into a dance. On the Continent he met with immediate success and a real revolution took place in the skating world. England, ever conservative and disinclined to adopt new ideas, received his skating coldly and it was not until quite recent years that the International style was generally practised in this country. Once it got a firm footing it went ahead with leaps and bounds until at the present day ninety-nine out of one hundred skaters have adopted it.

Even now one hears the expression " Continental Style." There is no such thing. There are two schools of skating, the English, which is by far the oldest and which was evolved and perfected in this country, and the International, which is a style common to the whole world and which no one country can claim as its baby.

Since the days of Jackson Haynes there has been an enormous advance in skating, not only in technique, but also in figures and movements that are done on the ice. Salchow, Hügel, Grenander, and many other giants of the skating world, have all produced figures and steps which have become famous, and are the basis on which the present-day skater is building his programme. It remains to be seen if the modern champions are going to advance the art as their predecessors did.

CHAPTER VIII

PRELIMINARY STAGES

THE hard but successful method of the savage of teaching her children to swim by simply chucking them into the water and letting them get on with it has much to recommend it when starting a child to skate. Lessons at the early stage are apt to bore children. It is better to make them fend for themselves. They will get their skating legs quicker by ragging about on the ice than by commencing with serious skating lessons. The time to start lessons is after they have found their feet and not before.

If, however, the beginner is of an age when staggering about by himself is not appreciated, the aid of an instructor must be invoked, but the moment the pupil has sufficient confidence to try alone, the instructor ought to be dispensed with, as a good skating balance can only be obtained by individual effort and the employment of an instructor at the first stage merely retards progress.

As omelettes cannot be made without breaking eggs, so it is impossible to learn to skate without having falls, and the beginner whose main object is to avoid falling will take a long time in finding a skating balance.

The first thing to do is to learn the art of falling. When balance is lost, never struggle against a toss. It is much better to relax, and then it will be found that a cropper is not a serious affair, and the first step has been mastered, the novice having gained confidence and learnt that it is possible to fall without serious injury.

A bad crumpler is usually the result of a violent struggle on the part of the skater to regain his balance. Muscles are tightened, and he hits the ice stiff and tense, instead of just letting himself flop.

The skater's next endeavour ought to be to learn to strike correctly and make each stroke even. When there is music the beginner always finds that he can get round the rink much easier, and this is simply because he instinctively tries to keep time and his steps are therefore more even than when there is no band.

When music is not available it will be found quite helpful if the skater counts One two three, One two three, like the old-fashioned dancing master, and tries to make each stroke occupy a bar of supposed music.

The strike should be taken from the side of the skate and never from the toe. Get the weight well over the skating foot and then push off with the side of the skate, allowing the striking, or in skating language the unemployed leg, to come off the ice with a side and backward motion, and not a direct kick back. The skating leg ought to be bent at the commencement of the stroke, gradually straightening, and the unemployed swung forward slowly so as to get it in position to permit of the weight being got over the skate in order to commence the next stroke. Whatever is done, avoid making one long and one short stroke. Try and make your strokes as long and even as possible. Once the skater has mastered these simple movements and is going to begin learning an edge, the aid of an instructor ought to be obtained.

At the very beginning of the skater's career it is impossible to develop any bad habits, but once the initial stage is over it is essential that a good style should be cultivated and correct instruction is of the greatest importance.

CHAPTER IX

TRAINING AND EQUIPMENT

THE difficulty of training for skating is the comparatively short season during which ice is available. Even
if there is an artificial rink there are only six months
during which it is possible to practise. It is, therefore, of the
utmost importance to have some method of keeping fit during
the rest of the year.

Training should be divided into two distinct parts : First,
the skating season when ice is available and the remaining
portion of the year when some other means must be found to
keep the skater's muscles in condition. Polo, cricket, tennis,
in fact all other sports and games, can be indulged in during
the whole year by going on tour. This is unfortunately denied
to the skater.

There are certain parts of the body used in skating that no
other sport will keep fit and pliant. This especially applies
to the ankles and hips, and as much valuable time is lost if
the skating muscles and sinews have to be got into condition
at the commencement of every season, a little time given daily
during the summer months to a few simple exercises will be
found most beneficial.

The following four exercises occupy very little time and will
be found of great assistance in keeping fit :

Exercise No. 1.

Put on an old pair of boots with skates attached. Stand
with feet close together, and gradually bend the ankles over
until the edge of the soles of the boots touch the floor. Then
come up into the upright position again. Raise one foot off
the floor and let the other ankle bend over until the side of
the boot touches the ground, coming slowly up to the upright
position. In the second part of this exercise the ankle should
be first allowed to bend outwards, and then the same motion
gone through by allowing it to bend inwards. When trying

112

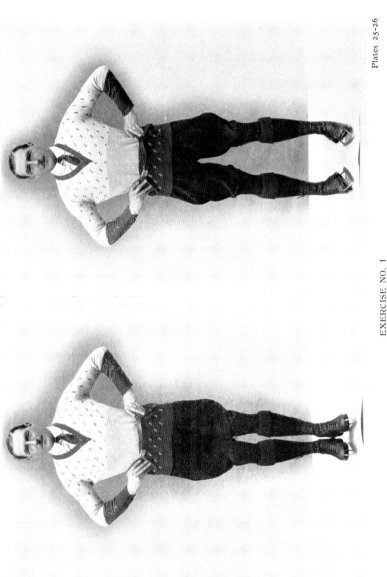

EXERCISE NO. 1

STANDING UPRIGHT WITH FEET TOGETHER, THE ANKLES ARE ALLOWED TO BEND OVER UNTIL THE SIDES OF THE BOOTS TOUCH THE FLOOR, ANKLES ARE THEN STRAIGHTENED UP UNTIL ORIGINAL POSITION IS ATTAINED. THE MOTION MUST BE GRADUAL AND NOT JERKY. KNEES TO BE KEPT STRAIGHT.

Plates 25-26

Plate 27

EXERCISE NO. II

SPREAD EAGLE POSITION, KNEES PERFECTLY STRAIGHT, BODY UPRIGHT, BACK HOLLOWED, HEAD
WELL UP.

Plate 28

EXERCISE NO. III. FIRST POSITION

BALANCE LEG STRAIGHT, UNEMPLOYED RAISED UNTIL KNEE IS IN LINE WITH HIP, TOE POINTING DOWN.

Plate 29

EXERCISE NO. III. SECOND POSITION

UNEMPLOYED LEG STRAIGHTENED OUT UNTIL THE WHOLE LEG IS IN LINE WITH THE HIP. BALANCE
LEG MUST NOT BE ALLOWED TO BEND. BODY TO BE KEPT UPRIGHT

Plate 30

EXERCISE NO. III.   THIRD POSITION

UNEMPLOYED LEG SWINGING ROUND.   NOTE THAT DURING THIS MOVEMENT THE UNEMPLOYED
LEG IS STILL HELD IN A STRAIGHT LINE WITH THE HIP, AND THE BALANCED LEG REMAINS PER-
FECTLY STRAIGHT.   AS THE LEG SWINGS ROUND, THE LEFT SHOULDER IS DRAWN BACK, SO THAT
THE BODY PIVOTS FROM THE WAIST.

Plate 31

EXERCISE NO. III. FOURTH POSITION

UNEMPLOYED LEG IS PASSED RIGHT BEHIND, AND RIGHT SHOULDER HAS COME FORWARD. THE
BALANCE FOOT HAS NOT ALTERED POSITION DURING THE WHOLE MOVEMENT, AND THE UNEMPLOYED
LEG HAS NOT BEEN ALLOWED TO DROP, BUT HAS BEEN HELD IN A STRAIGHT LINE WITH THE HIP ALL
THE TIME.

the second part it may be found difficult to keep balanced whilst standing on one foot. Rest a hand on the back of a chair for the first few days and gradually try to do the exercise without this support.

Exercise No. 2.

Get the legs into the spread-eagle position, i.e. feet turned out so that a straight line can be drawn from toe to toe. Knees perfectly straight. Heels not less than two feet apart. Back well hollowed and head held up. When starting this exercise it will be necessary to rest a hand on the back of a chair to keep balanced. The position should be held from ten to fifteen seconds.

Exercise No. 3.

Balance on one foot, raising the other leg until the knee is in a straight line with the hip. Now straighten out the leg so that the toe and hip are in a straight line. Gradually swing the leg from the forward position until it is directly behind you. During the movement the leg must be kept perfectly straight, and not allowed to sink nearer the floor. The knee of the balance leg must not be bent.

Exercise No. 4.

Stand on one leg, push the other out in front so that the toe is in line with the hip. Hold this position and gradually sink down as near the floor as possible. Eventually it will be found that it is quite easy to get right down into what is known as the teapot position.

N.B.—Skates are not worn for Exercises Nos. 2, 3 and 4.

Personally, I have found these four exercises invaluable. In fact, I owe it to them that I am still able to skate. Some years ago I had an accident which tore every muscle and nerve from the knee to the ankle, and after I was able to walk the doctor whom I consulted told me that my skating days were over. I did not like to give up without at least making some kind of an effort, so I started trying what exercises in my room would do, and now find that my leg causes me very little inconvenience.

One important point in training, which most people overlook,

H

is that it is not necessary to have ice to practise school figures. Every skating turn and position can be executed in a room without skates. When using this method of training it should always be carried out in front of a large mirror, so that ugly and cramped positions can be noted and corrected. It will be found most useful when the stage of trying the more advanced figures, such as Rockers and Counters, is reached. When there is no movement it is easier to get the body into the correct position to execute the turn, and to have the body in the right position is the great secret of figure-skating. The various movements should be practised until they are quite automatic. It will then be found that when they are tried on the ice falls will be fewer and turns carried out in that effortless manner which is always a sign of a first-class skater. Now comes what is by far the most difficult part of the skater's training—arm and hand movements. It is invariably easier to train the legs to execute graceful movements than the arms. This applies specially to the British nation. Somehow or other an Englishman is always self-conscious when it comes to using his hands and arms in anything but a scrap. One of the chief reasons that we as a nation do so badly in skating championships is, I think, that little or no attention is paid to this part of the skater's training. The graceful use of the arms play quite an important part even in school figures, but it is in free skating that their correct use means so much. This is amply proved by all the recent championships. Our representatives do quite well in the set figures, but are hopelessly outclassed when it comes to free skating, the execution of the foreign competitors always being far more polished. This is where the mirror will help in training, but better still the dancing school. A course of ballet-dancing lessons will be of immense help, not only will it teach the correct use of hands and arms, but it will also give that lightness and delicacy of movement which is only seen on the ice when watching the performance of a champion.

At the beginning of the season when starting to train on the ice, the first thing to do is to select the teacher you wish to train under, and, if possible, do not chop and change. Although it is quite possible to train alone for any test or competition, it is a long and tedious performance and much valuable time is wasted.

Plate 32

EXERCISE NO. IV

FIRST POSITION OF EXERCISE IS EXACTLY THE SAME AS SHOWN IN PLATE 28, POSITION 1.   SECOND
POSITION OF EXERCISE IS AS SHOWN IN PLATE 29, POSITION 2.   FROM SECOND POSITION SLOWLY
SINK DOWN UNTIL POSITION AS SHOWN IN PLATE 32 IS ATTAINED.   DURING THE EXERCISE THE
UNEMPLOYED LEG MUST BE KEPT IN A STRAIGHT LINE WITH THE HIP, TOE WELL POINTED FORWARD.
BALANCE FOOT TO BE KEPT FLAT ON THE GROUND.   FROM POSITION SHOWN IN PLATE 32, GRADUALLY
STRAIGHTEN UP, STILL HOLDING UNEMPLOYED LEG STRAIGHT IN FRONT, UNTIL ORIGINAL POSITION
IS GAINED.

The ideal skating coach is one who takes the trouble to develop each pupil's individual style. Great skaters cannot be turned out by mass production methods, but the natural style of the person being trained should be perfected. The average teacher has one method which he applies to everyone, and this is a hopeless way of being taught. Great care should therefore be exercised in making the selection of a coach. Remember that it is the practice put in between the lessons that counts. Lessons should never last more than half an hour, and notes which can be referred to while practising should always be taken.

A mistake which is very often made, especially by beginners, is the skating of one figure on and on without stopping. The initial starting from rest is very often the hardest part, and as all tests and competitions lay down that a figure shall be skated three times on each foot, it is better when practising to carry out the following method : Start—skate the figure three times on each foot—stop and start again.

A considerable number of figures have to be skated starting first with the right foot, and secondly with the left. Do not forget to practise these figures both ways ; as many people find, although a figure when starting with the right foot is quite easy to skate, it is far from easy when it has to be started with the left.

Take every opportunity of practising free skating movements. The continual skating of school figures is apt to get the skater into a cramped style.

Briefly, the object to aim at when training is, first, general fitness and the getting into condition of the skating muscles, so that at the end of the school figures, the free skating can be gone through with plenty of fire and dash ; second, that the necessary figures should be skated, not only with true tracings and graceful carriage, but also with little or no apparent effort.

There is also one other useful aid to training, and that is the slow-motion cinematograph. The great objection to this is the expense, but if the skater can manage to have slow-motion pictures taken, first of an expert and then of himself, carrying out the figures which he desires to learn, he will find that many valuable tips as to correct position can be obtained.

Equipment.

When starting to choose skates and boots, how few except the experts know how to go about it. Now, although it may be the bad workman who blames his tools, it is equally true that it is impossible to do a good job when using wrong implements. It is only courting disaster if figures are attempted when wearing a pair of hockey skates.

Skates.

There are four distinct types of skates, each being specially designed for its own style of skating, i.e. the English school, the International school, speed skating and ice hockey. If more than one branch of skating is going to be taken up seriously, suitable skates for each style should be obtained.

As the curves in English skating are very much larger than those demanded in the International figures, the English skate must have a larger radius and broader blade. International skating, with its smaller circles, requires a skate with a smaller radius, the blade should be narrower and also hollow ground. For modern skating it should have a turned-up toe with small saw-like teeth. Toe spins and pivots are much used in free skating and the teeth on the toe of the skate make these movements much easier to execute, and also do not take chunks out of the ice like a pointed skate. For racing, a specially long skate is necessary. The hockey skate has to be light. The frame is usually made of aluminium with a very narrow, sharp steel blade which enables the player to stop and turn at high speed. I have known many people use the English type of skate for International skating, simply because the International style is so often wrongly called Continental, and they jump to the conclusion that the skates must therefore be of foreign manufacture. There are several British firms which make the International type, and the patriotic person need not handicap himself by using a wrong design.

Boots.

Boots are another most important part of the skater's equipment. It is better to have them made to order by an experienced firm. Ready-made boots are rarely satisfactory. When trying on a pair of skating boots always do so over the exact weight of stocking that will be used when skating. If bandages or ankle supports of any kind are necessary, they should be worn when the boots are being fitted. The following are the points to which attention should be paid. Lacing ought to commence at the toe-cap. A new pair of boots when laced up tight should have a gap of about an inch between the sides. The leg of a skating boot always stretches with use, and if it laces up so that the edges touch to commence with, in a short time the boot will have stretched so that it will not give the necessary support to the ankle. The tongue should be wide enough to permit of this gap being left to start with. It ought also to be padded. If ankles are tender and inclined to chafe, a section of rubber sponge placed under the tongue will relieve the pressure. Stockings or socks worn for skating are thicker than those used for everyday wear. The skating boot is therefore slightly larger in the foot than the ordinary boot. I mention this to show the necessity of buying the boots before the skates.

Ice Hockey.

There is more equipment required for this game than any other sport on the ice. To start with, the boots should have ankle protectors. Shin guards are not absolutely necessary, but it is advisable to wear them, as a blow from the Puck might cause a nasty wound. Shorts are usually worn, so that the knees have to be protected. Elastic knee-caps having rubber piping similar to that used on cricket gloves are the best. Gauntlet gloves should also be worn. The goal-keeper is even more elaborately clad. Shin guards are not sufficient, so wicket-keeping pads are used. Special protection must also be given to the body. This takes the form of a quilted apron reaching from the chest to just below the stomach. This equipment is very necessary in first-class ice hockey as a hard shot at goal might easily cause a serious injury if the goal-keeper was insufficiently protected.

Etiquette.

Certain laws, both written and unwritten, are continually being broken by skaters, and it will usually be found that it is pure ignorance of their existence that causes the offence to be committed. I think, without doubt, that skating through another person's centre is the most common crime committed on the ice. If the occupier of the centre has a quick temper, the offender will probably hear all about it, but, as in ninety-nine cases out of a hundred, he hasn't the faintest idea that he has done anything wrong, he will simply think that he has got in the way of someone with a disagreeable temper and never imagine that the black looks and curses are justified by his having committed a major ice sin. When skating a figure to a centre, the skater has the courtesy of the ice, and no one should skate over any portion that his figure may cover. Centres should be arranged so that the various figures may be practised without clashing. If a portion of the rink is not roped off for the practising of figures, it is always understood that centres are to be taken up in the middle, leaving the sides for beginners and those who wish to practise other movements than turns and circles to a centre.

CHAPTER X

THE ENGLISH AND INTERNATIONAL SCHOOLS OF SKATING

MUCH has been written and many hard words have passed between the supporters of the two schools of skating.

The followers of the English style consider the International style unmanly and affected, and the International skaters say the English school is stiff and ungainly.

Unfortunately, the English school is practically dying out. Its followers are few and far between, and it says a great deal for their enthusiasm that it keeps going at all.

I think that it is a mistake to try and prove that either school of skating is superior to the other. Both have their good points, and it is not because of any inferiority that the English style is on the wane.

In English skating the carriage has to be upright with the body held stiffly like a soldier standing to attention. Arms are carried by the side of the body and there is no using of the unemployed leg. Turns have to be done with a sharp flick, giving the appearance of a squad doing old-fashioned ceremonial drill. Figures are skated very large and are not started from rest.

The skating of combined figures is greatly gone in for. Four skaters take up position and a board is placed on the ice which forms the centre where the skaters converge, and execute the turns that are called by whoever is taking command of the figure being skated.

Good combined skating is exceedingly interesting and far from easy. It is essential that all four skaters are of the same standard. If one of the team is even a little worse than the others, the four will be ruined, as the stronger skaters have to skate down to the standard of the weakest members of the team. Combined skating occupies a very large ice surface. On an

ordinary indoor rink there is little room for anybody else if a
combined figure is being skated.

The difficulty of getting a four in which all the skaters are
first class and the large amount of ice that it is necessary to
supply for the skating of four people are the two greatest
drawbacks to the English style of skating.

International School.

This style differs from the English, in that figures are not
skated nearly so large, but they have to be started from rest.
The unemployed leg, instead of being not used, becomes a
most important factor, and the arms are not held stiffly by
the side of the body.   Turns should never be jerked, but skated
with a rhythmic sway.   The whole essence of the International
school is grace.   It is not merely the putting down of a correct
tracing on the ice, but the skating of the tracing correctly with
graceful execution.   There are many more things to think of
in modern skating.   The graceful use of the arms and the
unemployed leg is a study in itself.

In the English school, after figures, there is only combined
skating, whereas in the International there is both free skating
by the individual and pair skating.   Music has no play in
English skating, but for free and pair skating it is essential.
There is also much more scope for individuality.   From the
skater's point of view there is the interest of building up a
programme, inventing new steps and movements and selecting
the music to which they are best suited.   As a spectacle it is
infinitely more interesting to watch.   Even when the programmes skated by various performers contain many of the
same movements there is always the different method of inter-
pretation.   Just as a piece of music is rendered in a different
manner by each player.

It is much easier to get a well-matched pair than a good four,
and greater pleasure can be got out of skating to music than
without it.

Fashions and tastes may change, but in skating there is little
likelihood of the English school becoming really popular again.
It will always have a certain number of devotees, but the
majority will follow the school which has the greatest variety
and where music and grace count for so much.

CHAPTER XI

FIGURE SKATING

THE various circles and turns which are skated to a centre are known as School Figures.

These set figures are according to their difficulty classified into three grades—first-class figures, second-class figures, third-class figures ; and from this schedule the figures for the various N.S.A. Tests and Competitions are selected.

The figures for the three Tests never alter, but in Competitions any figure may be taken so long as those selected are not of a higher standard than the competitors are expected to skate.

The main object of most people when starting skating is to learn how to waltz as quickly and with as little trouble as possible. Unfortunately, there is no short cut and the elementary figures, or what might be called the Five-Finger Exercises of skating, must be mastered first.

If higher ideals are aspired to and there is a desire to become a really first-class performer, a good deal of time must be devoted to figures, especially at the commencement of the skater's career. I do not mean by this that figures and nothing but figures should be practised all the time. Even in the early stages the practising of spirals is beneficial. It prevents the novice from becoming bored, and also helps him to get into the way of skating his figures in a nice easy style.

One mistake which is always made by the beginner is that he thinks the skating foot is the most important member. This is entirely wrong. It simply draws the tracing on the ice, and the unemployed leg and shoulders are the important members which cause the skating foot to describe the desired turn or circle. It is impossible to emphasize this point too much. Get the body into the correct position by the use of the shoulders and unemployed leg, then the skating foot simply must execute the turn. It is therefore of the greatest importance that from the very beginning the skater should pay attention to skating the simple eights and turns with correct position. As more difficult figures are attempted so the importance of correct positions increase. If a nasty toss is taken it is inclined to affect the nerves and make the skater funk the turn, and all the real crumplers occur when a difficult figure is tried with the body in the wrong position.

Although a figure, to be correctly skated, must be started from rest, it is a mistake to begin learning a new figure in this way. It is better to carry out the following sequence :

First, master the turn or circle without bothering about its being skated from rest or to an exact centre.

Second, practise to control it to a centre, but do not start from rest.

Third, practise the figure correctly, starting from rest and controlling it to a centre.

When commencing the third phase an actual centre should always be used for eights. If the figure contains a turn there should be three points marked on the ice. The following diagram illustrates the way a figure should be laid out :

Outside Forward Eight.

Position taken up at point A. Starting on right foot, the circle is continued until the skater is in a position to commence at point A with the left foot and complete the figure.

Circle No. 1 should correspond in size to circle No. 2 and if a straight line were drawn from B—C this should divide the two circles into four equal parts.

Three Turn.

Here we have a figure not composed of a simple circle, but containing a turn. This necessitates three points being marked on the ice. A, the position from where the figure has to be started ; B, the point where the turn has to be made with the right foot ; and C, where it has to be made with the left.

Points A, B and C all to be in one straight line, and the line
B—C again divides the figure into four equal parts.

The figures used in these diagrams are two of the most

elementary ones, but the method described applies to all
figures.

When the figures can be skated accurately with the aid of
these marks, they should finally be practised without any
definite centre or marks to indicate where a turn should be
made.

The great difficulty lies in correctly putting down the first
tracing. If this is done, the second and third tracings are
comparatively easy.

In Tests and Competitions where the placing of a centre
on the ice is not allowed, a good tip when taking up your
position to skate the figure is to make a note of two points—
the corresponding pillars of a rink, for instance, and skate the
figure with them as a guide.

Starting.

The initial strike off from rest should be made with the side
of the skate, and not with the toe. Striking off with the toe
will not only lose you marks, but will also tend to make the
skating of the figure jerky and unbalanced.

Use of the Unemployed Leg and Shoulders.

Each circle of a figure eight, whether skated outside edge,
inside edge, forward or back, is divided into two distinct phases.
When eights are skated on the forward edges, the unemployed
is behind the skating foot to start with and finishes up in front
of it. If they are skated on the back edges, the position of the
unemployed is exactly opposite, in front of the skating foot to
start with and behind it to finish.

It is the transition of the unemployed from position No. 1
to position No. 2 that is so important. All jerky or violent

movements must be avoided, and the motion should be smooth, like the swing of a pendulum. As the unemployed leg comes from the first to the second position the shoulders must be allowed to move round with it. It is the co-ordination of this leg and shoulder movement that makes smooth skating. If the leg and shoulder movement is not synchronized exactly, correct balance and a true edge cannot be kept. While this change of carriage is taking place, all that happens to the skating leg is that the knee, which is bent to start with, is allowed to straighten up slightly during the forward movement of the unemployed, and then bend again when the movement is complete. This slight straightening and bending of the skating knee is necessary to permit the comfortable changing of the body from a forward to a back balance, and is hardly perceptible to the eye, but is clearly seen in a slow-motion picture.

The Change of Edge, which is a figure that embraces both the outside and inside edges, is an excellent one to illustrate the importance of the unemployed. When learning this figure there is always the feeling that the initial strike will never supply enough energy to complete it. There is no necessity to make a violent strike to commence with. Sufficient pace can be obtained and the change from outside to inside, or inside to outside edge made by using the unemployed leg correctly. Just before the point where it is desired to make the change of edge, the unemployed is allowed to swing forward. The swing should be from the hip, and remember that it is a pendulum movement and not a kick. If the movement is at all jerky or violent it will not only throw the skater off his balance, but it will also retard, instead of increase, his speed. The unemployed should pass close to the skating foot and only just in front of it. It should then swing back to its full extent. The shoulder comes forward with the leg, and during this forward movement the knee of the skating foot straightens, bending again as the leg swings back. The head is turned to the left as the skating knee bends. Here there are three movements to synchronize—the bending of the knee—the backward swing of the unemployed—and the turning of the head to the left. These are the movements of the skater when the change of edge is being skated. Right foot leading : outside forward change to inside forward. When the Figure is being

skated, Left foot leading, the movements are exactly the
same with the exception of the head, which in this case is
turned to the Right.

Arms and Hands.

When skating after the English school the arms and hands
do not present any great difficulty, as they always retain the
same position—close to the skater's side. This holding of the
arms, like a soldier standing to attention, is one of the reasons
why English skating is inclined to look clumsy and stiff when
compared with International.

In the International style, where grace is of so much account,
they play quite an important part. Nothing is uglier than to
see a figure skated with the hands carried too high or with arms
which are stiff and awkward looking. When the hands are
changing position they should always be carried below the
level of the skater's waist with the arms slightly bent at the
elbows. The palms of the hands should be turned towards
the ice with the wrists a little bent back, hands not clenched
or stiff. Every movement must be like a dancer's, graceful
and rhythmic.

Head.

This might be summed up in five words : Look where you
are going. It sounds as if it would cause little trouble to the
skater. Nobody when walking along a street who wished to
turn left or right would do so without turning his head in the
desired direction. When it comes to skating this seemingly
natural desire appears to depart, and I have found a large
number of people when learning carry out every movement
correctly but steadily refuse to allow the head to turn with the
body. They get it into the correct position to start with, but
when direction is changed they stick grimly to the original
pose. Another common fault, and this is not confined to the
novice, but is often seen in the experienced performer, is the
allowing the head to drop and the keeping the eyes fixed on
the ice. This is caused by the desire to superimpose the turns
accurately. One quick glance is sufficient to locate where the
first turn has been made, and there is no need to skate with
downcast eyes throughout the whole figure. Remember always
to keep the head up.

Style.

From the very beginning a good style should be cultivated. Bad habits are easy to acquire and difficult to get rid of. It is not sufficient just to put down a correct tracing, although it may be the most important part as regards marks. Remember that good style and graceful execution come a very close second. All cramped or crouching positions must be avoided. The carriage of the body should be upright, with the back well hollowed. Arm and leg movements smooth and rhythmic. Although figures ought to be skated as large as possible, it is a great mistake to sacrifice grace for size. Time spent in acquiring the art of skating figures in a graceful and easy manner is never wasted. The best method of attaining perfection is to study the various positions in front of a mirror.

Plate 33

AN ICE GYMKHANA AT ST. MORITZ

H. GRENANDER, THE EX-AMATEUR CHAMPION SKATER OF THE WORLD, FINISHING A SPIN.

CHAPTER XII

TESTS AND COMPETITIONS

THE National Skating Association draw up the rules and regulations under which all tests and competitions are carried out.

The National Skating Association in their turn act in conjunction with the International Skating Union, which body is supreme in the skating world.

The great difference between a Test and a Competition is that in a Test a stated amount must be scored, whereas in a Competition the winner is the competitor who obtains the most marks.

Tests.

A minimum of two out of a possible six marks must be obtained in each figure, and the total scored in all the figures set must add up to a certain amount.

Take, for instance, the third N.S.A. Test. The highest possible marks that can be obtained in the set six figures is thirty-six, and the competitor must obtain not less than twenty marks from each Judge in order to pass. So considerably more than pass marks must be averaged in order to qualify for the badge.

Failure to obtain minimum marks in any one figure prevents the competitor from passing, even though the average scored in the other figures is greater than the total number of marks required to pass the Test.

All figures must be started from rest, and the required turn or circle skated three times on each foot. If a loop was one of the set figures, five perfect loops and one obvious crosscut would fail, but six indifferent loops (i.e. three on each foot) might obtain a pass mark.

When a competitor fails to obtain the necessary minimum in any figure, the Judges have the right to allow him to reskate it.

The N.S.A. has divided its Tests into three classes : third, bronze medal ; second, silver medal ; first, gold medal.

The following are the figures laid down for these Tests :

THIRD-CLASS N.S.A. TEST

(INTERNATIONAL STYLE)

Compulsory Figures

Eight	.	.	.	Rfo—Lfo	.	.	.	.
Eight	.	.	.	Rfi—Lfi	.	.	.	.
Eight	.	.	.	Rbo—Lbo	.	.	.	.
Change	.	.	.	(a) Rfoi—Lfio	.	.	.	.
				(b) Lfoi—Rfio	.	.	.	.
Threes	.	.	.	RfoTbi—LfoTbi	.	.	.	.

R = Right.	f = Forwards.
L = Left.	b = Backwards.
T = Three.	o = Outside.
	i = Inside.

Each figure may be marked up to a maximum of 6 points. In marking, there shall be considered, firstly, correct tracing on the ice ; secondly, carriage and action ; thirdly, approximately accurate covering of the previous traces in repeating the figure ; fourthly, size of the figure.

In order to pass, a candidate must obtain a minimum of two marks in each figure and an aggregate of 20 out of the maximum of 36 marks. These marks must be obtained from each Judge. Judges may use half-marks.

SECOND-CLASS N.S.A. TEST

(INTERNATIONAL STYLE)

Compulsory Figures

Figure.						Factor.
Eight	.	.	.	Rbi—Lbi	. .	2
Change	.	.	(a) Rboi—Lbio	. .	2
			(b) Lboi—Rbio	. .	2
Three	.	.	(a) RfoTbi—LbiTfo	.	2
			(b) LfoTbi—RbiTfo	.	2
Double Three	.	.	RboTfiT—LboTfiT	.	1
Change Three	.	(a) RfoiT—LboiT	. .	2
		(b) LfoiT—RboiT	. .	2
Change Three	.	(a) RfioT—LbioT	. .	3
		(b) LfioT—RbioT	. .	3

Plate 34

EXHIBITION OF FREE SKATING

AN ARTISTIC FINISH BY MISS DIANA KINGSMILL.

Figure.		*Factor.*
Loop . . .	RfoLP—LfoLP . . .	2
Loop . . .	RfiLP—LfiLP . . .	2
Loop . . .	RboLP—LboLP .	2
Loop . . .	RbiLP—LbiLP . . .	2
Bracket . .	*(a)* RfoB—LbiB . . .	3
	(b) LfoB—RbiB . . .	3
One-foot Eight .	*(a)* Rfoi—Lfio . . .	2
	(b) Lfoi—Rfio . . .	2

R = Right.
L = Left.
T = Three.
LP = Loop.
B = Bracket.

f = Forwards.
b = Backwards.
o = Outside.
i = Inside.

Each figure may be marked up to a maximum of 6 points. The marks given for each figure are multiplied by the factor of value for that figure. In order to pass, a candidate must obtain a minimum of 2 marks out of 6 in each figure, and an aggregate of 130 out of the maximum of 234 marks.

FREE SKATING

The candidate will be required to skate a free programme of three minutes' duration.

This will be marked :

(a) For the contents of the programme (difficulty and variety) up to a maximum of 6 marks.

(b) For the manner of performance up to a maximum of 6 marks.

In order to pass, a candidate must obtain 7 marks for (a) and (b) together.

The marks for Compulsory Figures and for Free Skating must be obtained from each Judge. Judges may use half-marks and quarter-marks.

FIRST-CLASS N.S.A. TEST

(INTERNATIONAL STYLE)

Compulsory Figures

Figure.		*Factor.*
Rockers . .	*(a)* RfoRK—LboRK . . .	4
	(b) LfoRK—RboRK . . .	4
	(a) RfiRK—LbiRK . . .	4
	(b) LfiRK—RbiRK . . .	4

I

Figure.					Factor.
Counters .	(a) RfoC—LboC	.	.	.	3
	(b) LfoC—RboC	.	.	.	3
	(a) RfiC—LbiC	.	.	.	3
	(b) LfiC—RbiC	.	.	.	3
Three—Change	(a) RboTfioT—LbiTfoiT		.	.	3
—Three .	(b) LboTfioT—RbiTfoiT		.	.	3
Loop—Change	(a) RfoLPfoiLP—LfiLPfioLP	.		.	4
	(b) LfoLPfoiLP—RfiLPfioLP	.		.	4
—Loop .	(a) RboLPboiLP—LbiLPbioLP			.	5
	(b) LboLPboiLP—RbiLPbioLP			.	5
Bracket—Change	(a) RfoBbioB—LfiBboiB .		.	.	4
—Bracket .	(b) LfoBbioB—RfiBboiB .		.	.	4

R = Right.	C = Counter.	f = Forwards.
L = Left.	LP = Loop.	b = Backwards.
RK = Rocker.	B = Bracket.	o = Outside.
		i = Inside.

Each figure may be marked up to a maximum of 6 points. The marks given for each figure are multiplied by the factor of value for that figure. In order to pass, a candidate must obtain a minimum of 2 marks out of 6 in each figure, and an aggregate of 203 out of the maximum of 360 marks.

FREE SKATING

The candidate will be required to skate a free programme of four minutes' duration.

This will be marked :

(a) For the contents of the programme (difficulty and variety) up to a maximum of 6 marks.

(b) For the manner of performance up to a maximum of 6 marks.

In order to pass, a candidate must obtain 7 marks for (a) and (b) together.

The marks for Compulsory Figures and for Free Skating must be obtained from each Judge. Judges may use half-marks and quarter-marks.

THIRD-CLASS N.S.A. TEST
(ENGLISH STYLE)

(a) A forward outside three on each foot, the length of each curve being 15 feet at least. The figure need not be skated to a centre.

(*b*) The four edges, outside forward, inside forward, outside back, inside back, on each foot alternately for as long as the Judges shall require, the length of each curve being 15 feet at least on the forward edges and 10 feet at least on the back edges.

(*c*) A forward outside eight, the diameter of each circle being 8 feet at least, to be skated three times without pause.

THE SECOND-CLASS ICE FIGURE SKATING TEST

(ENGLISH STYLE)

(*a*) A Set of Combined Figures including at least three of the following figures numbered 1, 2, 3, 4 and 5.

1. Forward, Turn, meet.
2. Once back—and Forward, meet.
3. Once back—and Forward, about—and Forward, circle, Turn, Inwards—and Inside, off meet.
4. Twice back, off meet—and Forward, Turn, meet.
5. Twice back, meet—and Back, out—and Forward, Turn, about—and Forward, meet.

And (*b*) three further figures, to be " unseen " and of a simple character to test the candidate's knowledge of Calls and power of placing figures on the ice.

The whole set (*a*) and (*b*) to be skated with a partner who shall be selected by the Judges and may be one of themselves, and the candidate must throughout show his ability to combine with such partner.

(*c*) The following edges on each foot alternately for as long as the Judges shall require : namely—

1. Inside back, each curve being 20 feet at least.
2. Cross outside back, each curve being 12 feet at least.

(*d*) The following figures skated on each foot : namely—

1. Inside Mohawk, the length of each curve being { R 30 feet at least   .   .   .   .   .   . { L
2. Forward inside Three, the length of each curve { R being 40 feet at least   .   .   .   .   . { L
3. Forward outside Three, the length of each curve { R being 50 feet at least   .   .   .   .   . { L

(*e*) The following complete Eights skated to a centre three times without pause :

1. Inside Forward Eight, diameter of each circle to be 10 feet at least.

2. Outside Back Eight, diameter of each circle to be 10 feet at least.

3. Forward inside Three, the length of each curve being 15 feet at least.

4. Forward outside Three, the length of each curve being 15 feet at least.

5. Forward inside two Threes, the length of each curve being 10 feet at least.

6. Forward outside two Threes, the length of each curve being 10 feet at least.

7. Back outside two Threes, the length of each curve being 10 feet at least.

(f) The following figures skated on each foot : namely—

1. Forward inside " Q," the length of each curve being 30 feet at least . . . . . . { R L

2. Forward outside " Q," the length of each curve being 30 feet at least . . . . . { R L

3. Back inside " Q," the length of each curve being 25 feet at least . . . . { R L

4. Back outside " Q," the length of each curve being 20 feet at least . . . . . . { R L

THE FIRST-CLASS ICE FIGURE SKATING TEST
(ENGLISH STYLE)

In the following list of figures the word " three " means a 3 turn.

SECTION A

This section consists of the combined figures in Parts I and II : the Judges may also give such simple calls as they think fit, to enable the candidate to recover his position, to alternate the feet, etc.

The figures in both Parts I and II shall be skated with another skater to be selected by the Judges, but if there are only two Judges, neither of them shall skate.

Each call must be skated at least twice, beginning once with the right foot and once with the left.

Subject to these conditions, the calls shall be skated in such order and with such repetitions as the Judges may, while the set is in progress, direct.

To pass this section the candidate must satisfy all the Judges in the manner in which he skates each set considered as a whole, and also in the manner in which he skates each individual call, and in the ability he shows throughout both Parts I and II of combining with his partner.

In the absence of a specific instruction to the contrary it is optional for a candidate to make strokes from a backward edge to a backward edge with feet open or crossed.

The Judges may pass a candidate in Part I, notwithstanding a reasonable number of errors on his part in the course of the set, provided that he ultimately skates all the calls to their satisfaction, and in Part II, notwithstanding errors, provided that the candidate has shown competent skill in skating unseen calls.

Part I

R. 1. Twice back—and Forward, Turn—and Inside, inwards, Turn, off meet.

R. 2. Back, Turn, out—and Inside, circle—and Once back —and Forward, three Turns, inwards—and Back, meet—and Back, two Turns, circle—and Forward, two Turns, meet.

R. 3. Twice back—and Forward, Turn, about, Change, meet.

L. 4. Forward, Turn, out—and Inside, about, circle—and In-side, Once back—and Back, about—and Back, off meet.

L. 5. Forward, Turn, Change, out, about, circle—and In-side—and Once back inwards—and Back Inside, centre Turn, Change, out, about—and Forward, meet.

L. 6. Twice back—and Back Inside, Turn, inwards, Mohawk, meet.

L. 7. Forward, Turn, out—and Back Inside, circle—and Inside, Mohawk, inwards and Back, centre Change, Turn, meet.

R. 8. Forward, Turn, circle—and Back Inside—and Once back—and Forward—and Inside, Turn, inwards, Turn, centre Change, meet.

R. 9. Inside, Turn, Change, out—and Back Inside, about, circle—and Forward, Mohawk—and Forward, in-wards, two Turns, pass, meet.

L. 10. Twice back, around of Turn—and Forward, Mohawk, inwards, two Turns, off pass, meet.

L. 11. Inside twice back—and Inside, inwards, Choctaw, centre Turn—and Forward, meet.

R. 12. Forward, Change, Turn, Change, Turn, circle—and
      Forward, Turn, Change, circle—and Forward,
      about, Change, Turn, off meet.

Part II

A set of not more than six or less than four " unseen "
figures of moderate difficulty in order to test the candidate's
knowledge of calls and power of correct placing.

This set must include Rockers, Counters and Brackets.

SECTION B

No candidate shall be judged in Part II of this Section until
he has passed in Part I.

The Judges may allow a candidate any number of attempts
at a given figure which they consider reasonable.

Part I

The figures, turns, Mohawks and Choctaws of this part must
be placed close to, and on the near side of, an orange or other
fixed point on the ice.   They must all be skated on each foot
to the satisfaction of the Judges.

The curve before and after the turn or change of foot must
be 40 feet long at least.

		FOR THE USE OF THE JUDGES
		Three.
		ROB, LOB, RIB, LIB.
		Rocker.
Threes	Outside back,	ROF, LOF, RIF, LIF.
	Inside back.	ROB, LOB, RIB, LIB.
Rockers,	Outside forward,	Counter.
Brackets,	Inside forward.	ROF, LOF, RIF, LIF.
Counters	Outside back,	ROB, LOB, RIB, LIB.
	Inside back.	Bracket.
		ROF, LOF, RIF, LIF.
Mohawks,	Outside forward.	ROB, LOB, RIB, LIB.
Choctaws	Inside forward.	Mohawk.
		ROF, LOF, RIF, LIF.
		Choctaw.
		ROF, LOF, RIF, LIF.

Inside Back Eight.

The complete Eight must be skated three times without pause. The figure need not be commenced from rest.

Part II

To pass in this part a candidate may select not more than one figure in each group, and must score 45 marks at least. A selection once made by a candidate must not be altered.

No marks shall be scored in respect of any one-footed figure unless it is skated on each foot, and the number set against each figure represents the maximum that can be scored for that figure.

A candidate shall not score for any figure on which he shall not have obtained at least half-marks.

EIGHTS

In marking these figures the Judges will take into consideration the general symmetry of the figure, and the approximate equality of corresponding curves.

In each figure the complete eight is to be skated three times without pause.

The figures need not be commenced from rest.

In groups D and E the turns and choctaws respectively are to be made on the near side of the centre.

The following turns are to be skated to a centre on alternate feet :

Group A

	Max.
Outside back two threes	4
Inside back two threes	13
Outside forward bracket	6
Inside forward bracket	4

Group B

Outside forward two brackets	6
Inside forward two brackets	10
Outside forward bracket, three	9
Inside forward bracket, three	5
Outside forward three, bracket	4
Inside forward three, bracket	12

Group C

	Max.
Outside back two brackets	14
Inside back two brackets	11
Outside back bracket, three	16
Inside back bracket, three	8
Outside back three, bracket	5
Inside back three, bracket	14

Group D (Figure 1)

Outside forward rocker	8
Inside forward rocker	4
Outside forward counter	8
Inside forward counter	4
Outside forward centre choctaw and inside forward centre choctaw (Figure 2), beginning on each foot . .	4
Outside forward mohawk and inside forward mohawk to a centre (Figure 3), beginning on each foot .	4

REVERSE Q'S

The turns and changes are to be made on the near side of fixed points determined by the candidate; the distance between these, and the lengths of the first and last curves, are to be each not less than 50 feet beginning on forward edges, 35 feet beginning on back edges.

Group E

	Max.
Outside forward three, change	2
Inside forward three, change	3
Outside forward rocker, change	3
Inside forward rocker, change	3
Outside forward bracket, change	5
Inside forward bracket, change	4
Outside forward counter, change	5
Inside forward counter, change	3

Group F

Outside back three, change	5
Inside back three, change	8

Max.

Outside back rocker, change	6
Inside back rocker, change	8

Group G

Outside back bracket, change	16
Inside back bracket, change	8
Outside back counter, change	16
Inside back counter, change	8

GRAPE VINES
Group H

Single, each foot leading	2
Double forward	3
Double backward	3
Pennsylvania	5
Philadelphia	6

The third-class Test is composed entirely of School Figures. In the second and first-class Tests, in addition to the Figures there is a period of Free Skating.

The bronze medal presents little difficulty, and anyone ought to be able to pass it at the end of a season's skating. There is a great difference between the bronze and silver standards. In the silver (counting the figures that have to be skated right and left foot leading) there are eighteen figures as compared with the six in the bronze Test. There is also the three-minutes' Free Skate.

The standard of accuracy demanded by the Judges is much greater, and on account of its length the physical strain is considerable. The skater must not get discouraged if after getting through his third N.S.A. he finds at the end of the following season that he is still a long way off from second-class standard.

Gold medallists are few and far between. The figures set are extremely difficult and the standard demanded is high. Much hard practice has to be gone through before the first-class Test is attempted.

Competitions.

Here the skater is not, so to speak, competing against Bogey, but against other entrants. He gets no chance of re-skating a badly done figure, and if he takes a toss, even although it is caused by a bad patch of ice, he cannot get up and start skating again, but is given credit for the portion of the figure skated before the fall.

If during the figure the skate of the unemployed leg should touch the ice, either to prevent a fall or to gain impetus, no marks are scored for that complete tracing. But if the ice is touched accidentally during the first circle, the skater can continue and get marks for the second and third turns.

Nerves are a tremendous factor in Test and Competition skating. Even experienced skaters find that there is a nervous strain which, if it is not kept well under control, will prevent the competitor from doing himself justice.

The feelings of the novice going up before Judges for the first time are difficult to describe. Knees seem incapable of supporting the body, and there is the dreadful sensation of being rooted to the spot and unable to move. As experience is gained the nervous strain becomes less, but is never really eliminated.

A useful plan before going up for the Test is to get a competent Judge to give you a dress rehearsal. If there is any figure you are at all doubtful of, ask him to be particularly strict in the marking of it. When the marks are added up you will see how many, if any, you have in hand. It is no good going in for a Test with the idea that the odds are against your passing. Having been judged unofficially by an expert, and finding that he has given you sufficient marks to pass, goes a long way in helping you to get rid of your nerves.

Never commence a figure until you are sure your Judges are ready, and continue to skate it until you are told to stop.

When skating in a Competition it is always better, if possible, to go quietly through the figures just before entering the enclosure. This gets the body into the right swing, and also acts as a good nerve sedative.

Before starting a figure, make quite sure that you have taken up a position giving yourself plenty of room to lay down the necessary tracing. If you see a nasty-looking patch of ice, take care that none of your turns will come anywhere near it. If necessary, move off and take up another position. Nothing is more demoralizing than finding that you are trying to lay down a tracing on a faulty surface.

Judging.

The judging of a Test is a comparatively easy matter as compared with a Competition.

In Tests the required standard is definitely laid down and the Judges have only got to see that those going up obtain the necessary number of marks. It does not matter if one person gets just sufficient to pass and another has a handsome margin. Here it is purely a case of qualifying.

Competitions give the Judges an infinitely harder task. It is now not a case of each competitor having to reach a certain standard, but of settling who is the actual winner.

For the Judges' guidance, the N.S.A. lay down the following points in sequence of importance :

1. That the tracing of the figure required is correctly set out on the ice.

2. The style in which it is skated.

3. The super-imposition of the turns or circles.

4. The size of the figure.

Free Skating.

An equal number of marks are given for the contents and execution of the skater's programme.

COMPULSORY FIGURES

ABBREVIATIONS

R = Right.	b = Backwards.	T = Three.	RK = Rocker.
L = Left.	o = Outside.	LP = Loop.	C = Counter.
f = Forwards.	i = Inside.	B = Bracket.	

Figure.	No.	Description.	Factor of Value.

Curve Eight

1.	Rfo—Lfo	1
2.	Rfi—Lfi	1
3.	Rbo—Lbo	1
4.	Rbi—Lbi	2

Change

5a.	Rfoi—Lfio	1
b.	Lfoi—Rfio	1
6a.	Rboi—Lbio	2
b.	Lboi—Rbio	2

Figure.	No.	Description.	Factor of Value.

Three

	7.	RfoTbi—LfoTbi	 1
	8a.	RfoTbi—LbiTfo	 2
	b.	LfoTbi—RbiTfo	 2
	9a.	RfiTbo—LboTfi	 1
	b.	LfiTbo—RboTfi	 1

Double-Three

	10.	RfoTbiTfo—LfoTbiTfo	. . . 1
	11.	RfiTboTfi—LfiTboTfi	. . . 1
	12.	RboTfiTbo—LboTfiTbo	. . . 1
	13.	RbiTfoTbi—LbiTfoTbi	. . . 2

Loop

	14.	RfoLPfo—LfoLPfo	 2
	15.	RfiLPfi—LfiLPfi	 2
	16.	RboLPbo—LboLPbo	 2
	17.	RbiLPbi—LbiLPbi	 2

Bracket

	18a.	RfoBbi—LbiBfo	 3
	b.	LfoBbi—RbiBfo	 3
	19a.	RfiBbo—LboBfi	 3
	b.	LfiBbo—RboBfi	 3

Rocker

	20a.	RfoRKbo—LboRKfo	. . . 4
	b.	LfoRKbo—RboRKfo	. . . 4
	21a.	RfiRKbi—LbiRKfi	 4
	b.	LfiRKbi—RbiRKfi	 4

Counter

	22a.	RfoCbo—LboCfo	 3
	b.	LfoCbo—RboCfo	 3
	23a.	RfiCbi—LbiCfi	 3
	b.	LfiCbi—RbiCfi	 3

Figure.	No.	Description.	Factor of Value.

One-foot Eight

	24a.	Rfoi—Lfio	 2
	b.	Lfoi—Rfio	 2
	25a.	Rboi—Lbio	 3
	b.	Lboi—Rbio	 3

Change—Three

	26a.	RfoiTbo—LboiTfo	 2
	b.	LfoiTbo—RboiTfo	 2
	27a.	RfioTbi—LbioTfi	 3
	b.	LfioTbi—RbioTfi	 3

Change—Double-Three

	28a.	RfoiTboTfi—LfioTbiTfo	. . . 1
	b.	LfoiTboTfi—RfioTbiTfo	. . . 1
	29a.	RboiTfoTbi—LbioTfiTbo	. . . 3
	b.	LboiTfoTbi—RbioTfiTbo	. . . 3

Change—Loop

	30a.	RfoiLPfi—LfioLPfo	 2
	b.	LfoiLPfi—RfioLPfo	 2
	31a.	RboiLPbi—LbioLPbo	. . . 3
	b.	LboiLPbi—RbioLPbo	. . . 3

Change—Bracket

	32a.	RfoiBbo—LboiBfo	 3
	b.	LfoiBbo—RboiBfo	 3
	33a.	RfioBbi—LbioBfi	 3
	b.	LfioBbi—RbioBfi	 3

Three—Change—Three

	34a.	RfoTbioTfi—LfiTboiTfo	. . . 3
	b.	LfoTbioTfi—RfiTboiTfo	. . . 3
	35a.	RboTfioTbi—LbiTfoiTbo	. . . 3
	b.	LboTfioTbi—RbiTfoiTbo	. . . 3

Figure.	No.	Description.	Factor of Value.

Double-Three—Change—Double-Three

	36a.	RfoTbiTfoiTboTfi—LfiTboTfioTbiTfo	3
	b.	LfoTbiTfoiTboTfi—RfiTboTfioTbiTfo	3
	37a.	RboTfiTboiTfoTbi—LbiTfoTbioTfiTbo	4
	b.	LboTfiTboiTfoTbi—RbiTfoTbioTfiTbo	4

Loop—Change—Loop

	38a.	RfoLPfoiLPfi—LfiLPfioLPfo	4
	b.	LfoLPfoiLPfi—RfiLPfioLPfo	4
	39a.	RboLPboiLPbi—LbiLPbioLPbo	5
	b.	LboLPboiLPbi—RbiLPbioLPbo	5

Bracket—Change—Bracket

	40a.	RfoBbioBfi—LfiBboiBfo	4
	b.	LfoBbioBfi—RfiBboiBfo	4
	41a.	RboBfioBbi—LbiBfoiBbo	5
	b.	LboBfioBbi—RbiBfoiBbo	5

CHAPTER XIII

FREE SKATING

IN all except very junior tests and competitions there are so many minutes allotted to free skating. Here the skater is not bound by any rules or regulations as to what he has to do on the ice. He has the right of choosing whether he will skate to quick time or a waltz. He has no partner to consider, so can go all out, and the more individuality he can put into his skating the better. There are many orthodox free-skating movements that are used by everyone, but a programme will always be improved if it contains special steps, provided they are gracefully executed.

As in pair skating, half the battle is giving a display that will please the eye. It is therefore most important when building up a programme that movements should be selected to suit the individual skater. Any movement that feels in the least awkward or cramped to the skater must be at once cut out.

Temperament is another factor that has to be thought of. Many people when starting free skating are self-conscious and skate their exhibitions with downcast eyes and awkward arm movements. This is a fatal fault, and unless it can be overcome the free-skating programme will never be successful, no matter how difficult the contents may be.

Without music free skating would lose all its charm. To the person who does not love dancing there is little interest, but to those whose bodies respond to music there is no more delightful or fascinating kind of skating.

It is this temperamental difference which makes it practically impossible for the first-class exponent of figure skating to be a really first-class free skater, or the free-skating expert to excel at figures.

The rule is laid down by the N.S.A. that in competitions and tests which consist of a combination of set figures and free skating the total marks allowed for free skating must not exceed two-thirds of the total marks allotted for figures. Free skating is therefore relegated to a position of secondary importance. I do not think that this is to the best interests of skating in general. It would be better to cut the free skating out of the first and second N.S.A. tests altogether. Let there be three tests for figures only and institute three new tests for free skating. I do not mean by this that the free skater can do without the trouble of learning figures. Figures must be mastered in order to free skate, but they can be looked upon as the five-finger exercises and need not be skated with the same perfection demanded in figure-skating contests.

The continual practising of school figures is apt to get the skater into a cramped style of free skating, and this should be avoided at all costs. Rocker and counter-Rocker turns are much used in exhibition skating, but to look effective they must not be skated in school figure style.

It must always be remembered that in free skating one is dancing, and although the feet are doing the steps, the arms also play just as important a part as they do in a dancing exhibition on the stage.

Although free skating is considerably more difficult than pair skating, there being no partner to give one confidence or that tiny bit of assistance when executing a turn which, although it may not be visible to the spectators, is all important to the skater, it has, however, this advantage, that many movements are possible which cannot be combined gracefully in a pair skate. Programmes, therefore, can be more varied and individual.

In competition an equal number of marks are allotted for the difficulty of the movements skated and the style in which they are carried out. It is therefore obvious that nothing can be gained by producing an exhibition that contains figures which the performer cannot skate in good style.

The method of working up a programme is just the same as in pair skating, start with easy movements, and as they are perfected, gradually add more difficult steps.

The present-day tendency to produce spectacular and sensational exhibitions is all very well for the chosen few who are at the top of the skating tree, but if the average individual waits until he can give a show containing hair-raising jumps and spins, he will probably give up the idea of ever becoming a free skater long before his programme is fit for production, and

CAPT. DUFF-TAYLOR AND MISS HOLT FIGURE SKATING AT MÜRREN

NOTE POSITION OF UNEMPLOYED KNEE—WELL TURNED OUT.

Plate 35

simply learn enough to scramble through any tests that may
be gone in for. If, however, a simple exhibition is first produced, he is bound to get interested in this branch of the art
of skating. There is nothing more amusing than the thinking
out and inventing of new steps. Free skating has no limits and
the invention of new movements is not the prerogative of the
expert, but is well within the powers of the novice.

When practising a programme the following are points to
which attention should be paid :

1. Perfect timing to the music, and arranging that the various
movements are so linked up that each step flows into the next
without loss of rhythm.

2. Avoid doing too many figures in one part of the rink,
and endeavour to cover as much ice as possible.

3. Make a careful study of the positions of the arms and
unemployed leg, so that all changes of poise will appear
graceful.

4. Plan the programme so that the finish will coincide exactly
with the time-signal. There is nothing that rattles the skater
more than finding he has finished his programme before the
time-signal goes, and he has to continue. He either loses his
nerve completely and stops, or endeavours wildly to improvise.
In either case the result is disastrous.

5. Skate the exhibition boldly and at a good pace.

Much can be learnt by watching expert exponents and trying
to model one's style on their lines, but it must always be borne
in mind that the great free skaters of the world are invariably
great individualists, and a style that may be suited to one person
is entirely unsuited to another.

As in pair skating, let graceful execution be your watchword.

K

CHAPTER XIV

PAIR SKATING

FIGURES are necessary and are the basis of all skating. Waltzing and ten-stepping are pleasant, but the greatest pleasure of all can be got out of pair skating.

It gives the most scope for graceful movements. It is possible to have an infinite number of programmes, both orthodox and unorthodox. All the school figures can be brought in and there is no dancing step that cannot be performed on the ice.

At present to waltz and ten-step are the popular skating achievements, but this is only because pair skating is so little gone in for. Everlasting skating of the ordinary waltz and ten-step can become monotonous, but pair skating never.

A skating programme is the production of the individual skater's brain. Ready-made programmes can be obtained, but these are never so satisfactory as the ones which are worked out by the couples themselves. Half the pleasure is the building up of an exhibition, thinking out new steps and new combinations of movements. The skater can let his originality have full swing, and is not tied down by rules and regulations as to what the programme has to contain.

I think that the reason it is not more popular is the mistaken idea that it is difficult.

There are any amount of junior and senior waltzing competitions, and couples, good, bad, or indifferent, will always be found ready to enter. Unfortunately there are few pair-skating competitions, and those who enter are amongst the first flight of skaters. Their programmes are naturally of an ambitious order, containing difficult and intricate figures, and this is apt to give the impression that pair skating is only for the first-class performer. This is entirely wrong, and any couple who are up to third-class standard can put together a simple programme.

Like every sport, you have to divide skaters into two classes, those whose ambition is to win competitions and championships, and those who have not got the competition complex and do not want to undergo all the nerve-strain that training and competing entails.

It is to skaters who belong to the second category that I would like to show how much pleasure they are missing if they do not have a go at this branch of skating.

Do not start off with the idea that difficult turns are necessary. Graceful execution is more than half the battle. A simple exhibition that is well skated and perfectly timed to the music is much more pleasing, both to the performer and to the spectator, than one containing difficult movements done in a jerky and uncontrolled manner.

There is another important point to remember, and that is turns that cannot be done alone with any degree of certainty become quite easy when done with the aid of a partner. Take a Rocker, for instance. Nearly everybody finds this a difficult figure to do alone, but perfectly easy when skated in a pair. As a finger under the chin of a person who is a bad swimmer will keep him afloat, so it is with skating. The slightest touch at the psychological moment just makes all the difference, and turns that it would be impossible to attempt alone become quite simple when done with a partner.

To make a success of pair skating there must be a skating partnership, not necessarily the until-death-do-us-part kind, but a definite arrangement that the couple will stick together as far as skating is concerned. It is hopeless to keep chopping and changing.

Having fixed up a pair, the next step is to commence building a programme. Do not be too ambitious to begin with. Keep to simple movements, and do not have too long an exhibition. Concentrate on the execution until each movement can be skated to perfection, and the various figures so connected that the whole programme goes with a swing. When a simple exhibition can be skated really well, then is the time to introduce more difficult figures, gradually working it up and lengthening the time until a really first-class performance is produced.

The building up of a free-skating exhibition is intensely interesting, but it must be gone about in the right way. It is not merely the selecting of so many figures and dance-steps and rattling them together. The various movements must be chosen, so that there is not only variety, but each movement must be so arranged that the transition is smooth and the skaters never get out of time to the music. It is this linking up of the different steps that is difficult and makes or mars the performance. No matter how well each individual movement may be skated, if they are badly connected together the result will be a poor and ragged performance.

Take the general composition of a programme. To begin with, momentum must be got up so that skating can be commenced at a good pace. An easy start for the pair-skating novice is, join hands as for ordinary skating, lady on the gentleman's right. Both start forward with the left foot, doing three long strokes and four very quick ones. This gets up plenty of speed, and the programme can be started with a strong inside forward edge on the right foot, changing without any use of the unemployed to an outside forward right. In this movement the lady leads, the man's right hand just touching her waist.

Now comes the padding, and steps have to be selected so that the skaters will cover all the available ice. Having completed the opening movement, join hands as for ordinary skating and skate a strong outside forward left, then outside forward right, changing to inside right. The man now turns an inside forward three, passing in front of his partner, the lady continuing on the inside right ; the movement being completed by both skaters doing an outside forward left and holding it until they are facing the same way as when the figure was started. The man is now on his partner's left and the step is reversed, lady doing the man's step. Repeat once more and the couple have now arrived at approximately the point where the programme was started, the lady being on the man's right. Next, something has to be put in which will bring the pair round the rink in an anti-clockwise direction. The position of the arms has to be changed, the man's right arm being placed round his partner's waist, and holding her right hand so that it rests just above her hip ; left hands being held in front. Both skaters chassé to the right, chassé to the left, Jackson Haines' turn, left feet are lifted up in front, swung behind and placed on the ice ; right feet are now lifted and swung back, and the bodies allowed to turn so that right inside forward can be skated. The right chassé is now skated with the lady on the left and slightly in advance, and during the left chassé she passes back to the original position for the Jackson Haines' turn. Repeat this three times, and the pair will be about three-quarters way down the rink. The simplest way to carry on from this point is when the inside right is skated and the lady

JUMPING

Plate 36

DEMONSTRATION OF A GOOD JUMP ON THE PART OF PHIL TAYLOR.

has moved to the left, hands are changed, man holding lady's right hand with his left. Three quick steps are done, the man jumping from left forward to right outside back, and the couple go into the ordinary waltz. Waltz down to the foot of the rink and continue until the centre of the rink is reached. As the man is skating outside back right, and the lady the left outside forward, he allows her to pass under his left arm, the unemployed legs are raised into high spiral position, the man's right hand holding the skate of the lady's right and the lady stretching out to hold the man's left skate with her left hand. The man's left and lady's right hands touching and being held straight above them. Hold this double spiral as long as possible. When the pace is getting slow, the couple part, lady skating an inside forward right, man continuing on the back outside right. The lady now turns an inside forward three on the right, and both skaters, putting the left toe on the ice, skate a pivot, the pivot being so timed that when finished the pair are side by side and facing their audience. Hold the finish of the pivot for two or three seconds, then both skate inside forward right, man taking lady's left hand with his right, outside forward left, cross right over left, and letting go hands skate the outside forward three, cutting away quickly with the left foot in front of the right to inside back left, when hands are joined again and the figure repeated. Having skated the figure twice, the pair join hands as for ordinary skating when doing the inside forward right, chassé, outside forward left, the lady doing a drop three and the man a mohawk turn, left feet are then lifted up in front and swung behind, placed on the ice on not too deep an inside back edge. Now a quick step, placing the right behind the left on the outside back edge, cutting away smartly to inside back left, and commencing once more on the inside forward right. The partners will have now changed places, and the man skates the drop three while the lady does the mohawk. (Note.—When commencing this figure lady should be on her partner's right and hands are not let go during the movement.) The two last movements should be so timed that the skaters are now nearing the top of the rink, in order that a figure which will bring them down to the centre can be skated.

As the pair skate the inside forward right instead of the chassé, the man skates a straight edge on the left, his partner straighten-

ing up from inside right to straight edge on the right. The
couple are therefore going down the rink, man on left straight
edge and lady on right straight edge. The pair are facing each
other, unemployed legs held in high spiral position, arms
stretched wide, man's right and left hand touching his partner's
left and right. Hold this position for a few yards, and then
the pair part, the man changing from left straight edge to left
outside, and the lady to right outside. These edges are held
for three-quarters of a circle, when the man skates right outside
forward and his partner left outside forward, straightening up
to a straight edge as they meet. Both now skate the mohawk
turn, and immediately after the turn the man skates a drop
three with the right and his partner a drop three with the left.
The man now skates forward right and the lady forward left.
The pair meeting, man left forward straight edge and lady
right forward straight edge. The pair are now once more
going down the rink on a straight edge. The mohawk turn
and drop three are again skated, and the partners meet going
up the rink, man right straight edge and lady left straight edge.
The pair now turn together with a counter-Rocker movement
from forward straight edge to back straight edge, which is held
until the top of the rink is nearly reached. The unemployed
toe is placed on the ice and both stop together on the points
of their skates. Three quick steps are taken on the points of
the skates, the skaters then coming on to an inside right forward ;
outside forward left is then skated together, mohawk turn, left
feet picked up in front and placed behind the right on the inside
back edge. (Note.—Up to this point of the figure the pair do
not let go hands.) Now, letting go hands, each skate forward
outside right, holding the edge until they again face their
audience, together a short step with the left and a large inside
forward circle, outside forward left, mohawk turn, finishing
the programme with a pivot side by side.

Although all the movements in this free-skating programme
are simple and well within the capabilities of any person up to
third-class standard, if it is smoothly skated and well timed to
music the result will be quite a pleasing exhibition.

Once a pair have mastered their first modest display, it is
wonderful how new ideas spring to life, and the easy programme
is worked up until it contains intricate and difficult steps.

There is one golden rule that must always be borne in mind :
Never sacrifice grace for difficulty.

CHAPTER XV

DANCING, WALTZING AND ACROBATIC SKATING

DANCING

IT is a mistake to imagine that the Waltz and Ten-step are the only dances that are suitable for the ice. Although pair skating and free skating are the setting of various figures and movements to music and so can be looked upon as dancing on skates, this is by no means the limit. There is no dance that cannot be carried out on the ice.

Several years ago the Lancers was one of the most popular dances in Canada, yet in this country how often have skaters attempted to get up a set. The idea that a square dance is bound to be difficult and can only be done by first-class performers, is wrong. As a matter of fact, they are easier than either the Waltz or Ten-step. All that is necessary for the skating of Lancers is to be able to skate outside forward, outside back, and do a three turn. Not a very high standard of skating. Every figure of the Lancers as danced in the ball-room has been worked out and adapted to the ice. I do not propose to give the various figures here, but anyone who is interested in this kind of skating can find all the figures, etc., worked out in a little book called *Dancing on Skates*, by Colonel H. V. Kent, R.E. The first glance at the diagrams in this book may rather give the impression that complicated movements have to be mastered, but closer study reveals the fact that simple edges and a three turn are all that is necessary. It is obvious that a certain amount of rehearsing must be done before the dance can be carried out perfectly, but much pleasure is to be got out of these rehearsals, and I think that it is a great pity that rinks do not encourage this kind of skating more, as I am certain that it would be most popular.

The skating revival which is taking place in this country and has led to the erection of so many artificial rinks makes possible the holding of ice spectacles, and although a proper ice ballet

requires not only much rehearsing, but also first-class skaters
if it is really going to be efficient, there are many other dances
besides the Lancers which are well within the capabilities of
the novice, provided sufficient time is given to rehearsals.

There is also another point in favour of these dances. Simple
though the movements required may be, they must be gracefully executed and skated in time to the music. Their practice,
therefore, is always training the novice to skate with rhythm,
and this is of great assistance to him in his ordinary skating.
Lancers, etc., make a very good turn in an ice cabaret, and give
the beginner a chance of performing in public. There is no
art in which there is more nervous strain than skating, and until
the nerves can be kept under control the skater will never do
himself justice when performing before an audience. The
more chances he has of skating in public, the less he feels the
strain. If square dances were attempted oftener, I feel sure
that they would be most beneficial to all who took part in them.

WALTZING

The popularity of the ball-room is gradually being super-
seded by the more varied attractions of the ice-rink. In this
era of swift movement there is more thrill to be obtained from
the flying movements of an ice waltz or ten-step than from the
monotonous foxtrot danced in a crowded space.

There is no dance that cannot be done on the ice, but by
far the most popular is the ordinary waltz. It is always possible
to get a partner for this, whereas the more complicated dances
require careful rehearsing with the same person.

There is one golden rule when starting to learn to waltz.
Do not try to run before you can walk. It is not necessary to
be able to skate three turns and outside back eights to a centre
in order to waltz, but it is essential that a three turn should
be skated without assistance as well as the forward and back
outside edges.

It takes a very short time to master these elementary movements, and waltzing on no account should be attempted before
this has been done. Many people ruin their waltzing by
starting too soon and getting a friend or instructor who is a
strong skater to pull them round, fondly imagining that if they
do this they will avoid the drudgery of learning to do a turn
alone. It is impossible to learn to be even a moderate waltzer

in this way. Look at any rink during the waltzing interval, and you will always see several couples who, instead of dancing, appear to be engaged in a wrestling match. There is no doubt what the trouble is. One of them cannot do the waltz step alone, but is depending on the support of the partner.

Another fault which is the invariable result of attempting to learn in this way is that, instead of the couple dancing close together, they will hold each other at arm's length. If one of the partners require support, there is always the feeling that at any moment he or she will trip up and the fear of taking a bad toss always develops this ugly style of holding.

The actual waltz step is simplicity itself—a forward curve on the outside edge, a three turn, after which the other foot is placed on the ice and the outside back edge skated. This step is done by both lady and gentleman and is combined in the following manner :

Gentleman : Forward outside Right—Three turn—Back outside Left—Forward outside Right—Forward outside Left —Three turn—Back outside Right—Forward outside Left— Forward outside Right, etc.

Thus the man, turning the three on the right foot to commence with, afterwards turns it alternately Left and Right, and skates the back outside edge once to the two forward edges.

Lady : Back outside Left—Forward outside Right—Three turn—Back outside Left—Back outside Right—Forward outside Left—Three turn—Back outside Right—Back outside Left, etc.

The lady skates the back outside twice, turning the three each time she skates the forward curve.

Briefly, the gentleman skates twice forward and once back, while the lady skates twice back and once forward.

The best way to practise the waltz step alone is to repeat the step twice with each foot, i.e. Right forward curve—turn— Left outside back. Repeat this, and when the Right outside is skated for the third time do not do the turn but skate a long outside forward with this foot and start Left outside forward, doing the step twice with the left foot leading. In this way both Right and Left turns are carried out, and if practised in this manner the movement does not occupy much ice, which will be found convenient when skating on a crowded indoor rink.

It also gets the skater into the way of waltzing more or less to a figure eight.

Starting.

The pair skate forward, lady on the gentleman's right, gentleman's right hand holding lady's left. This position is held for a few steps, just long enough to enable the couple to get the time of the music and so commence on the right beat. The lady now turns a three with the left, dropping on to the right outside back, her partner skating left outside forward. The gentleman now holds his partner exactly as for the ballroom waltz, and the step is commenced, man right forward, lady left back.

The step which has been already described is skated until the end of the rink or waltzing enclosure is reached. The pair have now to turn the corner and come up the other side. This is done by the man turning the three every time with the left foot if the waltz is being skated round the ordinary way of the rink, and on the right if it is being skated the reverse way, until the corner has been turned when the ordinary step is again resumed. This is the simplest way of getting round the end of the rink. There are several others, such as the man skating a forward rocker on the right or left, but these methods should not be attempted until the skaters are fairly proficient.

Waltzing the Reverse Way of the Rink.

During a waltzing interval, couples must all waltz the same way round. The usual way is against the clock, but waltzes are very often skated with the clock. It sounds as if this would not make any difference to the skaters, but except for experts the steering is much more difficult when the waltz is skated the reverse way of the rink.

Always be careful when you start that you do so the right way round. If a couple start the wrong way, even for one step, it will cause endless confusion.

Steering.

This is the man's prerogative. He must indicate clearly to his partner each turn that he is going to do, and she must follow. There is nothing more trying than to have a partner who will not answer the helm. It not only makes the couple look ragged and out of control, but it will most certainly lead to crashes. Bad steering on the part of even one couple can spoil a waltz for every other pair on the rink.

It is the man's part to be ever on the *qui vive* and guide his partner so that they neither touch nor interfere with any other couple, and it is impossible to do this if the lady insists on having a say in the matter. The best partner is one who has enough confidence in the man's steering to close her eyes and let herself go.

In order to steer well, the man must hold his partner, not at arm's length but closely, so that he can indicate clearly and quickly any change of direction.

Waltzing Competitions.

The most important part is the final stage where the selected pairs have to waltz an eight round chairs or posts placed on the ice.

Each couple is given two preliminary canters, one waltzing the ordinary way, and the other the reverse way round the rink. During the preliminary rounds the judges select so many of the best performers, and the real tug-of-war begins with the waltzing of the eight.

The following diagram shows how this should be done :

One important point to remember is that each circle of the eight should consist of the same number of steps. The easiest way to skate a symmetrical figure is to do three steps to both circles.

Starting at point A with the right foot, the first turn is done at B, the second at C, and the third at D. After the third turn, the couples should be in such a position that when the forward outside left is skated by the man it will start at point A, and turns will be done at points E, F and G. Points C, A, F should be in a straight line. Point D should be equidistant and in line with B, and E with G.

Each chair has to be skated round three times, so this means a total of nine steps, right foot leading, and nine, left foot leading.

In order to control a waltzing eight accurately, it is essential that the couple should start exactly midway between the posts or chairs. If the start is not central, the circles are bound to be of unequal size.

The best way to make your circles correspond is to skate so that each chair or post marks the central spot of its circle. A simple way of starting is to skate a few steps forward side by side. The lady now turns a three with the left, dropping on to the right outside back, which should be so timed that her next stroke, i.e., outside back left, will commence at point A. This enables the pair not only to start dead central, but it also lets them get into the swing of the music, and so get off on the right beat.

Music.

For ordinary waltzing the old-fashioned tunes are best, especially those which have a marked beat.

Some people prefer to waltz a quicker time than others, so it is always as well before starting to skate round the chairs in the final stage of a competition to let the band play a few bars before a start is made in order to see if they are keeping the time you wish to skate to. Nothing looks uglier than a couple skating out of time to the music, and the waltzing will always suffer if the skaters are trying to keep a time to which they are not used.

ACROBATIC SKATING

During the last few years a form of skating has crept in which can be most accurately described as acrobatics on the ice. This type of skating is rarely attempted by amateurs, but the professional is going in for it more and more every year.

We live in an age in which the public want thrills. Although there is nothing more beautiful than a good pair-skating exhibition, full pleasure cannot be got out of the spectacle unless the audience has some knowledge of the art of skating, and they will not get that catch-of-the-breath feeling that audiences of the present day demand.

ACROBATIC SKATING

MR. PHIL TAYLOR, THE FAMOUS ENGLISH SKATER, IN A GRACEFUL ATTITUDE AT ST. MORITZ. HE IS SEEN WEARING SKATES ON STILTS, AND CLAIMS
TO BE THE ONLY SKATER TO STUNT ON THEM.

Plate 37

As the professional depends largely on putting up shows which the general as well as the skating public are willing to pay to see, he must therefore try and invent various stunts which either look or are dangerous.

A friend of mine who is a very fine skater was once giving an exhibition, and in the middle of his programme, when executing a difficult turn at a very great pace, he caught his foot in a crack in the ice, which caused him to take the most unholy crumpler. The pace he was travelling at made him shoot right up in the air, do a kind of dive, hit the ice with his chest, bounce to his feet again and continue skating. Although pretty badly shaken he was too old a hand to lose his head on account of a fall, however bad, so went on with his programme to the end. In the evening, when the various exhibitions were being discussed, a lady turned to me and said : " I think So-and-so's skating simply wonderful, especially that marvellous dive. I wonder how he learnt it ? Do please ask him if he will do it again to-morrow."

It is this desire to see something in which the performer takes, or looks as if he takes, an odds-on chance of breaking his neck that has brought stunt skating into favour.

Graceful execution, which is the essence of the art of skating, does not enter into acrobatics, but pluck and exceptionally good balance are necessary even for stunts which are not actually dangerous.

The dancing of an Apache dance, where the partner is swung about and hurled violently to the ice, is not a feat in which there is any real danger. There is, however, a considerable amount of risk in the skating of turns and pirouettes on a pair of high stilts, or in the jumping of long rows of chairs or barrels. Strictly speaking, it is not skating, but a means of providing thrills on the ice for those who desire them.

CHAPTER XVI

ICE HOCKEY

THAT ice hockey is the finest game in the world is perhaps too sweeping a statement, but it is certainly well up in the list.

There is no game that is faster or more open. It demands great physical fitness on the part of the players, as well as perfect combination. In fact, it is typically a game to appeal to the Briton.

Unfortunately the English climate does not provide suitable winters for open-air rinks, and this means that ice hockey in England has to be played on indoor rinks. It is, of course, quite possible to play first-class ice hockey on artificial ice, but it can never be really satisfactory unless the rink is only used for this purpose. To attempt to amalgamate ordinary skating and ice hockey on the same rink will never be a success, and the only way it can be done is to arrange that all the matches and practice games take place during the last session. After a game the ice is unskatable for figures. The unfortunate hockey player is therefore never looked upon with much favour by rink authorities in this country, and finds great difficulty in getting ice preserved for practice.

Another disadvantage of playing on an indoor rink is the lighting. A hockey puck is not a large object, and if the lights are not specially arranged it is difficult and very often dangerous for the goalkeeper.

We have to turn to Canada to see the game in perfection. There it is the national winter sport, and there the finest players in the world are produced.

In spite of all the handicaps under which the game is played on this side of the ocean, it is nevertheless steadily gaining in popularity. During the last two years skating has had a revival, and this has led to the erection of more artificial rinks, so that it is gradually getting more possible to reserve ice for practice.

Twenty years ago practically nobody thought of going abroad for winter sports. Nowadays everybody seems to go to Switzerland or some Continental country where winter sports can be indulged in.

Ice hockey can be played in Switzerland under ideal conditions. It is possible to provide special rinks where practice games can be played at any time without interfering with figure skating, and, although at present we cannot compete with teams from Canada, there is little doubt that a time will come when we shall at least be able to give our Canadian cousins a good run for their money.

There is one curious thing about ice hockey, and that is there is no regulation as to the length or width of the rink to be used. Championship matches are played at the Palais de Glace, Paris, which is a circular rink and entirely unsuitable for the game. Even in Canada there is no uniformity and rinks are of various sizes.

The ideal ice-hockey rink should be 185 feet long by 85 feet wide, and the ice surface should never be less than 170 feet by 70 feet.

The rink ought to be surrounded by boards at least 3 feet 6 inches high. Low boards slow up the game by allowing the puck to get out of play too often and they are also a source of danger to the players.

The following are the rules for the game as laid down by the Ontario Hockey Association of Canada :—

RULES OF THE GAME

Players.

1. The game is played on ice by teams of six men on each side wearing ice skates, with a puck made of vulcanized rubber, 1 inch thick all through, 3 inches in diameter, and weighing not less than $5\frac{1}{2}$ ounces and not more than 6 ounces. The players to be designated as follows : Goalkeeper, right defence, left defence, centre, right wing, left wing. In addition to the players mentioned, each team may use two extra players as substitutes, but there shall not be more than six players a side on the ice at any time during the match.

A substitute goalkeeper shall also be allowed, but this substitute shall not play any other position but goal, and any substitution to be made only at the end of a period, except

in case of injury, as hereinafter provided for. In case of a
penalty to a goalkeeper he shall be replaced by one of the
players who are on the ice at the time the penalty is inflicted.

Sticks.

2. Hockey sticks shall not be more than 3½ inches wide at
any part and not more than 54 inches in length to the heel,
and not more than 15 inches long at the blade.

Goal.

3. A goal is placed in the middle of each goal-line composed of official goal-nets supported by two upright posts,
4 feet in height, placed 6 feet apart, and at least 5 feet, preferably 10 feet, from the end of the ice. The goal-posts shall
be firmly fixed. In the event of a goal-post or net being
displaced or broken, the referee shall ring his bell, and the
game shall not proceed until the post or net is repaired. It
shall be the duty of the referee before each match to measure
the goals. A dark distinguishing line shall be drawn on the
ice between the goal-posts.

Match.

4. Each side shall have on the ice a captain, who alone
shall have the right to speak to the referee on any question
in dispute. The visiting team shall have the choice of goals.
In case of a game on neutral ice the referee shall toss for
choice of goals.

5. The teams shall play three periods of twenty minutes
each, a ten-minute rest being allowed at expiration of each
period. The duration of championship matches shall be one
hour, exclusive of stoppages. The team scoring the greater
number of goals in that time shall be declared the winner of
the match. If at the end of that time the game is a draw,
ends shall be changed, and after ten minutes' rest the match
continued for ten minutes, each side playing five minutes from
each end, and if neither side has then scored a majority of
goals, additional similar periods of ten minutes shall be played
in the same way until one side shall have scored a majority of
goals, with a five minutes' rest after each ten minutes of play.
No match shall continue for more than thirty minutes' (actual
play) overtime. In case either club should decline to play

Plate 38

INTER-VARSITY ICE HOCKEY AT ST. MORITZ

CAMBRIDGE GOALKEEPER HAVING A WARM TIME, AND SHEWS THE NECESSITY OF KNEE PADS, ETC., TO PREVENT DAMAGE TO PLAYERS.

in any of the necessary extra periods, it shall be declared a loss for that team.

Time-keepers.

6. Two time-keepers shall be appointed, one by each captain, before the commencement of the match, whose duty it shall be to keep an accurate account of the time of each game, deducting time for stoppages in the play, and the time-keepers shall report to the referee by ringing a gong any variance in their time, and the matter shall be at once decided by him. The referee also shall appoint a time-keeper, who shall keep the time of penalized players, and shall direct them to enter the game. He shall also keep the score, including the names of the players scoring the goals. When, in the referee's opinion, a neutral penalty time-keeper is not available, the referee may appoint a representative of each club to act as penalty time-keepers. The time-keepers shall be under the control of the referee. A gong shall be kept for their use. A penalty imposed on any player shall not commence until said player has reported to the penalty time-keeper. The duration of the penalty shall be measured in actual playing time, exclusive of stoppages.

Referee.

7. There shall be only one referee for a match, but the Executive may appoint an assistant in addition to the regular referee, and in no case shall he belong to either of the competing clubs, and he may be an amateur or professional. They are to enforce the rules, adjudicate upon disputes or cases unprovided for by rules, appoint or remove goal umpires ; control the time-keepers, keep the score, announcing each goal as scored, and at the conclusion of the match declare the result. The puck shall be considered in play until the referee or his assistant stops the game, which they may do at any time, by sounding a whistle or ringing a bell. The referee's decision shall be final, and there shall be no appeal.

Score.

8. A goal shall be scored when the puck shall have passed between the goal-posts from in front and below the top of the net. If the puck strikes the iron cross-bar at the top of the net and bounds over the bar the referee shall not allow a goal

L

to be counted. For the better guidance of officials the puck must be wholly inside the goal-line between the goal-posts to count as a goal.

Goal Umpires.

9. There shall be one umpire behind each goal ; he shall inform the referee when the puck has been put into the goal from the front, but the decision of the referee as to the scoring of the goal shall be final.

Face.

10. The game shall be started and renewed by the referee ringing his bell or calling " Play " after dropping the puck in the centre of the ice between the sticks of two players, one from each team, who are to face it. The left-hand side of the players who face the puck shall be towards the opponents' goal, and they must keep the blades of their sticks on the ice until the referee drops the puck. After a goal has been scored the puck shall be faced in like manner in the centre of the ice.

Off-side.

11. (a) A player shall ENDEAVOUR always to be on his side of the puck. A player is off-side when he is in front of the puck or when the puck has been hit or touched or is being skated with, by any of his own side behind him, namely, between himself and the end of the rink near which his goal is placed.

(b) A player being off-side is put on-side when the puck has been hit by or has touched the dress or person of any player on the opposite side, or when one of his own side has skated in front of him, either with the puck or having played it when behind him.

(c) Since a player who is off-side may be put on-side as provided in clause (b), the referee shall not stop play unless the player offends against the following clauses (d) or (e) of this rule.

(d) Persistent failure to be on-side shall be designated as loafing and penalized as a foul.

(e) If a player when off-side plays the puck or annoys or obstructs an opponent THE REFEREE SHALL STOP THE PLAY AND THE PUCK SHALL BE FACED where it was last played before the

ICE HOCKEY AT ST. MORITZ

THE PHOTO SHOWS MAJOR PATTON, THE LIONS' GOALKEEPER, MAKING A GREAT EFFORT TO SAVE.

Plate 39

off-side occurred. THE DELIBERATE MAKING OF OFF-SIDE PLAYS
SHALL BE PENALIZED AS A FOUL.

(*f*) Despite the foregoing clauses a player on the defending
side is not to be considered off-side within a space of 60 feet
out from his own goal-line and extending to the side of the rink.
A line parallel to the end of the rink shall be drawn across the
ice of the rink to designate this distance. Within the space
between this line and his end of the rink a player on the
defending side, even though in front of the puck, may take a
pass from or play the puck as it bounds off his goalkeeper or
the end of the rink or netting or is passed by any of his team
mates.

(*g*) Players on both sides shall be on-side when they and the
puck are between the goal-line and the adjacent end of the rink.

(*h*) On all face-offs every player must be on his own side
of the puck.

Note.—NEW DEFENCE AREA is defined as follows : On all rinks
200 feet or over in length a line is to be drawn 60 feet from the
goal-line ; on all smaller rinks the ice to be divided into three
equal sections BETWEEN THE GOAL-LINES. Distance behind
goal-posts must be at least 5 feet ; ideal distance 10 feet. In
the new 60-foot area the old rule applies, viz. no off-side for
the DEFENDING TEAM. All rinks must be marked with defence
lines as shown at head of page overleaf.

Knocking-on.

12. The puck may be stopped with the hand, but not carried
or held or knocked on by any part of the body. A player
must not throw the puck or shove it along the ice with his
hand or kick it deliberately. This rule does not apply to any
player of the defending team back of the 60-foot line except
in regard to throwing the puck. The goalkeeper is the only
player who may throw the puck, and he may throw it to the
corners behind the net.

Charging, Tripping, etc.

13. No player shall raise his stick above his shoulder or throw
it along the ice. Charging, tripping, collaring, kicking, cross-
checking, or pushing shall not be allowed. And the referee
must rule off the ice, for any time in his discretion, a player
who, in the opinion of the referee, has deliberately offended

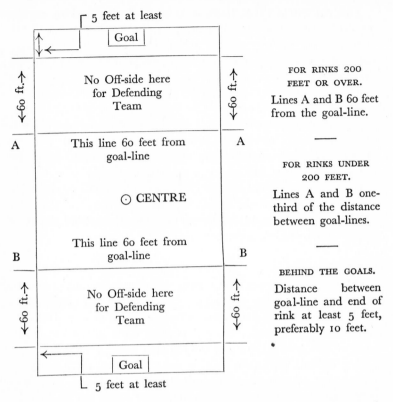

For rinks 200 feet or over, lines A and B are 60 feet from the goal-line. For rinks under 200 feet, lines A and B are one-third of the distance between goal-lines. Behind the goals, the distance between goal-line and end of rink is at least 5 feet, preferably 10 feet.

against the above rule. If a player makes any unfair or rough play, or disputes any decision of the referee, or uses any foul or abusive language, the referee may rule him off for the remainder of the game or for such time as he may deem expedient, and no substitute shall be allowed. If, in the opinion of the referee, a defending player has deliberately committed a foul to prevent a score, he shall not stop the play until that play has been completed.

Definition of Body-Check.

Note.—A fair body-check shall be when a player bodies an opponent with the hip or side of the body when standing still or skating at a slow rate of speed. If, however, a player is skating fast or uses his knee or elbow, it will be considered charging and be penalized accordingly. There shall be no body-checking within 5 feet of the boards.

This rule means that there is to be no body-checking on the forward line. The only players permitted to use the body in checking are players on the defending team when they are back of the 60-foot line, but there must be no charging by these players.

When the Puck leaves the Ice.

14. When the puck goes off the ice behind the goal-line it shall be brought out by the referee to a point 5 yards in front of the goal-line, on a line at right angles thereto, from the point at which it left the ice, and there faced.

When the puck goes off the ice at the side it shall be similarly faced 3 yards from the side.

When the puck hits the referee, play shall cease and the puck faced where the accident occurs.

Goalkeeper.

15. The goalkeeper may stop the puck in any position or manner he wishes, but shall not throw or hold it, and no other player of the defending side, other than the goalkeeper, shall, during the play, lie, sit, kneel or slide along the ice in front of the goal. The goalkeeper may wear pads and a face protector, but must not wear a garment such as would give him undue assistance in keeping goal. The maximum width of the goalkeeper's pads while lying flat must not exceed 10 inches. The referee must rule off the ice for at least one minute a goalkeeper who infringes this rule, and must rule off the ice, for at least two minutes, any other player on his side who has offended against this rule. When a goalkeeper is ruled off, the player who takes his place shall have all the privileges of the goalkeeper and shall be considered as such.

Change of Players.

16. In addition to the extra goalkeeper referred to in Rule 1, two extra players may act as substitutes on each team during a match (making nine players altogether), and a change of players may be made at any time by the substitute or substitutes reporting to the referee, when that official has stopped the play, but must not get on the ice while play is in progress ; such substitute or substitutes must be all ready to play and must take his or their position without delaying the game.

The player for whom the substitution is made must also leave the ice promptly when the substitute appears. In case of injury to the goalkeeper an extra substitute may be allowed, but he must play in goal and in no other position. The substitute goal-tender can only be used at the end of a period, or in case of injury, as aforesaid. Should any player be injured during the match, break a skate, or from any accident be compelled to leave the ice, his side shall immediately put on a substitute to equalize the teams, and the match proceed until such time as the player so compelled to retire because of the accident is ready to return. Should more than two players of one team (exclusive of the goalkeeper) be compelled to retire because of accident, the opposing side shall drop a man to equalize the teams. No player shall resume play until he has received permission from the referee to go on. In event of any dispute, the matter shall at once be decided by the referee.

Note.—If on any occasion it is found that a team is playing too many men, the said team shall forthwith be forced to drop the extra player or players and be penalized by being forced to drop another player for the period of two minutes ; and no goal shall be counted as scored by the offending team while the extra player or players are on the ice.

Stoppages.

17. Should any match be stopped by the referee by reason of any infringement of any of the rules or because of an accident or change of players, the puck shall be faced again at the spot where it was last played before such infringement, accident or change of players shall have occurred.

BOBBING

BY H. C. AND H. M. MARTINEAU

CHAPTER XVII

BOBBING

THE history of Bobbing may be said to date from about 1890 when a certain Mr. Wilson Smith first had the idea of tying together by means of a plank stretched between them two " luges " or small sleighs. This he used to convey himself and others down the snowy slopes of St. Moritz and on to the frozen lake. Naturally the idea of competition soon arose and it was not very long before organized races were being held between different teams. These took place on the roads, and it is on record that great difficulty arose among the newly-formed band of Bobbers owing to the hostility of the local people, who were using the road for the purpose of transport, and who used on many occasions to draw their laden sleighs to the side of the road when the sportsmen wished to pass them on their descent.

It did not take very long for some sort of sleigh, made especially for the purpose of carrying several people, to be devised, and though at first it consisted merely of a set of wooden runners tied to each end of a plank, the principle as applied to the perfected modern bobsleigh remains the same.

If the front set of runners were to be fixed rigidly to the plank in the same way as those at the back, it is obvious that there would be no means of steering and that the bob would merely go in a straight line until it upset. So the front set was made movable by means of strings tied to the front ends of the runners, so that the person sitting on the bob and pulling them would be able to guide its course. Thus corners could be negotiated, provided that the speed was not sufficient to cause centrifugal force to make the bob turn over outwards at the corner.

Next, the passengers began to realize that they might serve some more useful purpose than mere dead-weight cargo. By leaning inwards, i.e. towards the centre of the corner, and thus throwing their weight as much as possible out of the bobsleigh and on the inside runner, they discovered that it

was possible to negotiate the corner a great deal faster than
if they merely sat upright without moving on the bob.

The Brake.

The man at the back of the bob had two iron spikes screwed
on to the end of the bob which dug into the snow and which
could be operated independently.   By using them both together
he could check the speed if he or the steerer thought the bob
was going too fast.   By operating them independently, and
applying the inside one on a corner on the same side as the
crew were leaning, the effect was to partially retard the bob
on that side and so tend to swing it around the corner.   Thus
if the corner went round to the left, the crew would lean as far
over to the left as they were able to, and the brakesman might,
if the speed warranted it, apply the left-hand brake.

The position of brake was, and has remained, a very important one.   His responsibility is next, and almost equal to
that of the steerer.   He must know his driver and understand
his particular methods of steering and cornering.   There
should be perfect co-ordination between them, as indeed must
exist throughout the whole crew if the best results are to be
obtained and fastest times made.   But the brake, as we will
now call that member of the crew who occupies the position
on the back of the bob, is especially privileged.   The other
members of the crew must hold themselves as rigidly as possible
in the bob in order to try and prevent themselves from swaying
and so altering the position of their weight.   This is very
important, as even the slightest movement of one of them in
the wrong direction will very often produce a skid.   Nor must
they ever lean at the corners until they receive the order from
the steerer or his brake, whatever has been agreed upon beforehand.   When they do lean, the more they do so together, the
more help they will be able to give their steerer.

One of the great urges in man's mind throughout the ages
has been the lust for speed, and the first bobbers were naturally
always thinking of how they could go faster and faster.   So
gradually arose the theory of the " banked " corner.   By this
is meant a corner, shaped like a saucer, raised around the outside edge so as to slope inwards towards the centre.   Up till
then their only race track had been the ordinary roads.   These
were naturally as level at the corners as they were on the

straight. Consequently centrifugal force would make the bob skid outwards or overturn if these were taken too fast, and although good crew leaning and judicious application of the brake might help to some extent in counteracting this, yet speeds were, comparatively speaking, bound to be very limited. By "banking" the corner the tendency of the bob to skid outwards or overturn on the outside runner was counteracted by the angle of the slope. So that the steeper the slope, the greater the speed at which the corner could be negotiated. The next step was to acquire a piece of land on which a special road or run could be made and this principle put into operation. At first the runs were crudely built. On the straight portions no particular attempt was made to roll the snow smooth and the corners were very "flat." That is to say that the banking was very little raised on the outside, and so the slope inwards was not very great. But still the principle had been understood and a beginning made, though at first the idea of sprinkling water on the snow so as to be able to build a corner and freeze it solid into any shape or angle of curve, was not properly made use of.

The surface of the old turn corners was composed merely of loose snow into which the runners of the bob often sank deeply. And perhaps for this reason it was the aim of the steerer to keep as low down on the banking of the corner as he could. In the same way as the leaning of the crew was of great assistance on the flat corners of the road, so on the banking of the run the effect of throwing their weight as far as possible out of the bob by leaning towards the inside of the corner made a tremendous difference to the height of the course the steerer was able to take without skidding. For an unintentional skid, where it is possible to get round a corner without doing so, always means loss of speed and time. Besides the fact, too often disregarded, that the nearer the top a driver goes around the corner, the bigger the radius of that sector of the corner will be. So he will actually have a greater distance to travel on his descent, and every little thing makes a considerable difference where split seconds are concerned.

Constructing the Run.

Now that I have said something regarding the system or, let me say, idea of bobbing, a few words would not be out of

place regarding the construction of the run before going into
more detail regarding team work, crews, and various kinds
of bobs.

In the first place, most of the runs in Switzerland are built
by Italians, who seem to be natural ice workers, with either
a Swiss or an English secretary over them. The runs are
usually built in sections so that beginners can travel, let us
say, half-way in order to learn the run, later in the season
another part being opened when the steerers have proved
themselves capable of negotiating the various turnings at greater
speeds. Generally the straight parts of the run are built first.
As the two straight pieces between the corner are built, then
by the aid of sticks placed in alignment, it is impossible to map
out the curve that you propose making. However, on most
of the big bob runs to-day a stone or earth wall is built, giving
the permanent curve which has been mapped out, like the
curve on a railway line. The workmen then begin to mould,
with snow and water mixed, a curve against the wall which
when frozen will form a complete block of ice and which
every night is watered and filled up until the right curve has
been attained. The height of the wall or bank is determined
more or less by the speed that is attained on arriving at that
corner. But it is so built that there is no maximum speed at
which a bob cannot get safely around. It is rather difficult
to explain myself, but what I wish to convey, is the fact that a
bob should be able to take a properly constructed corner at
any speed, without the slightest chance of a spill.

The straight parts of the run are constructed in the same
way, i.e. the snow and water mixed to a depth of about a foot.
The reason for this being so thick, is that in case a hole or
bump is made by the continuous descents of bobs it can be
filled up, or shaved off in order to have the track thoroughly
smooth again for the following day. Great care has to be
exercised in the making of these runs when you get three or
four, or perhaps even more, very quick turns following each
other, because as you probably go into this labyrinth of
turnings at a very great speed, the corners must be built so
that it is possible to go from one bend to the other without
in any way endangering the bob, owing to the fact that the
curve of one corner will not permit the bobs coming off it in
such a way that it can enter the next corner at the proper

CORNERING.

ABOVE—A VENTRE A TERRE BOBSLEIGH LEANING ON A BEND. NOTE POSITION OF 3, 4, 5.
BELOW—A VIEW OF A BOBSLEIGH GOING ROUND SUNNY CORNER AT ST. MORITZ.

angle. To give an idea of the curves that are built, I should like to mention the last corner of the run at Davos. You come into this corner at about 45 miles an hour. Once you have got into the turning you can take your hands off the steering and the corner will take you round of its own accord.

Steering and Crew Work.

Under this heading we have three different forms of steering and two different kinds of crew or team work. There is rope steering, the steering wheel, and lying down steering. On many runs before the War it was not possible to use a steering wheel owing to the fact that it would be much easier to make two or three very quick turnings in succession with rope steering than with the steering wheel, and I will, therefore, confine myself to dealing, for the moment, with the different methods in the order as mentioned above.

In rope steering there are two cords each attached to the end of one of the front runners, each on a pulley, so that you have absolute control on each runner if the ropes are held taut. One hard pull to the left, thereby turning the runner hard to the left ; whereas if it had been a steering wheel it would take longer to give it a complete revolution than to take one direct pull with the rope steering.

In teaching a novice to steer, the best advice you can give him is to keep to the centre of the course on the straight, and when he comes to a turning to the right or to the left, as the case may be, to keep well over to the side where the corner is so as to take the corner early, that is to say, get on to it where it first starts, then ride it well, i.e. steer a smooth and even course around it, and come off it as early as possible without engendering the bob to skid. Later on, the driver may or may not skid his corners at his own discretion in order that he may possibly gain a fraction of a second in time. This idea of skidding corners is open to a great deal of criticism. Many good drivers disagree with it on the plea that if they take the whole bend in a natural curve they will gain speed, whereas skidding the bob may take off a great deal of speed. I think that most drivers will agree with me that often, when a rough and bumpy passage has been made as against a very smooth one which to the crew and driver seems to be very fast, it may, on the contrary, be the rough passage that is the fastest. This, personally, I have noticed on very many occasions during my ten years as President of the St. Moritz Bobsleigh Club and I have had, I am sorry to say, many infuriated drivers coming to the top of the run, and telling me that the clock must be wrong and they cannot understand their slow time, as they had the fastest and smoothest passage they had ever made, as opposed to the man who has been seen going down and watched by spectators skidding and bumping the sides of the track and then made a wonderful time. I am not giving advice at this moment to the novice, to deliberately attempt the method of the rough passage in order to gain time, as this is contrary to all correct driving and would not be a very easy matter for him even if he wished to do so.

Wheel Steering.

Wheel steering is carried out in exactly the same manner as rope steering, except that, as I have said before, rope steering is more direct and therefore on some runs wheel steering cannot be used. For example, on the run at Davos where there are eight or nine very quick turnings in succession which it would not be possible to negotiate with wheel steering. However, on most of the runs it is a matter of preference which is used.

" Ventre-a-terre " or " lying down."

This was first brought to the notice of the bobbing world by Lord Carbury before the War, who believed that to keep the centre of gravity as low as possible would be a good thing. He produced this lying-down bob and ran it in several races, eventually being disqualified by the Committee after winning a race because he seemed to have a great advantage over the others, as he was the only " ventre-a-terre " bob running. However, after a little while the " ventre-a-terre " became an accepted type of bob and was driven by various other drivers during the War, as the run at St. Moritz was kept open by the Swiss for visitors during that time. Before the War the steerers and crews came up to train and race together the whole winter, and it was after the War, when people were only able to stay but a few weeks, that the " ventre-a-terre " bob was revived and came into its own. The idea being, that it was not necessary to have as well trained a crew, the centre of gravity being so low that the most important thing was for them to

RIGHT AND WRONG LEANING

ABOVE IS SEEN CORRECT LEANING OF A CREW WITH THE STEERER SITTING UPRIGHT, ALTHOUGH HE MIGHT BE LEANING ALSO.

BELOW IS SEEN HOW NOT TO LEAN. NOTE NO. 2 IS LEANING THE OPPOSITE WAY TO 3 AND 4.

hang on tightly. This, up to a point, was very true, and it did away to a great extent with the systematic training of the crews that took place before the War, and of course, during the post-war period, it was very convenient to be able to find someone who could go down at the last minute in a crew and really act as dead-weight, all he had to do being to hang on. Of course, when possible, you naturally trained your crew and therefore I do not wish to convey the idea that it is unnecessary to train a " ventre-a-terre " crew. Far from it. I really take it as very important because on a " sitting-up " bob, when a crew leant, they could exert a tremendous effect on the bob, whereas on a " ventre-a-terre " bob, with the crew lying down, on top of one another, their leaning outwards is very small, and therefore has not the same effect on the bob as it would in the case of a sitting-up crew. However, there are very few runs in the world where a " ventre-a-terre " bob is permitted, and now that the International Federation of Bobsleighs has forbidden them in all championship races I am afraid you will see very few " ventre-a-terre " bobs any more except for St. Moritz, which is their home and naturally can run their own private club races.

I have not as yet stated the number of the crew. This varies in many cases from four, five or six persons, and on boblets, which are a form of smaller bob, two or three. Before mentioning team work, I had better say that once you have collected a crew, or rather, hope you have, you must decide as to where you need the weight on the bob. This is determined by the fact that the weight must be evenly distributed all over the bob, taking into consideration your weight as driver and that of the brake, who must be a strong, heavy and active fellow. After you have balanced the bobsleigh evenly, then begins the training of the crew. The first instruction to the crew will be leaning, and after having decided who will give the command for the leans, the brake or the steerer, you give the following words of command, " Left, back—right, back." When the steerer gives " Left," the whole crew, including the brake, lean out as far as possible to the left all at the same time, and when the command " back " is given, they come back to the natural sitting or lying position, again all at the same time. Let me add that if this is not done together and with great precision it may mean the skidding of the bob and a very nasty spill.

Also, if the bob is going at a great speed, it may make a whole difference as to whether the driver will be able to take the next bend with certainty.

Sometimes the crew may get the command " Left, right, left," which means to say that they will be travelling through a labyrinth, and in order to make these turnings the driver must add three very quick " left right lefts " in order to enable him to take the corners in the proper manner. On a good many occasions, not unlike the young recruit, I have seen a crew when given " left " lean " right," thereby upsetting the whole bob. This of course came about owing to the crew not being properly trained, and therefore it is not an unusual occurrence in the morning to walk into one of the steerer's rooms and see, sitting on the floor, the crew practising their leanings. Great responsibility is held by the member of the crew who is acting as brake, because he may see something which the driver does not, and by leaning suddenly on his own he can correct any mistake on the part of the driver. I have seen, on a good many occasions, a driver when coming out of one of the big turnings make a bad mistake, which has been immediately corrected by the brake by lifting the whole of the back of the bob and putting it into a new position. This is perhaps best explained by likening it to a man riding a bicycle and lifting the front wheel while he is going along. However, this sort of thing can only be done by the most expert of brakes.

Previously I mentioned that the brake of the bob must be a strong, heavy and active fellow, one of the reasons for this being his liability to have to try and correct any mistakes the steerer may make and also because on him depends the starting.

There are two methods of starting a race. One is a " standing " start where all members of the crew are on the bob before starting. The other method is the " flying " start, which means to say that the brake has to push the bob and get it under way as quickly as he possibly can, thereby getting up as great a speed as possible within a few yards, and at the same time having to jump on the bob when it is travelling almost faster than he can run. Very often, especially in the case of sitting-up bobs, two of the crew will push. For instance, when there are five people on the bob, No. 1 being the steerer, Nos. 4 and 5 give the push, and as No. 4 jumps on, so No. 5, being the

SITTING UP

LEANING WHILE TAKING A CORNER HIGH UP ON THE BANK.

VENTRE A TERRE

TAKING A BEND. NOTE THE POSITION OF BRAKE.

Plates 44-45

brake, would go on pushing, until he thought it advisable to
jump on. As much as two seconds on a run may be gained
by getting a good start. Therefore, always choose a man
who is a sprinter as your brake. On some runs it is necessary
to apply the brakes a good deal, as the descent is so rapid
that it would be impossible to negotiate the corners without
doing so. On other runs this is hardly necessary except
possibly, as I have said before, to help bring the bob into a
certain position by only using one of the side brakes. On other
runs braking is not allowed at all, sawdust being put down
30 or 40 yards in front of various corners to the depth of 3 inches
according to the speed of the run, to slow the bob up sufficiently
to take the corner.

There are two sorts of bobs which come under the International Federation of Bobsleighing. One is an iron bob, the
other is a wooden bob. On some runs where the wooden bob
is used, the iron one would be quite useless. For instance, at
Chamonix, which is an ice run without a thin covering of
snow, the wooden bobs are in use, whereas at Davos and St.
Moritz, where an iron bob takes a minute and a half to go
down, a wooden bob will take 5 minutes, the reason for this
being that over the ice 2 inches of stamped snow are placed
and tracks are cut by the first bob going down. These are
kept to as far as possible by all the bobs, thereby getting down
to the ice, which, of course, makes the bob go faster. A
wooden bob would not have the weight of the iron bob and
naturally would run along the top of the snow, and even if it
were able to keep to the tracks it would always be being slowed
up by snow that did not affect the heavier bobs. I cannot
give the exact reason why a wooden bob on some of the runs
should be slower, because we once weighted a wooden bob
up to the same weight as an iron bob at St. Moritz, and even
though the width of the runners of both bobs was the same,
the wooden one still took a great deal longer to go down.
On all the runs in French Switzerland the wooden bob is used,
even though the runs are more or less the same type as those
in the Engadine.

TOBOGGANING

BY LIEUT.-COL. J. T. C. MOORE-BRABAZON, M.C.

CHAPTER XVIII

TOBOGGANING

IT has always struck me as surprising that although the conditions in Switzerland have been for centuries the same as they are to-day, no one invented the ski as a sport until quite recently ; on the other hand, the luge stretches back into the immemorial past, although it was again left to Englishmen to develop the riding of it into the sport it has now become.

The Cresta Run.

It is more than forty years ago that the late Major W. H. Bulpett used the valley behind St. Moritz to build the track down into Celerina known as the Cresta. At first, races were held sitting on luges, but as time went on the type of toboggan was improved as well as the track. From the sitting position it was found advantageous to lie head foremost upon what is now called a "skeleton," and the course has become year by year more definite and standardized, and to-day instead of being a snow run, it is one solid piece of ice from start to finish.

Tobogganing takes place on various runs in Switzerland, but most of them are bob runs, used for skeleton races. There is no great ice run existing to-day except the Cresta, consequently for all interested in this sport St. Moritz is the Mecca, and it is upon the Cresta, as embodying all that is known about tobogganing, that I wish to discourse in this article.

It may seem odd to-day, but it is an undoubted fact that much of the present prosperity of winter sports, and of St. Moritz in particular, is due to the fame that the Cresta Run early acquired for itself, and it is a wholesome thing that to-day, when the supercilious look upon St. Moritz as a type of night-club town, tobogganing on the Cresta, of all winter sports essentially a man's game, is in a more flourishing condition than it has ever been. It is, in the writer's opinion, one of the purest sports and one of the cleanest. It has the spice of danger without which nothing is worth while doing ; it does not require great muscle or an athletic frame, everyone stands equal with all others at the top of the Run in propelling force, viz. gravity. It is for the individual so to direct and manage his toboggan while descending to go as fast as, or faster than, anyone else. Let me say right at the beginning that riding is an art that requires a long apprenticeship and is not learnt easily. The greatest experts still differ on methods of riding. Here is a new " shop " as technical as that of golf or fishing, and as exclusive.

When I say that this sport starts at 9 a.m. in the morning, which is not a time when many people are about at St. Moritz, it will be appreciated that riders really do it because they love it, and not because of any plaudits from a crowd. Except for a few enthusiasts the audience at that time in the morning is composed of one or two Engadiners only, who are there on official duties. Yet, frequently, on arrival at nine o'clock I have found myself, on putting my name down to claim a run, about the twentieth on the list.

It will be appreciated that to-day this sport is as flourishing and more so than it has ever been, in addition to which, although no advertising takes place, I find real interest in the doings on the Cresta in every walk of Society in England. It is a sport founded by the English and, although we have, I suppose, on the whole won most events on it, there are some very honourable exceptions and it must always give us pleasure to remember that probably the most distinguished figure and the best rider that ever descended the Cresta is Colonel Thoma-Badrutt, a Swiss, who (although no longer riding) is responsible for the building of the Run year by year. Some technical details of the Run would perhaps be of interest to my readers in order that they may visualize an image of what the Run consists. (See plan.) Let me say, therefore, that the Run starts high up at St. Moritz, it descends 514 feet, it has no less than ten very definite corners, called " Banks "—First, Second, Thoma, The Rise, Battledore, Shuttlecock, Stream, Bulpetts, Scylla, Charybdis, which must be negotiated, the average gradient is 1 in 7·7, the steepest gradient is 1 in 2·8, the maximum length is 1,320 yards, which has been done in no less than 58 seconds.

When judging speed, however, let it be clearly understood

THE START

LOOKING DOWN FROM THE TOP.

BATTLEDORE AND SHUTTLECOCK

LOOKING UP THE RUN.   RIDER ON SHUTTLECOCK.

that a lot of the time is wasted from the pure speed point of view in that a standing start is always made, and that the acceleration at the beginning is not enormous in view of the fact that the gradient at the start is slight. Recent tests have shown that the finishing speed is over 77 miles per hour, and when it is borne in mind that your eyes and nose are within a few inches of the ice, it will be appreciated that the sense of speed is felt keenly by the rider. At the same time, as an old rider, and I think everyone will agree with me, the finish is not as a matter of fact the most thrilling part, the seconds during which one is struggling round some of the corners like a fly on the ceiling, notably round Shuttlecock, are the most thrilling, and yet the speed there is only between 35–45 miles per hour.

The track is built in three separate parts, the lower part first, then about two-thirds of it, and then the completed track. This lends itself very admirably to learning to ride in a progressive way in view of the fact that it becomes increasingly difficult to ride, the farther up the slope one starts. The lowest part, that is from Stream, a distance of about 564 yards, is generally open at Christmas-time, the second part (from Junction) opens at the beginning of January, and the Top is open generally at the beginning of February. Local conditions, due to the fall of snow, etc., vary these dates from year to year, but those given are roughly what one can expect.

There are two outstanding, and two only, races run every year, although there are of course numerous handicaps that are arranged to give everyone a chance. The two great races are the Curzon Cup, formerly known as the Ashbourne Cup, which is held from Junction, generally at the end of January, and the Grand National, held from the Top about the second week in February, which closes the season. It is difficult to say which one can be represented as the blue ribbon of the track, perhaps riding from the Top should be looked upon as the great race, but unfortunately it is held so late in the season, as a rule, that few competitors remain, and for many years it has not been so representative a race as the Curzon Cup from Junction. Riders, I think, will agree also that, although riding from the Top is a magnificent exhibition of control and courage, it yet lacks the " fineness " of riding from Junction and the race is won or lost in both, on the two great Banks of Battledore

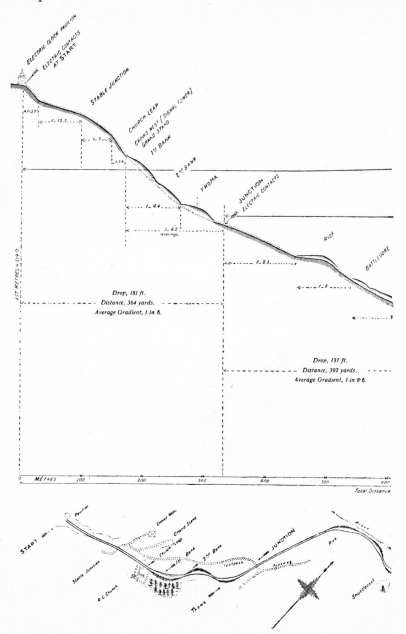

FIG. XVII.

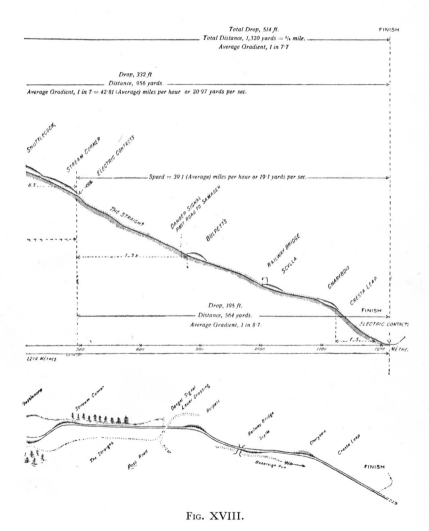

FIG. XVIII.

and Shuttlecock. If riding from the Top introduced new
problems to be faced which overruled these two great corners,
the position would be otherwise, but I do not believe such is
the case. Detailed timing has clearly proved to me that,
although a certain advantage may be derived from fast riding
on the first three Banks, the problem presented by Battledore
and Shuttlecock still dominates the time to such an extent as
largely to eliminate the earlier occurrences. I am stating this
as my own opinion, and I daresay there will be many riders
who will disagree with me.

The history of the Cresta it is not my province to describe,
I have alluded to some incidents in its career, but it is more as
we find it to-day that we are concerned with than its develop-
ment up to the present time. To any student of form, however, the St. Moritz Tobogganing Club issues every year a book,
which can be obtained from the Secretary, which gives details
which it would be but redundant to include in this work. I
have myself now ridden the Cresta for over twenty years, and
it may therefore be of interest for me to give my opinion (for
what it is worth) on the merits of the great riders of the past.
As an old Harrovian I am aware of the words " There were
wonderful giants of old," and consequently I feel bound to
remark immediately that I believe the standard of riding to-day
is every bit as good as it has ever been, and the great names
of the past if they were present to-day in the full flush of
youth would have to go as hard as they knew how in order
to win.

A point I must warn enthusiasts against is comparing the
time of one year against the time of another year. It is true
that to the uninitiated the course looks the same and is the
same year after year, but only the rider knows how entirely
different it is to ride. Recently, under the direction of Colonel
Thoma-Badrutt, the course has been very beautifully built and
consequently the times have become progressively faster.
Recently the record from the Top was lowered to 58 seconds,
yet no one could say really that 58 seconds on a perfect track
was a more meritorious run than a time of 61 seconds a few
years ago. It is the same thing in riding from Junction, times
of 46 seconds are common to-day, whereas a few years ago the
best time of the year was 48·5, which, on the present track,
would be almost third-class riding.

FROM THE TOP
FROM CHURCH LEAP ON TO FIRST BANK.

SHUTTLECOCK
COMING ON TO THE GREAT BANK.

Plates 48-49

E. Thoma and J. A. Bott were two of the most distinguished
riders of years ago, and although I never saw him, Major Bertie
Dwyer has always been quoted to me as a very first-rate
exponent of the art.   It is interesting to note that in the year
1901 Captain Trenchard, now Lord Trenchard, ex-Chief of
the Air Staff, won the Cresta Freshmen's Cup.   Of Bott and
Thoma, although Bott's name appears in the records as having
won the Grand National five times and the Ashbourne Cup
three times, Colonel Thoma's record is even more remarkable
as he won the Ashbourne Cup six times and the Curzon Cup
once, making seven in all, as well as one Grand National and
dead-heating in another.   They were indeed two giants who
stood out in their day.   In more recent times, before the War,
the rivalry of an American named C. E. Bacon and Lieutenant
V. F. Gibbs of the Royal Navy, was very keen and I must say
that I have never seen better tobogganing than in the duels
between these two.   Gibbs, who was later killed in the raid on
Zeebrugge, I do not believe ever had a fall, he was undoubtedly
the safest rider that I ever saw and his command of his toboggan
when riding forward, even on such difficult Banks as Battledore
and Shuttlecock, was quite uncanny.   Bacon was more dashing
and perhaps as fast, but without reliability and, as reliability
is of the essence of Cresta riding, he could not quite compare
with Gibbs.

Since the War riding has been in and out, and there have
been no dominating figures, though the riding has been fast.
N. Marsden stands out as a very distinguished, graceful and
finished rider, but, at his best, I think Lord Northesk would have
beaten anybody as not only had he great knowledge and
command of tobogganing, but his start was one of the most
astounding I have ever seen.   Except from the Top starting
plays a very important rôle in tobogganing, it is a difficult
thing to hold a toboggan on the ground with two hands and
at the same time run fast while pushing it, yet this acrobatic
feat is performed by everybody with varying degrees of success,
but such a position did not seem in any way to incommode Lord
Northesk who got more kick and speed into his start than
anybody.   I do not want, however, to decry his excellent riding
on the course by giving the impression that his success was due
to his start alone, as when riding from the Top the start does
not play such an important rôle as when riding from Junction,

yet some of Lord Northesk's most distinguished performances have been from the Top.

Before passing to a more detailed description of the Cresta and how to ride it, it would be ungracious not to pay a tribute to those who, year after year, have devoted so much time, effort and organizing power to the success of this wonderful Club, situated at St. Moritz.   First and foremost, apart from our tribute to Colonel Thoma-Badrutt as a great rider, it has been due to his love of the sport and of the Run, and to his tremendous knowledge of the whole subject, that we are provided to-day, year by year, with an even more perfect course.   He has of course the advantage of living at St. Moritz and of being always there in the winter, he is a perpetual Vice-President of the Club and, although never conspicuous, he is always there behind the scenes to help with his advice. The Club have paid him the honour, which it is hoped will last for ever, of naming Third Bank after him.   Mr. Leland Littlefield was also a great patron for many years of the Cresta, and for two years he was President when the Hon. F. Curzon was unable to come out ; nobody took a keener interest in the organization and detailed work than he did and his death in 1924 was a grievous loss to the Club.   The Hon. Francis Curzon, donor of the Curzon Cup, is also one to whom the Club owes a very deep debt of gratitude.   A very keen though never a very great rider, nobody has played a more important part than he in keeping the Club up to that high standard which it enjoys to-day.   Much of the work he does is not spectacular, but the Club would not be the successful institution it is, had it not been for his untiring zeal and enthusiasm for the cause.

Two secretaries of the Club will always be remembered as of outstanding personality and ability, and let me say that the duties of the Secretary are very much wrapped up with the success of the sport in general.   The amiable figure of the late A. N. Ranney stands out in my mind, for a long time the beloved Secretary of the Club.   With his fur collar and high boots he ordered us about for many years with firmness and tact, and under his direction everything went smoothly.   In latter days Captain Boddam-Whetham has proved himself one of our most successful secretaries ; he early appreciated the fact that the Secretary is the Executive Officer of the Club, solely responsible for the lives of the riders and the safe running of the track, and that under these conditions it was his duty to give orders and the duty of riders instantly to obey. Besides possessing these military qualities which, although sometimes resented by the inexperienced, are very much appreciated by those who know, he was singularly successful with the help of the President on the difficult financial side and the preservation of a reserve fund for the future.

The Cresta, on the whole, has been very happy in its personnel, and the author cannot help saying that though he has indulged in many sports in his life, he has never found himself in competition with a keener and better collection of sportsmen than are to be found riding the Cresta. When it is remembered that it is an international medley and that you never know what language you have to speak to the rider who walks up with you, it is indeed a high tribute to the sport what a happy family all the riders soon become. St. Moritz has much to be proud of in its winter sports, but I feel sure that in its heart it is most proud of its Cresta Run which has no rival and is unique throughout the world.

II

As has been said in the previous section, the Cresta is open in three successive stages, from Stream, a distance of 564 yards, from Junction, a distance of 956 yards, and from the Top, a distance of 1,320 yards.

It is my intention to envisage the reader as being new to tobogganing in all its branches, yet wishing to take up the sport, and consequently I must look upon him as a pupil unaware of the most rudimentary knowledge which I will endeavour to impart to him. Some things will be common to riding from each stage such as Equipment, and consequently a detailed description of what is wanted is a most suitable subject with which to start this section.

EQUIPMENT

As to clothes, nothing very ornate is required. I have always found three sweaters and plus-fours as good as anything; breeches are not as good as they seem, as they definitely impede running at the strained angle required at the start. Boots should be stout but not heavy. Before you are allowed down the Run you must be equipped with rakes screwed on to them,

with a bridge coming over the toe. In addition, there should
be three spikes on the sole of the boot in order to get a kick-off
from the ice. Too much attention cannot be paid to one's
boots, as they are the sole method you have of accelerating
and of retarding and you will early find that braking is required, sometimes very urgently. There is one point about
the rakes which I think is useful and that is not to have the
spikes of the rakes sticking out too much on the inside of the
foot, the spikes should start pointing forward, not inward.
The reason for this is that if you have the spikes pointing
inwards you are very liable to catch your legs on them when
running, with the most painful results, and also it is sometimes
necessary and comforting when riding the Cresta, to trail a foot
flat upon the ice when rounding a Bank, and this cannot be
done without raking if they project on the inside.

Knee-pads.

Knee-pads are essential. They are first of all required when
jumping on one's toboggan, and also very often when you are
full back on your toboggan you will find that a lot of
your weight is on your knees, and unless they are adequately
protected this delicate part of one's anatomy becomes seriously
hurt. Concentrate on seeing, also, that knee-pads do not slip
down as they always tend so to do.

Elbow and Hand-pads and Crash Helmet.

Elbow-pads of a substantial nature are essential, and hand-
pads. The hand-pads should have steel saucers on them in
order to protect the knuckle from the side, and finally it is
now compulsory to wear what is called a crash helmet. The
writer was instrumental in introducing this as a compulsory
article of clothing and there is no question but that it is essential
to wear this, as a fall in the Run (as compared with a fall over
the Run) is now comparatively innocuous, whereas formerly
it led to very serious concussion. The writer once, due to a
hole in the ice on Third Bank, now Thoma, and his toboggan
jamming in it, shot forward and slid head over heels, sometimes on his face, sometimes on his back, hitting the side of
the track with every part of his body from Third Bank to the
middle of Shuttlecock. This is a distance of some 300 yards
and yet he did not receive a serious bruise or scratch, entirely

due to the fact that a helmet automatically keeps your head
from receiving injury from the side, and also your face just off
the ice. Cases in which the helmet has saved people from
serious injury are so numerous and acknowledged so universally
by all that I am glad to say the use of it is now compulsory.

The Toboggan.

Garbed, as one can imagine, rather like a knight of old, one
is now ready, except for the toboggan. Toboggans, like all
things, have changed and have advanced, but the modern
instrument consists of a padded plate of about 18 inches broad
and about 2 feet long which slides upon the main toboggan,
which is about 4 feet long. The runners we will not worry
about, except to say that the distance they are apart, the steel
they are made of, and the bow which they have, all contribute
different characteristics to your running. A modern toboggan,
however, as good as anything upon the track, can easily be
acquired at no great expense. I introduced myself a toboggan
embodying a spring between the main frame and the sliding
platform with which I had considerable success, but although
I quickly offered it to every other rider to copy and to ride,
it has not found great favour, although I cannot help saying
that it is incomparably more comfortable to ride. It requires,
however, a good deal of experience in other ways as it is
extremely sensitive. The runners of the toboggan are smooth
and should be highly polished, but towards the end—for about
the last 4 inches—they end in a deep groove. This groove
should be kept very sharp, and its function is to prevent side-
slipping at corners. The normal position of the rider on the
toboggan on the straight is forward, when his weight is evenly
balanced on the runners ; when, however, a corner is reached
his weight is shifted to the after part of the toboggan by sliding
the seat back. On doing this the weight is on the groove, when
the nose of the toboggan can be swung either to the right or
to the left, and it is by this procedure that steering occurs, the
toboggan being unable to side-slip.

Our first adventure down is to be from Stream. It will be
noticed that a thin piece of cotton is stretched across the Run,
and that you are instructed to start 10 feet behind it. On
breaking this first contact the clock will be started, at the bottom
you will break another contact which will stop the clock. The

clock, which was presented by Mr. Littlefield, is electrically
operated and is remarkable in that it ticks in tenths. Few
clocks have so quick moving an escapement as this, most tick
in fifths. The thing which riders do not appreciate enough is
the distance traversed per second. It will be appreciated that
when pushing the toboggan over the line you are not going at
more than 5 miles per hour, whereas at the finish (as I have
already said in a previous chapter) you are going about 80
miles an hour. It is interesting to work out what these speeds
mean in distance per second, or better still in tenths of seconds.
At the speed of 5 miles an hour, a tenth of a second = 9 inches ;
at 80 miles an hour one-tenth of a second = 12 feet. Therefore,
from the point of view of gaining time, if at the start you can
gain 9 inches, it is equivalent to gaining 12 feet at the finish.

The Start.

Here lies the importance of quick starting. The rules have
it that you may not start farther back than with the nose of the
toboggan 10 feet behind the line. If you are right-handed you
will stand on the left of the toboggan, seeing that the sliding
seat is well forward, you will grasp it with both hands, locking
it to the toboggan by your hands, and run (crossing the tape)
until you have got up your maximum speed, then still holding
your toboggan you will throw yourself prone upon it. This
may sound a simple operation, but it is one requiring no little
agility and a certain amount of gymnastic ability, and great
experience is required in order to jump on fast and, what is
as essential, true. It will be realized that the last push must
be a straight one and that you must pitch on to your toboggan
on the right place upon it, the right place being perfectly
straight as an arrow fore and aft and with your chin projecting
about a foot ahead of the cross-bar at the forward end of the
toboggan. The elbows should be well in and up, the body
as straight as a die, and the legs together, slightly in the air
so as not to touch the ice.

You are now off, and one of the most difficult parts of
tobogganing is before you, which is keeping a straight course
when going slowly. It is comparatively easy to steer when
going fast, but the first 80 yards from the start is always a
difficult time in which to control the toboggan. All toboggans
have a pernicious habit of wishing to go either to the right

Plate 50

TOBOGGANING EQUIPMENT

THE AUTHOR FULLY EQUIPPED, SEATED ON THE SPRING TOBOGGAN THAT THREE TIMES WON HIM
THE CURZON CUP.

or to the left when going slowly, and to obviate this, should you find yourself drifting, say, to the left, incline your head and put your body as much as you can on the right-hand runner (Plate 51). This will slightly correct the tendency. Should you actually be about to hit the side of the track it is best at all times to do this with your elbow, which is padded for the purpose, rather than with the end of the toboggan, covered by your hand. Sometimes it pays not to touch with your elbow or your hand, but this is only under advanced conditions and when the angle at which you are about to hit is very slight.

Acceleration will be occurring the whole time and for a beginner it is wise to start trailing your feet so as to diminish the acceleration. You will now be rapidly approaching what is known as The Road with your first corner before you, namely Bulpetts. Every corner which you come to should be taken as early as possible, so, to take Bulpetts, get your toboggan running straight but well to the left-hand side of the track and, as you actually come to the corner, push yourself back on your toboggan. Bulpetts is a corner to the right, therefore leave your left hand forward and bring your right hand back under your weight. You are now on the grooves of the toboggan and if you move the front of it, the toboggan must steer as you are on the grooves. The moment you come on to the corner, push with your extended left hand the front of the toboggan down slightly, this will take you round the corner, and the moment you are round, take your right hand from where it is and place it forward again. Pull yourself on your sliding seat as far forward as possible, and you will have tackled your first corner.

After about another 80 yards there is another corner called Scylla, which bears to the left. Still trailing your feet, go through the same operations as before, keeping this time well to the right before the corner, taking your left hand back, and pushing the nose of the toboggan well down on the corner. You will now have negotiated Scylla. Another 50 yards and you meet another bend to the right called Charybdis. Charybdis is a bank which, later on, you will treat with great respect as you meet it at great speed as a rule. Negotiate it in the same way as Bulpetts, after which you will find the track drops down very steeply to the finish and no great difficulty exists after Charybdis, all you have to do is to ride forward

N

and keep the centre of the track. At the bottom of the dip you will break the contact and your first time will be recorded. From then on the track rises very quickly and bears to the left. The moment you have crossed the line go back on your toboggan, leaving your right arm forward as the finishing bank bears to the left, rake hard, and you will find yourself coming to rest all safe and sound, after your first run down the Cresta.

Some years ago the finish used to be perfectly straight, but one was going so fast that one could not stop jumping into the air at the end which was painful, and damaging to the toboggan. Now Colonel Thoma-Badrutt has swung the track to the left which does not increase the difficulty of riding but which makes a better finish and saves about 100 yards of walk up, a very considerable thing.

Notice well that we have concentrated on going down the Run without trouble, and the sort of time you will have recorded against you will be about 37 seconds for your first time down. Do not be worried in any way at the length of time taken, the cracks will have been going down in 30 seconds and you have a lot of time to make up, but there is one golden rule of the Cresta which is " Never hurry, until you are familiar with every part of it, and never frighten yourself." If you frighten yourself going down the Cresta it will delay you for many subsequent runs. The whole thing at first is alarming, I confess it. I have done it so many years that one would imagine I should not be alarmed any longer, but the first time each year I go down I am always alarmed even now, and it is not until you get familiar with the whole feeling and get rid of fear that you can impose your will on your toboggan. Good riding consists of nothing else but imposing your will on your toboggan, and only thus can fast times be obtained.

Continue to go down in exactly the same way once or twice, after which you will find that for the three Banks at the bottom of the Run, that is for Bulpetts, Scylla and Charybdis, you will no longer find it necessary to rake at all. After this you will find that it is no longer even necessary to go back on your toboggan, but I maintain that it is necessary even in the early days that you should be familiar with going back on your toboggan, because it is the way to get out of difficulties and should be learnt at the earliest stage rather than from higher up.

In a few days if you are keen, enthusiastic, and young, you

will find yourself starting fairly well, going down without going back on your toboggan, and without raking, yet you will find yourself a second or so slower than the cracks. You have got to get down to their standard and this can only be done by practice and by riding the corners as you wish to, leaning at the right time and taking them without any form of skidding, which is the bugbear of the Cresta. So often one comes off a Bank not quite true, which means with a slight drift, and the moment this occurs you are losing time very badly.

I have seen riders get in as many as eight practice runs in the morning from Stream, and consequently it is a part of the Run which should in no way be neglected by the beginner so as to get all the experience possible in starting, which is so important later on. Also you gain experience in riding the three Banks at the bottom which have to be negotiated at a higher speed from farther up, and with which acquaintanceship and familiarity is required if they are to be taken efficiently.

Practice from Stream generally goes on until about the first week of January, after which the Run is closed from Stream and starts higher up from Junction.

RIDING FROM JUNCTION

Riding from Junction is probably the most subtle and the most difficult from the point of view of speed of any riding on the Cresta. The start is similar to the start from Stream in that the slope is not very pronounced and all the difficulty of a quick start and keeping straight for the first 80 yards is common to both runs, but we have now to face the great problem of the Cresta, namely the negotiations of the two great corners, Battledore and Shuttlecock. Get into your head a definite and wholesome respect for the Cresta ; so many people after riding from Stream think that they know all, whereas they have not begun to know anything, and it is not until they are good riders from Junction that they can be called riders at all.

Approach riding from Junction with the humility of a beginner or else the Cresta will get it back on you every time. Falls over Shuttlecock may be quite innocuous ; I have seen one man take six running and not get a bruise, but, on the other hand, sometimes a simple fall will cause very grave damage, as it is difficult to get away from one's toboggan, and when it hits you, weighing as it does some 80 lb., the results are not pleasant. Approach riding from Junction, therefore, with all caution and the determination in your mind not to hurry your times to start with but to concentrate on getting familiar with the whole feel of the thing and with the technique of the business, as also to avoid falls, because a fall puts you back very much from the point of view of self-confidence and time.

You have started your run from Junction, you are coming to a corner bending slightly to the right called the Rise. There is no rise, do not imagine therefore that you will slow up, far from it. This particular corner is built for higher speeds than that at which you are going ; it is built for riding from the Top, consequently it is banked much more than is necessary for the speed at which we attack it. Pay no attention to it, except to keep off it as much as possible by leaning the head and putting your weight on the right-hand runner. The moment you get on to the tail of it you will be faced with a sharp drop of about 10 yards right on to Battledore. Battledore is an extremely vertical and sharp Bank turning to the right, and is undoubtedly the key to the whole secret of successful riding. The attack on Battledore is, to my mind, the most emotional moment in the whole run, you have got back on your toboggan, your right hand is back, your left hand is leading, you are as near as possible to the left-hand side of the track, do not hesitate to rake hard. To come on to the Bank, get the nose of the toboggan slightly down so as not to come too high, but do not force yourself off the corner altogether ; keep, if you can, a long, low Battledore rather than a high, peaky one. I say " long " for this reason, that after Battledore you are coming to the great corner Shuttlecock, which is very nearly 180 degrees and which wants the highest skill in riding.

All corners should be attacked early, and it is more important to attack Shuttlecock early than any other, but it will be realized that it is impossible to do this unless you use Battledore—or rather, the tail of Battledore—to throw you up early on to Shuttlecock. As you come to the tail of Battledore you have got to indulge in a manœuvre which is quite difficult considering the speed at which you are travelling. You will remember that you have taken Battledore right back

AT THE TOP
THE AUTHOR STRUGGLING TO KEEP STRAIGHT JUST AFTER STARTING.

A SPILL OVER SHUTTLECOCK
NOTE THE STRAW TO FALL INTO

on your toboggan with your left hand leading, pushing the nose of the toboggan down, and with your right hand still under your weight on the runners. As you come off Battledore into the trough you have to take your right hand and put it forward and your left hand from forward and put it back, reversing your position. Now you have to steer round Shuttlecock, but do not make the fatal error of trying to avoid it, Shuttlecock has got to be taken and cannot be avoided. So many people on arrival at Shuttlecock push the nose of their toboggan down instantly ; this is a mistake, get up as high as you can on the first few yards. After taking about 10 yards of the first part of Shuttlecock, the critical part of the corner will be upon you and it is with this that you must deal with care. Keep the nose of the toboggan down and see that you do not get anywhere near the top of Shuttlecock, and if you are rightly placed upon your toboggan, no skid will occur and you should be master of the situation. Continue to rake with both feet, not spread out but very nearly together, they should not be separated by more than 2 feet if all is going well. After this there will come a very definite sensation to you which can only be felt and not described, that the crisis of the corner is over. The moment this occurs, you may stop riding back and may pull yourself forward and in this position you will be deposited quietly on to Stream, which is usually a corner which looks after you in the most motherly way and requires no riding except for a slight lean to the right. If it is built well it will deposit you true and well into the straight, after which you find yourself riding from Stream as you have already practised, but of course at a higher speed and the corners will have to be negotiated with care, so do not think you know all about them because you have done them from Stream. Pay great attention to them at first until they come easily to you, and let me remind you that they come very fast at you now and it is difficult to take them beautifully, as a good deal of riding is necessary to get on to them early and at the right place.

I have referred to Stream Corner being a motherly corner and looking after you ; of late years it has been built like this, but sometimes the tail of Stream is one of the most difficult spots on the course to negotiate, necessitating the use of the most advanced tricks to negotiate it. I have myself fallen

four times on the tail of Stream, and yet during the last few
years such a thing would sound incomprehensible. It is
necessary, therefore, the first time down from Junction not to
take any liberties, but to explore the position thoroughly to
see what new difficulties exist in the Run.

Your first time down from Junction, if you are a wise rider,
should register about 56 seconds. You have been raking the
whole way from Rise to the tail of Stream ; do not be frightened
of raking, remember that the track is made of ice and no raking
that you do impedes other people. Nobody on the Cresta is
upset at anyone raking, it disturbs no one, and does no harm.
There is a popular idea that raking damages the track ; this
is certainly true of snow tracks, but it is not true of an ice track
like the Cresta. Remember that nobody is annoyed at anyone
going slowly, what they are annoyed at is people being rash
upon the Cresta. You will get all the support and all the hints
and all the help from riders if you treat the Run with respect
and try at first to go slowly, but you will have little sympathy
from anybody if you try short-cutting at first and so come to
grief. Let me say again that there is no short cut to fast times
on the Cresta, only hard work and practice.

Continue to go down from Junction in the way I have
described until all the alarm on coming on to Battledore and
going on to Shuttlecock has disappeared, after which slightly
different tactics can be indulged in. First of all, you need not
go back on your toboggan until actually arriving on Battledore.
From Junction for very expert riders I do not believe it is
necessary to rake at all, the raking that takes place by first-class
riders is more to steer by than to diminish speed. The Run
of course is built in a different way each year ; I have seen
great riders like Gibbs take Battledore and Shuttlecock forward,
but nobody could do that as they are built at present, nor do
I think there would be any advantage in it. The expert rider
to-day goes back on entering Battledore and comes forward
after the crisis on Shuttlecock, but he goes round smoothly
and fairly low on both Banks and manœuvres himself to do,
what is so very difficult, which is to come off Shuttlecock without any skid and true on to Stream, to be poured into the
straight at an ever-accelerating speed. Every time you walk
up from the Cresta, watch the good riders, it is astonishing
what you can learn, but it is only after many trials down your-

self that you appreciate the amazing "fineness" of this astonishing art.

From Junction is held the great race of the year and by far the most popular race, the Curzon Cup. All riders doing a certain minimum time are allowed to compete on the first day, out of whom only the first eight compete on the second day, the race being the aggregate time of six courses. If in your first year you can become one of the Curzon eight you have done well. I do not wish to discourage anybody, far from it, but I have never seen a beginner become a really first-class rider in his first year. This is of little moment, however, as the Cresta has such an attraction that to have ridden it once necessitates coming back to ride it again.

RIDING FROM THE TOP

Riding from the Top is the climax of one's Cresta career. On the whole it is not so pleasing as riding from Junction, the long walk up is exhausting and tedious, added to which the whole course is invisible while one is waiting to start and consequently somewhat less attractive than riding from other points on the course. The view, however, from the Crow's Nest, situated about 150 yards from the start, is superb, the whole progress of the rider from start to finish can be seen. Timing takes place actually in the Crow's Nest, which is the nerve centre of the course.

When riding from the Top great caution is necessary as the slopes are very steep, and it is inadvisable to descend at all unless a good deal of experience has been acquired from Junction. The start differs materially from the start either from Stream or from Junction in that the slope is very pronounced and consequently the art of running with your toboggan is a good deal discounted, two short steps being all that is necessary in order to get well away. I would recommend a thorough overhaul of knee-pads and equipment and, anyhow to start with, the fitting of heavier and sharper rakes.

The first sharp slope does not continue for more than about 6 yards, after which the course is straight and very flat until a skyline approaches over which one can see nothing. This skyline occurs just after what is called Stable Junction, where there is a track across the course. After the first skyline, one approaches another which is of an alarming character, and is

known as Church Leap. It depends very much on how the
course is built, but for many years this slope was so steep as
to cause you actually to leave the ice for a distance of several
yards. I do not say that this will occur if you have raked from
Stable Junction hard, which one is well advised to do to start
with. Later, after becoming a little accustomed to riding from
the Top, raking is not necessary until just before Church Leap.
Church Leap deposits you upon First Bank, which is a sharpish
turn to the left. This is a very big bank, in fact the biggest
on the course, and tremendously steep.

On arriving on First Bank, fully back, it is necessary to rake
hard with the left foot and swing the toboggan well to the left
or there will be little chance of coming on to Second Bank
correctly. At no period during the Run does one feel so out
of control as on First Bank, one is literally a projectile with very
little control, but in spite of this one can somehow present
oneself at the right place on Second Bank.

Second Bank is a sharp turn to the right, hands must be
changed and an effort made to ride it low, as a high Second
Bank necessarily leads to a high Thoma which can be very
disastrous. On the tail of Second Bank, hands must be
changed again and Thoma attacked. Again attention must
be concentrated on keeping low, but once round it you come
forward and shoot across Junction at a very high speed. It
is to be noted that even fast riders will rake from Church Leap
till coming forward on Thoma. The amount of raking will
no doubt vary as experience is gained, but very hard firm raking
is essential to start with if disaster is to be averted, and it
would be unwise of me if I were to pretend that riding Church
Leap and the first three Banks is anything like child's play.
It is a very serious undertaking, requiring great command of
riding and self-confidence.

Rise is now approaching at a speed one is little accustomed
to, and even the fast riders do not go round it forward. It
is wiser to get well back on the toboggan about one-third of
the way round as velocity is now high, and the critical part
of the Run is still approaching, that is the attack on Battledore.
Remember that you are coming to this crucial corner at
a very much increased speed, and very severe raking is
demanded before getting on to it. A great deal of the
skill in making a fast time depends on how much raking is

required to get round Battledore and Shuttlecock. There is little doubt that the riding of Battledore and the beginning of Shuttlecock from the Top calls for different tactics as the speed is so high, but from the tail of Shuttlecock and down the straight I believe the speed reaches its maximum even from Junction, and that riding from the Top does not alter anything, so that from Stream onwards the course can be ridden as from Junction.

One of the difficulties of riding from the Top is the estimation of speed of the track each morning, as sometimes it is not necessary to rake very hard before Battledore and Shuttlecock, and at other times it is essential so to do in order to negotiate them. Constant practice is required before high speeds are attempted, as the Leap and the first three Banks are a very alarming experience and one which one must be accustomed to before concentrating on high speeds.

The season finishes with the Grand National run from the Top, which is a scratch race of three courses.

You will, by now, have been bitten by the intricacies of riding and from now on you will be talking " shop " the whole way up with your competitors, comparing notes, taking and offering advice. It is an easy thing to go down the Cresta, and it is a safe thing to do at a moderate speed, but the difficulty lies in knocking off the last few tenths of a second, and endless patience and great study is wanted to do this. Yet how important these tenths are I know full well, for I won once the Curzon Cup from that great rider, Marsden, beating him by one-tenth of a second in an aggregate of six courses. 12 feet ahead of him after six runs ! It shows, I think, the keenness of competition and the necessity of saving every particle of time and using every device imaginable.

There can be no question that riding from Junction is more popular than riding from the Top ; this may of course be largely explained by the following reasons : First of all, the extra climb to get to the Top makes it very difficult without very great effort to get more than three courses in, in one morning, added to which when at the Top, no portion of the Run is visible and one waits for one's turn quite unable to see what is happening at any point in the Run, whereas when riding from Junction the whole of the track is visible. When riding from Junction, interest never flags in the performance of others, in their descent, added to which one must not forget that riding from the Top is undoubtedly a much more serious business than riding from Junction. Unless one is a rider of skill there is little doubt, and it is undisputed, that it is a dangerous pastime and no one should go down unless he is familiar with tobogganing in all its branches, and a rider of experience and skill from Junction. This alone, I daresay, diminishes the number of riders that present themselves, added to which there is little doubt that even after safe descents one finds oneself very considerably knocked about ; many times on walking up I have found myself bruised in leg and arm and unable to account as to when or how such injuries had been received.

I do not, however, attribute the lack of popularity in riding from the Top to this cause, I attribute it rather, as I have said before, to the fact that it is so very late in the season. Also, one must remember that to ride well from the Top one must ride well from Junction, and to ride well from Junction necessitates at least a fortnight's hard work on the lower part. In that the Grand National occurs a fortnight after the Curzon Cup it means that to be a successful rider from the Top necessitates a visit to St. Moritz of over a month, which in these days when everybody has work to do is very difficult to arrange.

No one can claim to be a complete tobogganer until he has ridden fast from the Top. After all, it is the whole splendid thing with all its tribulations and no one who has ever done it can forget its thrills or regret that he has taken full part in what must always rank as the King of Winter Sports.

CURLING

BY ALEXANDER LORIMER

A WELL DELIVERED STONE

THE PLAYER HAS SOLED THE STONE NICELY AND HAS THE EYE FIXED ON THE OBJECT TO BE PLAYED FOR.

Plate 53

CHAPTER XIX

CURLING

HISTORY OF CURLING

LIKE one or two other games, the origin of the game of Curling has never been traced to its source. A good many writers have written books on Curling and have studied ancient books on the game in order to try and place the beginning, but without success.

The late Rev. John Kerr in his monumental book on *The History of Curling* gave extracts from various papers of different people, some of which say the game came from the Flemish people, others the Germans, and others that it started in Scotland. However that may be, the game does not seem to have been played in Scotland until the beginning of the sixteenth century.

In the beginning the stones with which the game was played were simply stones taken from the bed of a stream, not hewn in any way, but in order to throw them, holes were cut out for the finger and thumb, and these were evidently thrown along the ice.

The next stage in the evolution of the stones was when someone struck the happy idea of fixing a handle in them so that they might be more easily lifted and thrown. The handle at this stage was fixed into the stone permanently. Then there was no limit to the size and weight of a stone and they varied from 115 lb. per stone downwards. The record weight of stone was one called the Jubilee Stone weighing 117 lb. which belonged to and was played by one, John Hood, who died in January 1888.

The third stage in the evolution of the stones was when they were made circular by the stone-hewer, and a hole drilled in the centre for the bolt and handle. There was at this time such a great variation in the sizes and weights of stones that it became obvious to many curlers that there should be some limit as to size and weight, and that a maximum and minimum should be fixed. An announcement was published in the *N. B. Advertiser* of 26th May, 1838, calling a meeting in Edinburgh on 20th June, at which a dozen curlers turned up. Thereafter another meeting was called for 25th July, 1838, at which fifty members of Initiated Curling Clubs attended, and Mr. John Cairnie of Largs was elected President. The constitution of the Club was adopted on 15th November, 1838, and the Grand Club, as it was then called, became the governing body in connection with Curling, and drew up Rules and Regulations in connection with the game and fixed the maximum weight of a stone at 44 lb., including handle and bolt.

METHODS OF DELIVERING THE STONE

At present there are two ways of delivering the stone. One is from the Crampet which is shaped thus :

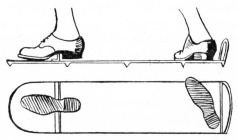

It is a long steel plate with a raised ridge at the back to rest the right foot against when delivering the stone. This is the method which most of the older curlers use who learned their Curling on open-air ice in the country before the advent of artificial rinks.

The younger generation of curlers are taking more now to what is called the Hack. This is usually placed just at the point of the crampet every time a hack player wishes to deliver his stone.

The hack is a brass or iron casting shaped thus :

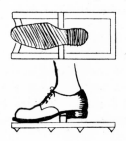

It is easy to carry about, and once one gets used to playing off the hack, to my mind one would not go back to playing off the crampet.

I have rather pronounced views on the advantages of the hack. To my mind, anyone playing off the crampet has his body badly twisted, his right foot is at right angles to his left which is pointing directly towards the tee at the far end of the rink. Of course some people have played this way all their lives and have become accustomed to it.

On the other hand, when playing off the hack as I do myself, my right foot is placed on the hack facing directly towards the far-away tee, my left foot and whole body are also facing the same way, and I get well down when delivering the stone. Thus the feet, the body and the head are all pointing in the direction in which the stone is to travel, and when one gets well down when delivering the stone I maintain that one gets greater accuracy in direction.

As in billiards most players get well down towards the level of the table to get their line and angle, and one is able to lay the stone down without wobbling it. No one knows how far such a stone will travel.

The stone should be held swinging from the hooked fingers and not the whole hand round the handle, the thumb on the top of the handle and pointing straight forward.

The swing back depends on the kind of shot one is going to play. In playing a heavy shot the arm swings back as far as possible so as to get the necessary impetus, but in ordinary play on fairly keen ice, very little backward swing is necessary.

The stone should be released practically at the finish of the forward swing just as the stone is making contact with the ice.

Every curler, with few exceptions, lays his stone absolutely flat on the ice. The wobble is sometimes put on to get distance, but one cannot get accuracy in this manner.

When the stone is leaving the hand, to get the " in turn," the hand and wrist are twisted in towards the body, thus making the stone rotate clockwise and drawing it while it is running from left to right. The " out turn " is obtained by the reverse motion, the wrist and elbow being twisted away from the body.

The most important thing is to keep your eye on your skip and play as nearly as possible to his broom.

There is nothing very special to recommend in the way of footwear. The most usual wear is snow-boots, goloshes or ordinary shoes with rubber soles.

There are quite a number of different kinds of stones and which are made to any weight or size so long as they conform to the Regulations of the Royal Caledonian Curling Club. The stone most used now is that made from the quarry on the rock of Ailsa Craig.

SOOPING

I am a great believer in Sooping, in spite of a book which was published recently on *Curling in Switzerland* and which seemed to indicate that there was not much advantage in Sooping.

Sooping polishes the ice and clears it of any small pieces of grit, tobacco ash, etc., which may be lying on it and at the same time makes the skip keep his eye on the running of the stone the whole time it is travelling.

In Winnipeg there is an Annual Bonspiel which lasts for about ten days, and nowhere in any country in which I have played have I seen such energetic Sooping. If it does nothing else, it keeps the various members of the rink on the alert, and ready to respond instantly to the commands of the skip. Many times also the skip is able to get his opponent's stone clear of the house if he soops vigorously after the stone has passed the centre line of the house.

SKIPPING

Skipping is no doubt the most important position in the game.

The skip, as a rule, serves his time like other people. Generally he starts leading and may do so for a year or two until his promotion to second player. He continues in this way working his way upward and gaining experience until he is ultimately chosen as a skip.

By the time he is elected a skip he should be pretty well conversant with the game and his duties.

The skip is the dictator and should maintain his dictatorship. Too many skips allow their players to congregate round the head and offer advice. This is contrary to the Rules of the Game and should be strongly discouraged. If the skip gives

A BAD DELIVERY

THE STONE WOBBLES TOO MUCH AND DOES NOT KEEP DIRECTION. THE PLAYER HAS NOT GOT DOWN FAR ENOUGH AND THUS IS APT TO OVERBALANCE

Plate 54

wrong directions, then he is responsible if his side are down. No player need blame himself if he plays to his skip's directions and things do not come up to expectations.

When the skip delegates his duties to his third player when his turn comes to play, he has no longer control over the directions, but if he is wise and has the slightest doubt as to how the head is lying, he should go up and look at it. Many a game has been lost on account of the skip not knowing exactly how the stones are lying after his opponent has played his stone.

The head looks very different from the far end to what it appears when viewed from the " Hog Score " or nearer. Do not discourage your team by losing your temper if your players do not do what you ask them to do. Every man in the team is doing his best, I have found, and he is as annoyed or more so than the skip if his effort is not successful. Give encouragement.

The skip is in charge of the game and should see that everything and everybody is ready to start at the appointed time. To my mind a very important point is to see that the stones are out on the ice in plenty of time. As a rule I like to have mine on the ice at least an hour before play to cool them. If the stones are brought straight from a locker on to the ice they are comparatively warm and when played are sticky to a certain extent, requiring more effort to put them up. Then as they gradually cool they become keener and the player is at sea as to the varying strength he requires to put into his throw.

See that your player thoroughly understands your directions and what you wish him to do.

TACTICS, ETC.

Every skip has his own idea of the game and how he is going to outwit his opponent. Only skill and experience can teach him.

The ideal is to have a first player who can place his stones on the front ring or as near it as possible, either in front or behind, and a little off the centre slide, on either side. From that you can start to build your head, but as the centre of the head is a fixed point, always try and keep your stones in front. In Bowls back stones are sometimes very useful as the jack may be trailed and bowls which are a long way behind may count.

In Curling it is different because there is always the opportunity
of raising your own stone into the house or putting your
opponent's stone right through.   Once you have your winning
stone in position begin to try and guard it, not in a dead straight
line if close, but staggered to some extent, which makes it
more difficult for your opponent to get at than if it were a
straight raise.   After that, steadily pile on your guards.

Strange things happen in a game, but if you are content to
score one or two per end and keep the other side from scoring,
you are doing well.   As a rule, a big head is either a bit of luck
or bad generalship on the part of the losing skip.

A BADLY DELIVERED STONE

THIS STONE WILL NOT TAKE BIAS AS IT IS ROCKY. IT WILL ALSO LOSE ANY TURN PUT UPON IT IN DELIVERY.

Plate 55

EXTRACT FROM THE CONSTITUTION OF THE ROYAL CALEDONIAN CURLING CLUB
By kind permission of the Council.

THE RINK AND THE RULES OF THE GAME

The Rink.

1. The length of the Rink for play, viz. from the Hack or from the Heel of the Crampet to the Tee, shall be 42 yards. The shortening of the Rink is provided for in Rule 21, but in no case shall it be less than 32 yards. *See* diagram, p. 212.

2. The Tees shall be 38 yards apart—and, with a Tee as the centre, a circle, having a radius of 7 feet, shall be drawn. Additional inner Circles may also be drawn.

3. In alignment with the Tees, lines, to be called Central lines, shall be drawn from the Tees to points 4 yards behind each Tee, and at these points Foot Scores 18 inches in length shall be drawn at right angles, on which, at 6 inches from the Central line, the heel of the Crampet shall be placed : when, however, in lieu of a Crampet a Hack is preferred, it shall be made 3 inches from the Central line, and not more than 12 inches in length.

4. Other Scores shall be drawn across the Rink at right angles to the Central line, as in the Diagram, viz. :

   (*a*) A " Hog Score," distant from either Tee one-sixth part of the distance between the " Foot Score " and the farther Tee.

   (*b*) A " Sweeping Score," across each Seven-Foot Circle and through each Tee.

   (*c*) A " Back Score," behind and just touching outside the Seven-Foot Circle.

NOTE.—In forming Rinks the Diagram on following page should be referred to.

The Rules of the Game.

5. All Matches shall be of a certain number of Heads, or Shots, or by Time as may be agreed on, or as fixed by an

Diagram to be drawn on the Ice and referred to throughout the Rules as

"THE RINK."

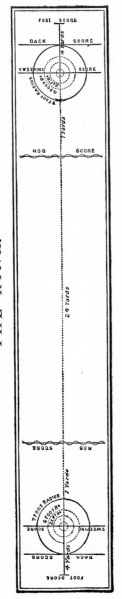

——— COMPULSORY

- - - - OPTIONAL

SCALE OF FEET

FIG. XXI.

DIRECTIONS

1. The Tees to be 38 yards apart.

2. Around each Tee draw a circle having a radius of 7 feet. [Inner circles may also be drawn.]

3. In alignment with the Tees, draw central lines to points 4 yards behind each Tee.

4. Draw scores across the Rink at right angles to the central line, viz.:—

   (*a*) The *Foot Score*—18 inches in length, 4 yards behind each Tee.

   (*b*) The *Back Score*—behind and just touching outside the 7-foot circle.

   (*c*) The *Sweeping Score*—across the 7-foot circle and through each Tee.

   (*d*) The *Hog Score*—distant from the Tee one-sixth part of the distance between the Foot Score and the further Tee.

N.B.—The length of the Rink for play is 42 yards (Sect. 1 of "The Rink"). It may be shortened (Sect. 21), but in no case shall it be less than 32 yards (Sect. 1).

   All measurements of shots shall be from the centre of the Tee to the nearest part of the stone.

Umpire at the outset. In the event of Competitors being equal, play shall be continued by all the Rinks engaged for one or more Heads, as may be agreed on, until the Match has been decided.

6. Every Rink of players shall be composed of four a side, each using two Stones, and no player shall wear boots, tramps, or sandals with spikes or other contrivance which shall break or damage the surface of the ice. The rotation of play observed during the first Head of a Match shall not be changed.

7. The Skips opposing each other shall settle by lot, or in any other way they may agree upon, which party shall lead at the first Head, after which the winners of the preceding Head shall do so.

8. All Curling Stones shall be of a circular shape. No Stone, including handle and bolts, shall be of a greater weight than 44 lbs. imperial, or of greater circumference than 36 inches, or of less height than one-eighth part of its greatest circumference.

9. No Stone shall be substituted for another (except under Rules 10 and 14) after a match has been begun, but the sole of a Stone may be reversed at any time during a Match, provided the player is ready to play when his turn comes.

10. Should a Stone be broken, the largest fragment shall be considered in the Game for that Head—the player being entitled to use another Stone, or another pair, during the remainder of the Game.

11. All Stones which roll over, or come to rest on their sides or tops, shall be removed from the ice.

12. Should the Handle quit the Stone in delivery, the player must keep hold of it ; otherwise he shall not be entitled to replay the shot.

13. Players, during the course of each Head, shall be arranged along the sides, but well off the centre of the Rink, as the Skips may direct ; and no one, except when sweeping according to rule, shall go upon the centre of the Rink, or cross it, under any pretence whatever. Skips only shall be entitled to stand within the Seven-Foot Circle. The Skip of the playing party shall have the choice of place, and shall not be obstructed by the other Skip in front of the Tee, while

behind it the privileges of both, in regard to sweeping, shall be equal.

14. Each player must be ready to play when his turn comes, and must not take more than a reasonable time to play. Should a player play a wrong Stone, any of the players may stop it while running ; but if the mistake is not noticed till the Stone is at rest, the Stone which ought to have been played shall be put in its place, to the satisfaction of the opposing Skip.

15. If a player should play out of his turn, the Stone so played may be stopped in its progress, and returned to the player. Should the mistake not be discovered till the Stone is at rest, or has struck another Stone, the opposing Skip shall have the option of adding one to his score and allowing the Game to proceed, or of declaring the Head null and void. If another Stone be played before the mistake is discovered, the Head must be finished as if it had been properly played from the beginning.

16. The sweeping shall be under the direction and control of the Skips. The player's party may sweep the ice from the Hog Score next the player to the Tee, and any Stone set in motion by a played Stone may be swept by the party to which it belongs. When snow is falling or drifting, the player's party may sweep the ice from Tee to Tee. The sweeping shall always be to a side, and no sweepings shall be left in front of a running Stone. Both Skips have equal right to clean and sweep the ice behind the Tee at any time, except when a player is being directed by his Skip. At the end of any Head, either of the Skips may call upon the whole of the players to clean and sweep the entire Rink. If objected to, this shall be subject to the approval of the acting Umpire.

17. (a) If, in sweeping or otherwise, a running Stone is marred by any of the party to which it belongs, it may, in the option of the opposing Skip, be put off the ice ; but if by any of the adverse party, it may be placed where the Skip of the party to which it belongs shall direct. If marred in any other way, the player shall replay the Stone.

(b) Should any played Stone be displaced before the Head is reckoned, it shall be placed as nearly as possible where it lay, to the satisfaction of the Skip opposed to the party displacing. If displaced by any neutral party, both Skips

Plate 56

THE SKIP

GIVING DIRECTIONS TO A PLAYER. HE MEANS HIS MAN TO PLAY THE " IN TURN " AND IS GIVING HIM ENOUGH ICE SO THAT IF THE BRUSH IS PLAYED
CORRECTLY THE STONE WILL DRAW IN AND COME TO REST WHERE HIS HAT IS.

should agree upon the position to which it is to be returned ; but if they do not agree, the Umpire shall decide.

18. No measuring of shots shall be allowed previous to the termination of the Head. Disputed shots shall be determined by the Skips ; if they disagree, by the Umpire ; or, when there is no Umpire, by some neutral person chosen by the Skips. All measurements shall be taken from the centre of the Tee to the nearest part of the Stone.

19. The Skip shall have the exclusive regulation and direction of the Game for his Rink, and may play last Stone, or any part in the Game he pleases, but he shall not be entitled to change his position when that has been fixed. When his turn to play comes, he shall select one of his players to act as Skip in his place, and take the position of an ordinary player. He shall not have any choice or direction in the game till he returns to the Tee as Skip.

20. If any player engaged in the Game shall speak to, annoy, taunt, or interrupt another, not being of his own side, while in the act of delivering his Stone, one shot for each offence may be added to the score of the party so annoyed.

21. If from any change of weather after a Match has been begun, or from any other reasonable cause, one party shall desire to shorten the Rink, or to change to another, and if the two Skips cannot agree, the Umpire shall, after seeing one end played, determine whether and how much the Rink shall be shortened, or whether it shall be changed, and his decision shall be final. Should there be no acting Umpire, or should he be otherwise engaged, the two Skips may call in any neutral Curler to decide, and his powers shall be equal with those of the Umpire. The Umpire shall, in the event of the ice appearing to him to be dangerous, stop the Match. He shall postpone it, even if begun, when the state of the ice is in his opinion not fitted for testing the Curling skill of the players. Except in very special circumstances, of which the Umpire shall be judge, a Match shall not proceed, or be continued, when a thaw has fairly set in, or when snow is falling and likely to continue during the Match, nor shall it be continued if darkness comes on to prevent the played Stones being well seen by players at the other end of the Rink. In every case of such postponement to another day the Match, when renewed, must be begun *de novo*.

22. Every Stone shall be eligible to count which is not clearly outside the Seven-Foot Circle. Every Stone which does not clear the Hog Score shall be a Hog, and must be removed from the ice, but no Stone shall be considered a Hog, which has struck another Stone lying in position. Stones passing the Back Score, and lying clear of it, must be removed from the ice, as also any Stone which in its progress touches the swept snow on either side of the Rink.

THE GRAND MATCH

1. A Grand Match shall be played annually in the open at the place fixed by the Annual Meeting. Clubs on the North side of the Forth and Clyde Canal shall be drawn against Clubs on the South side thereof. All Matches must give place to the Grand Match.

2. A Form of Return regarding this Match will be sent to all Local Secretaries, who shall in reply intimate to the Secretary of the Royal Club (1) the number of Rinks, if any, intending to be present from their Clubs ; (2) the names of the Skips ; and (3) the name and address of someone to whom notice of the date of the Match shall be sent, and who will undertake to communicate the same without delay to the Skips intending to compete. The Council shall make all arrangements for the ballot for opponents and for carrying out the Matches.

3. Every Local Secretary, in transmitting this return, shall, at the same time, remit Two Shillings and Sixpence for each Rink, failing which the Rink or Rinks shall not be entered for the Match.

4. If any Rink, entered to play at the Grand Match, fail to appear at the Match, they shall be liable, at the discretion of the Council, for a fine not exceeding £1, over and above the reasonable travelling expenses of the Rink against which they were balloted to play, upon a complaint being lodged by the Secretary of the opposing Club, unless the Rink failing to appear shall give the Council a satisfactory excuse for their absence.

5. Umpires shall be appointed by the Secretary. They shall perambulate the pond attended by flag-bearers while the Match is being played, and settle any dispute which may arise. Their decision in all cases shall be final.

6. The Challenge Trophy shall be awarded to the Club on

the winning side having the highest average majority of Shots per Rink. There shall also be awarded to the Rink of the winning Club which has the greatest majority of Shots four Gold Badges to be retained by them. In addition a second Trophy shall be awarded to the Club, on either side (other than the one which has gained the Trophy and Badges), having the greatest net majority of Shots. There shall also be awarded to the Rink of the winning Club which has the greatest majority of Shots four Gold Badges, to be retained by them. No Club shall be eligible for either Trophy unless it shall have at least Two Rinks forward. There shall also be awarded a Medal to the Club on the losing side having the highest aggregate of shots.

7. The Council shall settle all disputes that may arise in connection with the Trophies, or other prizes, and make arrangements for the proper custody of the Trophies.

8. The surplus Rinks, or Clubs which have not been successful in the ballot for places in the Grand Match proper, shall be drawn against each other, and shall form a separate Match called the President and President-Elect Match.

9. In the event of the Grand Match taking place on an Ice Rink, each player can only play once in the Match.

MEDAL COMPETITIONS

1. Three classes of Medals shall be awarded for Competition to Local Clubs, viz. (a) Provincial Medals ; (b) District Medals ; (c) Local Medals.

2. *Provincial Medals.*—A Medal shall on application be given to each Province on the occasion of its Competition.

3. *District Medals.*—All Local Clubs shall be drawn to compete for District Medals. Each Club is entitled to be drawn for a District Medal in the rotation of two years. In the first year of the rotation, all the Clubs shall be, as far as possible, arranged into pairs, an Umpire Club being appointed for each pair. When the List has been duly completed and numbered, it shall be decided by lot whether the odd or the even numbers shall be drawn for the Medals in the first year. In the second year of the rotation the other half of the List shall be taken, it being understood that before the same Clubs be again brought into competition three years at least must elapse.

4. (a) The Council shall arrange Local Clubs into pairs

to compete for District Medals, and shall appoint the Clubs that are to provide umpires for these Competitions.

(*b*) In arranging all District Matches, distance and other circumstances, including the relative number of Ordinary Regular Members (*vide* Rule 10), shall be taken into account.

(*c*) The Medal for Competition shall be sent by the Secretary of the Royal Club direct to the winning Club after receipt of the Umpire's Report.   One of the Representative Members of the Umpire Club, except as provided hereinafter (*vide* Rule 8), shall act as Umpire in the Match.

(*d*) Should the Council, owing to distance or any other cause, not appoint an Umpire Club, the two competing Clubs shall appoint an Umpire, who shall have the same power as if appointed by the Council. (*Vide* Rule 8.)

(*e*) In the event of one of the competing Clubs becoming defunct or ceasing to be associated with the Royal Club, the Council, along with the Umpire, shall choose some other Club to compete for the Medal. (Rule 12, " Medal Competitions.")

(*f*) Clubs which from their situation cannot be pitted against others sufficiently near, shall not be included in the ballot of the first year of a Rotation, in the prospect of other Clubs joining which might compete with them the following year ; but these Clubs may have Local Medals awarded to them for competition among their own Members. (Rule 11, " Medal Competitions.")

5. When two Clubs are drawn to compete for a District Medal it shall be the duty of the Club which appears first in the alphabetical list to initiate correspondence with the other, with the view of bringing off the Match, and to intimate to the Umpire the arrangements agreed upon.   If the two Clubs fail to agree as to the necessary arrangements, the Umpire shall, at the request of the Secretary of either Club, fix the day, the hour, and the ice for the Match, giving at least twenty-four hours' notice to the Secretaries of both Clubs.   (Rule 1, " The Umpire.")

Plate 57

A POOR HEAD

IT IS MUCH TOO OPEN AND SCATTERED THE PLAYERS SEEM NOT TO HAVE PLAYED TO THE SKIP'S BROOM AND HAVE ALL GONE WIDE.

6. If either Club fail to appear at the place and time appointed, without an excuse which is satisfactory to the Umpire or his Deputy, the Medal shall be awarded off-hand to the Club which does appear on the ice (Rule 11, "The Umpire"), and the Club failing to appear shall be liable for the travelling expenses of the Club against which they were to play.

7. When a District Medal has been awarded for competition, and no Umpire has been appointed by the Royal Club, the two Clubs shall appoint an Umpire, who shall have the same power as if appointed by the Royal Club, and should they fail to do so, the Medal shall be awarded to the Club willing to appoint an Umpire, by an Arbiter chosen in accordance with Rule 12, "Medal Competitions."

8. The Representative appointed to act as Umpire shall, in the event of his being unable, from any cause, to give notice of the Match, or to attend thereat, depute a Curler associated with the Royal Club, acquainted with the Rules, and not connected with either of the competing Clubs, to act in his stead ; but the Report of the Match to be transmitted to the Secretary of the Royal Club must be countersigned by the Representative. (Rule 4, "The Umpire.")

9. When two local Clubs agree on the day, the hour, and the ice, written notice to the Umpire shall be given in terms of Rule 5, "Medal Competitions" ; if, however, he or his Deputy should fail to attend at the hour fixed, the Clubs shall jointly appoint a duly qualified Curler to act for him, and the Umpire, so appointed, shall transmit to the Secretary of the Royal Club, along with the Report of the Match, his written authority for acting.

10. District Medals shall be competed for on the first favourable opportunity, and by at least eight players a side. If no arrangement in writing, fixing the number of players, is come to between the Clubs, that number shall not be less than one-half of the Ordinary Regular Members of the smaller Club, as appearing in the last published *Annual*.

NOTE.—Clubs having 16 Regular Players shall play 2 Rinks.

Above 16 and not more than 24			,,		3	,,
,,	24	,,	,,	32	,,	4 ,,
,,	32	,,	,,	40	,,	5 ,,
,,	40	,,	,,	48	,,	6 ,,

11. *Local Medals.—*

    (*a*) Medals may be awarded in special circumstances to Local Clubs.

    (*b*) Medals may also be awarded in the second year of Rotation to such Clubs as in the opinion of the Council are too far distant from other Clubs to compete for District Medals. (Rule 4, "Medal Competitions.")

12. (*a*) *Settlement of Disputes.—*Should any dispute arise between Clubs or Players owing to the Umpire's decision it shall be referred to an Arbiter to be appointed, failing agreement, by the Council.

    (*b*) The Arbiter's decision, though informal, if in writing, shall, except with respect to the Umpire's right of appeal to the Council, be final and binding on both parties.

    (*c*) The Council shall only have power to overturn the same if the procedure has been irregular. In all cases their decision shall be final.

    (*d*) Any complaint as to irregularity must be lodged with the Secretary of the Royal Club within ten days of the date of the award.

    (*e*) Should the procedure be found irregular, the Council shall set aside the award, and order the disputants to begin the reference anew.

RULES FOR LOCAL MEDAL COMPETITIONS

Point Game.

1. Competitors shall draw lots for the rotation of play, and shall use two Stones.

2. The measurement of the Rink for Point Play shall be in conformity with the provisions of Rule 1, "The Rink."

3. Two Circles, having a radius of 4 feet and 7 feet respectively, shall be drawn round the Tee, and a line through the centre of these circles to the Hog Score.

4. Every Competitor shall play 4 shots at each of the nine following points of the game, viz. Striking, Inwicking, Drawing, Guarding, Chap and Lie, Wick and Curl in, Raising, Chipping the Winner, and Drawing through a Port, according to the definitions and diagrams here given.

5. In Nos. 2, 6, 8, and 9, and at *Outwicking* when played, two Stones shall be played on the right and two on the left.

6. No Stone shall be considered *without* a circle unless it is entirely clear of that circle.

NOTE 1.—No scores made in Local Competitions shall be reported in the *Annual* unless these have been conducted under the above Rules.

NOTE 2.—Much time will be saved if two Rinks be prepared lying parallel to each other, the Tee of the one being at the reverse end of the other Rink ; every Competitor plays both Stones up the one Rink, and immediately afterwards both down the other, finishing thus at each round all his chances at that point.

DIAGRAM TO BE DRAWN ON THE ICE BEFORE PLAYING.

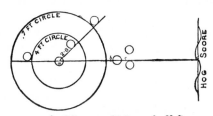

FIG. XXII.   *a-b* = 8 ft.   *a-c* = 10 ft.   *a-d* = 21 ft.

Placed Stones shown ●   Played Stones shown ☉

FIG. XXIII.   *Striking.*

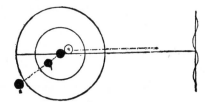

A Stone being placed on the Tee, if struck, shall count 1 ; if struck out of the 7-foot circle, it shall count 2.

FIG. XXIV.   *Inwicking.*

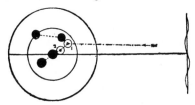

A Stone being placed on the Tee, and another with its inner edge 2 feet 6 inches from the Tee, and its fore edge on a line drawn from the Tee at an angle of 45° with the central line, if the played Stone strike the latter on the inside, it shall count 1 ; if perceptibly moves both Stones, it shall count 2.

Fig. XXV. *Drawing.*

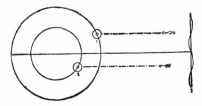

A Stone being played, if the same lie within or on the 7-foot circle, it shall count 1 ; if within or on the 4-foot circle, it shall count 2.

Fig. XXVI. *Guarding.*

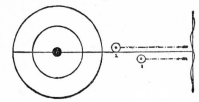

A Stone being placed on the Tee, if the Stone played rest within 6 inches of the central line, it shall count 1 ; if on the line, it shall count 2. It must be over the Hog, but must not touch the Stone to be guarded.

Fig. XXVII. *Chap and Lie.*

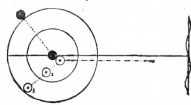

A Stone being placed on the Tee, if struck out of the 7-foot circle, and the played Stone lie within or on the same circle, it shall count 1 ; if struck out of the 7-foot circle, and the played Stone lie within or on the 4-foot circle, it shall count 2.

Fig. XXVIII. *Wick and Curl in.*

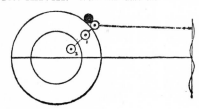

A Stone being placed with its inner edge 7 feet distant from the Tee, and its fore edge on a line making an angle of 45° with the central line, if the same be struck, and the played Stone curl on or within the 7-foot circle, it shall count 1 ; if struck, and the played Stone curl on or within the 4-foot circle, it shall count 2.

Fig. XXIX. *Raising.*

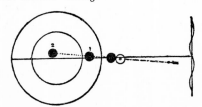

A Stone being placed with its centre on the central line and its inner edge 8 feet in front of the Tee, if it be struck into or on the 7-foot circle, it shall count 1 ; if struck into or on the 4-foot circle, it shall count 2.

Plate 58

SOOPING

SOOPING POLISHES THE ICE AND SWEEPS AWAY ANY STONE OR GRIT. THE SWEEPER NEAREST THE
CAMERA IS THE BEST, HE GETS DOWN TO HIS WORK BUT COULD SWEEP CLOSER TO THE STONE WITH
ADVANTAGE.

FIG. XXX. *Chipping the Winner.*

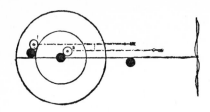

A Stone being placed on the Tee, and another with its inner edge 10 feet in front, just touching the central line, and half guarding the one on the Tee, and a third Stone being placed 4 feet behind the Tee, with its inner edge touching the central line, but on the opposite side from that on which the guard is placed, if the played Stone strike the Stone placed behind the Tee, it shall count 1 ; if it strike the Stone on the Tee, it shall count 2.

FIG. XXXI. *Drawing through a Port.*

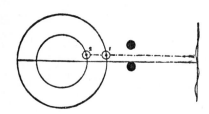

A Stone being placed with its inner edge on the central line 10 feet in front of the Tee, and another Stone on the opposite side and with its inner edge 2 feet from the central line, if the played Stone pass between these two Stones without touching either, and rest within or on the 7-foot circle, it shall count 1 ; if within or on the 4-foot circle, it shall count 2.

FIG. XXXII. *Outwicking.*

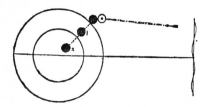

A Stone being placed with its inner edge 7 feet distant from the Tee, and its centre on a line making an angle of 45° with the central line, if struck within or on the 7-foot circle, it shall count 1 ; if struck within or on the 4-foot circle, it shall count 2.

This point is only played in the event of two or more competitors gaining the same number of shots.

If the competition cannot be decided by these shots, the Umpire shall order one or more of the preceding points to be played again by the Competitors who are equal.

THE UMPIRE

Besides the general superintendence of a Match, the power of settling disputed shots, and other questions that may arise in course of play, the duties and powers of the Umpire shall be as follows :—

1. He shall, at the request of the Secretary of either Club,

fix the day, the hour, and the ice most suitable and mutually convenient, giving at least twenty-four hours' notice to the Secretaries of both Clubs. (Rule 5, "Medal Competitions.")

2. He shall satisfy himself that the competing Clubs have paid their annual fees to the Royal Club (Rule 5, "The Grand Match"), and that all the Players are duly qualified, or have been previously agreed to.

3. He shall fix the terms of the Match (whether by Time, Shots, or Heads), if not mutually agreed upon by the competing Clubs. (Rule 5, "The Rules.")

4. He may depute a Curler associated with the Royal Club, acquainted with the Rules and not connected with either of the competing Clubs, to act in his stead ; but the report of the Match shall be countersigned by him. (Rule 8, "Medal Competitions.")

5. In the event of the Match being played on the ice of either of the parties (when the visitors may select the rinks), he may be called upon to approve of the ice and rinks upon which the Match is to be played.

6. He shall have power to decide whether it is necessary to shorten or change the rinks, should the Skips not agree. (Rule 21, "The Rules.")

7. He shall have power to postpone the Match, even if begun, when in his opinion the state of the ice, or the weather, is not such as to test the Curling skill of the Players. (Rule 21, "The Rules.")

8. He shall, in the event of the Competitors being equal, direct that play be continued by all the rinks engaged for one or more Heads, as may be necessary to decide the Match. (Rule 5, "The Rules.")

9. He shall, in all cases, call for objections from the losing party before awarding the Medal ; and if he shall find that neither Club has complied, or appears willing to comply, with the Rules, he shall return the Medal to the Secretary of the Royal Club and report the circumstances.

10. He shall, under the penalty of having his name struck off the lists of the Royal Club, at once forward a report of

A GOOD HEAD

A GOOD HEAD IS ONE IN WHICH THE STONES ARE FAIRLY WELL GATHERED TOGETHER ROUND THE CENTRE TEE, BUT SLIGHTLY IN FRONT. NEITHER
SIDE CAN THEN GET A BIG HEAD.

Plate 59

the Match to the Secretary of the Royal Club, giving the information required by schedule provided for that purpose.

11. He shall have the power to award the Medal off-hand to the Club which appears on the ice, should the other Club be absent without a reason satisfactory to him. (Rule 6, "Medal Competitions.")

12. He shall have the power along with the Council to appoint another Club to compete in the place of a defunct Club (Rule 4, " Medal Competitions "), or of one which has failed to satisfy the Umpire as provided above in Rule 2.

13. His decision in respect of all questions affecting the Match, unless appealed against (Rule 12, " Medal Competitions "), shall be final.

14. He may appeal to the Council against the award of the Arbiter. (Rule 12, " Medal Competitions.")

THE INTERNATIONAL MATCH

1. A Committee, consisting of seven representatives of Scottish Clubs and seven representatives of English Clubs, shall be elected annually at the Annual Meeting, who shall have full power to deal with the legislative and administrative affairs connected with this Match.

2. The Match shall be not more than thirty Rinks a side and not under eighteen Rinks a side, and the Rinks for the Competition shall be selected by the Scottish and English Representatives respectively, and invited to take part in the Game, and no Circular shall be issued asking general entries and no ballot taken for places. A few reserve Rinks shall also be selected in case of any unavoidable absences.

3. The Match shall be played annually on an Ice Rink to be chosen by the Committee, alternately in Scotland and England.

4. The Scottish Committee shall select one Member from the Scottish Representatives, and the English Committee one Member from the English Representatives, and they as a Sub-Committee shall meet once a year in Edinburgh to make the Draw and all other necessary arrangements.

5. There shall be no entrance fee for this Match.

P

A GLOSSARY OF CURLING TERMS

The Crampet .	A long steel plate with a raised ridge at the back against which one foot is rested while delivering the stone.
The Hack. .	A modern development of the crampet. It consists of a brass or cast-iron frame with a central ridge on which the right instep is placed while delivering the stone. Originally it was a cut or hack in the ice in which the player put his foot.
A Head . .	A group of stones round the centre tee.
The Hog Score.	A line drawn across the ice in front of each tee, distant from the tee one-sixth part of the distance between the Foot Score and the further tee. Every stone which does not clear the Hog Score shall be a Hog and must be removed from the ice, unless it strikes a stone already in position, in which case it remains where it lies.
The Skip . .	The Captain of the team whose word is law and whose instructions must, on all occasions, be most accurately obeyed.
Sooping . .	Sweeping the ice in front of the stone to polish it and to clear it of anything which may be lying on it.

WOMEN IN WINTER SPORTS
BY M. S. MADDEN

CHAPTER XX

WOMEN IN WINTER SPORTS

SNOW queens and ice maidens in long floating raiment, with pale faces and streaming locks, are familiar figures to us all from the fairy tales of our childhood. When women, half a century ago, first devoted themselves to winter sports in Switzerland their general appearance bore a close likeness to that of these legendary beings. They wore skirts reaching almost to their feet ; their hair and hats had to be kept in place by innumerable combs and pins, while long flowing complexion veils shielded their faces from sun and wind.

Photographs of these bygone sportswomen leave us literally amazed that our mothers and grandmothers were able to accomplish any sport at all, considering the tremendous handicap of their attire.

How different is the case of the snow and ice maidens of to-day ! Clad in the shortest and neatest of skirts, or in well-cut ski-ing trousers, with sun-browned faces, they have freed themselves from the trammels of dress and appearance decreed by fashion for the women of the 'eighties.

We shall have a good deal to say on the subject of winter-sport clothing in the course of this article, in the meantime it is enough to remark that a modern young woman's sport outfit is as sensible and workmanlike as that of the present-day young man.

With the discarding of unsuitable and hampering fashions, the part played by women in winter sport has become much more prominent than it used to be even a dozen years ago. In many branches of snow and ice sports, as practised in the High Alps, women can now vie on equal terms with men ; in other branches, especially of course in those sports which demand great physical strength or powers of endurance, it is impossible for members of the opposite sexes to meet on quite the same ground.

Sheer force of muscles does not, however, always rank first in snow and ice pastimes ; there are cases in which grace of action, sense of balance, quickness of eye or brain play an even more important part, and here it is that women have every chance to excel.

For the purpose of reviewing the share taken by women in winter sports it is not possible to consider snow and ice games under one general heading. Each individual sport must be treated separately, for each sport requires different qualities and makes a different demand upon its votaries.

We will accordingly begin by turning our attention to a sport in which women are acknowledged to reign supreme—Figure Skating.

No man has ever attained to the lightness or grace of a Sonia Henje, the sixteen-year-old Lady Skating Champion of the World. This dainty little Norwegian girl, placed first in the Olympic Winter Games of 1928, can skim over the ice like a piece of thistledown, dance light as a feather on the points of her skates, twirl, spin and jump with an abandon and grace such as no man or boy has ever yet attained on ice.

The average woman skater is undoubtedly more spontaneous and graceful than the average man ; she finds it easier to make turns and loops on one foot than does her more muscular brother ; her neck and arms and hands take the correct positions almost by nature, and she is troubled by none of that self-conscious awkwardness and fear of " looking an ass," which afflicts many a male skater when first he tries to cut figures on the ice rink.

In the International Figure-Skating Competition held this winter (1930) at St. Moritz, the figures set for women competitors were more difficult and carried higher marks than those set for the men. This fact speaks for itself.

In pair skating the woman often has the hardest part to perform, the jumps and twirls are generally hers, the man acting as " supporter."

MODERN DRESS

That a woman skater is almost invariably more attractive to watch than her male partner is, of course, partly due to her dress. Her usual skating attire is infinitely more picturesque in cut and colour than that adopted by men, except on the rare occasions when these appear in fancy costume. Nothing can be prettier than the swing of a well-made skirt or the dainty lines of a well-cut tunic. A few words of advice about what to wear on the ice rink. will not be out of place here.

The best-known Continental women skaters, such as Sonia Henje, Madame Yvonne de Ligne, Lady Champion of Belgium, and the noted Viennese and Hungarian skating stars, nearly always wear velvet dresses of some delightful art shade : Eau-de-Nil blue, tangerine red, beech brown and golden bronze being their special favourites. The dress may be made all in one piece with close-fitting bodice and sleeves and a short flared skirt. It is essential that cut and fit should be really good and the style adapted to the wearer. Frills and furbelows or anything else that gives an appearance of untidiness are best avoided.

The skater's skirt must be full, measuring from four to seven yards round the hem and not more than knee length. The bodice, while allowing enough freedom on back and chest, ought to fit tightly over the hips to keep it from twisting. The sleeves should reach to the wrists, finishing perhaps with a neat edging of fur. If the bodice and skirt are not made in one, it is wise to have them buttoned together or kept in place with a belt to prevent " gaps." It is important to have knickers and linings of the same colour as the skirt. If a jumper of different material is worn it is advisable that it should tone in colour with the skirt.

For headgear, velvet caps and cloth bérets always look neat and smart, but—since sunburn has become the vogue—many girls skate hatless on the sunny rinks of the Swiss Alps. As regards colours : bright tints or black look best against the snow ; greys, browns, drab and also white should be avoided.

Skaters are strongly advised to wear specially made skating boots without toecaps and seamed right up to the toe ; these can now be bought in London as well as abroad. Choose a soft leather that will not press the ankle too much. Felt padding allows the boot to be tightly laced ; extravagantly high boots do not look well and are uncomfortable to wear ; at the same time the boot should reach well up the leg. Fashions in stockings vary from season to season, but too pronounced a shade or pattern seldom is pleasing. Many skaters wear a

light pair of wool socks which need not necessarily show above
the boot.

For figure skating and waltzing " Continental " skates are
essential. These have rounded toes and a shorter radius than
the " English " skate. The " Salchow Mayer " and the
" Stille " skate, both of which can be obtained in London, are
some of the best-known blades.

English skating, once so ardently practised by pioneers of
winter sport in Switzerland, only survives now at a few centres,
notably at Morgins. The younger generation of skaters takes
little interest in the " combined figures " of this school and
much prefers the International style which allows its votaries
to waltz and ten-step and perform all sorts of fancy steps,
rigorously forbidden by the stricter English style. Although
there have been some brilliant women exponents of English
skating, it is undeniable that this style has always appealed
more strongly to the mere man.

SPEED SKATING AND ICE HOCKEY

If women are outclassed by men in English skating with its
long powerful strokes, still more is this the case in two other
branches of the art : Speed Skating and Ice Hockey. No
woman can race on equal terms against a man, and few women
ever attempt speed skating at all. Length of leg, as well as
strength of muscle, come into play here ; and the girl skater
is hopelessly outdistanced from the start.

So far ice hockey has found favour with very few women,
though there is no reason that schoolgirls should not play it
among themselves. Mixed matches, in which men and women
join, are unquestionably dangerous. Almost as well might
members of the fair sex join with men in a game of Rugby
football. Besides the deliberate " charging " of an adversary
permitted by the rules, the puck—the hard rubber disk used
instead of a ball—hardly ever goes out of play, with the result
that ice hockey makes a tremendous demand on the heart
and lungs. Even men players have to be relieved at frequent
intervals in this fast and furious game beloved of Canadians.

BANDY

Bandy, an older form of ice hockey, played with a ball
instead of a puck, is much more suited for women. It has,

however, gone almost entirely out of fashion in recent years at the Swiss resorts, the reason being that the post-war young woman has taken with extreme zest to ski-ing which leaves her little time to spend on the ice rink. Ski-ing can be learnt much more quickly and easily than skating, and it offers much greater variety to the beginner, as well as to the expert. To ski really well is not easy and requires hard work and much practice, but to ski sufficiently well for enjoyment is soon learnt. " Why stay on one patch of ice when you can roam the mountains ? " is a question often heard nowadays.

Few of the rising generation return any answer to their own inquiry save " Why indeed ! " They have felt the spell of the wild free mountains, the untrodden slopes, the unending reaches of virgin snow. Who can blame them for preferring the wide snowfields to the narrow confines of an artificial skating rink ?

SKI-ING

Any young and vigorous girl can learn to ski in a short time. It is advisable in this sport, as indeed in every other, to learn the right way from the very start. One or two lessons to begin with from an experienced ski instructor or a well-informed friend will make progress much more rapid and assured. It is very difficult to " unlearn " a bad habit and very easy to pick up a wrong method through want of teaching. In most Swiss resorts there are ski-ing clubs which organize classes for beginners, as well as tests and tours for the more advanced.

In no form of winter sport have women made greater progress in recent years than in ski-ing. The standard of women's ski-ing has improved almost beyond belief. Miss Sale Barker, Miss Doreen Elliot, Miss Freda Gossage are names well known in the ski-ing world. All these women have beaten men in Downhill or Slalom racing in open competition. Men ski-ers are and will always be superior in long-distance and endurance races as well as in ski-jumping. It seems doubtful whether women ought to attempt jumping on ski at all ; at any rate, it is a form of sport for the few. Slalom racing, on the other hand, in which quickness of eye and brain and deftness of action count for so much, specially appeals to the girl ski-er. In this form of the sport she can meet her brother on equal terms with some prospect of beating him. The famous Spanish

tennis star, Senorita Lili d'Alvarez, is one of the most daring
and skilful of Downhill ski-ers of either sex.   She can beat
many men at this game.   Recently she took part in a high
climb on ski, for film purposes, to the top of the great white
mountain, the Piz Palu above Pontresina.   The party consisted
of six men and two ladies, the women having to carry their own
ski and knapsacks.   No woman who is unable to do this should
attempt a high climb.   Some women climbers even carry ice
axes, but the cutting of ice steps is a man's work and women
should not attempt it.

It is probably in ski-ing more than in any other winter sport
that the alteration in the style of women's dress has had the
most marked consequences.   In the old days only a handful
of women were bold enough to defy convention and adopt
masculine dress for ski-ing and climbing.   Nowadays it is rare
to see a girl wearing a skirt when she is on ski.   The usual
ski-ing costume most generally adopted consists of dark blue
or black trousers which descend to the ankles and are laced
inside the ski-ing boot.   The coat or tunic is plainly cut, and
the suit is made of some waterproofed material such as gabar-
dine.   Bright colours are not in vogue among ski-ers of either
sex.   Dark blue is the most popular colour, a touch of lighter
hue being given by the Norwegian garters which keep the ends
of the trouser leg in place.

Norwegian ski-ing caps with ear-flaps for use when necessary
are very generally worn.   Regulation ski-ing boots with special
soles and attachments are indispensable for those who intend
to take ski-running seriously.   These can be procured in
London or abroad.   Thick strong ski-ing socks are worn with
these boots ;   lined waterproof ski-ing gloves should be part
of every ski-er's outfit.   As regards the actual ski, it is better
to obtain them in Switzerland under advice from some trust-
worthy ski instructor or experienced friend.   There are various
sorts of bindings ;   an inferior type may mean a sprained ankle
or broken leg, so let not the incipient ski-er be penny wise and
pound foolish in risking a doctor's bill for the sake of saving a
few francs by the purchase of cheap ski.   In most of the Alpine
resorts ski are let out on hire ;   here again caution is required
and beginners must beware of letting themselves be imposed
on by some persuasive-tongued hotel concierge or shop assistant.   If you are a novice, do not choose your ski by yourself

but have them chosen for you by someone who knows about the fittings.

A great deal may be learnt about ski-ing from the many excellent handbooks that have been published on the subject. It is always wise to combine theory with practice, and many valuable hints can be obtained from books. At the same time book knowledge can be dangerous if it is ill applied ; common sense and experience are both needed by those whose ambition it is to roam in winter amid the eternal snows of ice peak and glacier. Long expeditions must never be undertaken without a guide or thoroughly skilled and knowledgeable companions.

When setting out on a ski tour, whether long or short, the exact destination and probable hour of return should be given in case of accident. Novices must always beware of virgin slopes which may contain pitfalls of which they have no suspicion. More than once an incautious ski-er has been smothered or severely injured by disappearing through the snow into some unsuspected hollow, cut out by a hidden stream. It is a wise rule always to follow in someone else's tracks.

The danger of avalanches is one that every woman ski-er should carefully study. She can learn much through reading on this subject, and by using her eyes and ears she can pick up a great deal of practical " snow-lore " which will in time help to judge whether a slope is safe or not. Ski-ing demands a good deal of physical strength, and no one with a weak heart should attempt long tours or arduous climbs. The lives of a whole party have sometimes been endangered by a woman who attempts a climb or expedition beyond her powers. A knowledge of first aid is particularly useful to a ski-er, as minor accidents, such as a sprained ankle, disjointed knee or even slight concussion, are not infrequent, and help may be far off. It is well to learn how to convey down an injured ski-er who can only use one leg, and how to turn a pair of ski into a makeshift " toboggan " for the more severely injured. Women ought to know what to do in cases of faintness or of mountain sickness. Frostbite is another peril of the mountains which has to be guarded against. Cases have occurred of severe frostbite owing to the wearing of woollen gloves which are quite insufficient protection to the hands at high altitudes.

Knowledge of the right food to take on a long ski-ing expedition also comes within the woman's special province ; sustaining nourishment in a small compass is, of course, the thing at which to aim, and the usual chocolate bars and meat essences can be varied with some similar form of compact and easily portable foodstuffs. A thermos of strong hot coffee and a small flask of brandy are never amiss.

TOBOGGANING

Tobogganing is a sport that has somewhat gone out of fashion since women took so ardently to ski-ing. Even children can soon learn to guide a luge, that is, a wooden Swiss toboggan, or to steer a boblet, down a steep slope. But when it is the case of a perilous ice run, such as the famous Cresta at St. Moritz or the bob-runs at Murren and Caux, then it is quite a different matter. Few women have the cool nerve, to say nothing of the physical strength, to negotiate a fast ice run with sharp corners safely. In such sport the gift of imagination is a serious drawback, grace and lightness are of no avail.

The Cresta Run used to be open to women riders, but two years ago the Committee came to the conclusion that it was too dangerous for ladies, and since that date it has been rigorously closed to the fair sex. In the olden days, before the banks were so high and the pace so fast, there were a handful of expert lady-tobogganers who rode face foremost with the same cool presence of mind as men. These women were, as a matter of fact, rather exceptional, and few girls ever ventured to brave the descent of the Cresta from the Top.

LUGEING

Lugeing down a winding road or a steep hard snow slope is a very pleasant occupation when there is nothing better to do, but it requires so little skill that most young women prefer to devote their time to something else.

BOBBING

Nor is bobbing in much greater favour with the many. This is a sport which is rather apt to pall after a time. Women are not strong enough to brake or steer the large heavy bobs weighing several tons. Some girls indulge in boblet racing, and so long as there are prizes to be raced for and a chance of breaking the record of the run, they probably are keen for a season or two. After that one seldom seems to hear any more of their achievements. For a woman to form a member of a crew otherwise composed of men on a big racing bob is not, of course, by any means rare, but neither is it usual. Ski-ing and skating come easily first, and most girls regard tobogganing and bobbing with indifference, if not with a certain amount of contempt. The fashion may change, as fashions do, but such has been our experience of late years at various Swiss winter resorts.

TAILING

Tailing is a means of progression which deserves a few lines to itself. A line of toboggans are attached by ropes to the back of a sleigh and as the horses trot, especially when they swing round a corner, the luges swing to and fro more or less violently, so that it requires a very good sense of balance not to be hurled off into the snow. A tailing party is a form of amusement that appeals generally only to the new-comer or to the very young! It is rather an undignified proceeding, not at all suited to the mature, but, as may be imagined, it is a sport beloved of schoolgirls.

SKI JORING

Ski joring, which means being towed on ski behind a horse, is a much more serious pastime and one which needs very considerable skill. The ski-er has but little control over the horse which very frequently bolts, leaving his driver to catch him up as best he or she may. A more satisfactory method, except for the expert, is to get someone to mount the horse. Nowadays one often sees a girl on horseback with a man ski-ing behind. The reverse is also fairly frequently the case. Ski joring is usually practised on the snowy surface of a frozen lake. Since the introduction of motor-cars with chain tyres for driving on snow it has become much less popular on the valley roads. It is a very great strain on the arms, and altogether appears to be a sport best left to men owing to its literally " rough and tumble " character.

CURLING

Curling, which somewhat resembles Bowls on ice, is a game in which women may join on almost equal terms with men. It is, however, not given to many women to make a good skip.

The skip or captain of the team of four has to have a considerable amount of determination, plenty of cheery optimism, cool courage in a crisis, a sure eye, a steady hand and a temper that nothing can ruffle !   Added to this a thorough knowledge of the science of the game is required.   As a rule, in Switzerland women and men curl together in mixed teams.   Men undoubtedly not only make the best skips but also the best threes and fours.   The player who has to put down his stones last, or last but one, is very often asked to play a knock-out shot which needs a good deal of force, as well as a very straight eye.   A man's aim is almost sure to be better than that of a woman. Ladies, on the other hand, make admirable twos and leads. The lead or player who lays the first stones is required to place her shot in front of the " dolly " that marks the centre of the circle, in curling parlance the " House."   This requires a delicate and accurate touch, such as a woman can generally apply with success.   The second player not infrequently has to curl gently round in front of the stones already laid.   There is one woman curler, the well-known Mrs. Mannering Robertson of Grindelwald, who each year plays " as a man " with men in the Swiss Curling Championship for the Jackson Cup.   Her play ranks above that of many of the men, which shows that it is possible, if exceptional, for women to vie in this sport on terms of equality with members of the stronger sex.

Women, as a rule, play with lighter stones than men, the weight generally varying from 30 to 40 lb.   The average weight of women's stones is 33 lb., that of men's stones 36 lb., but in almost every club there are some men who prefer to use light stones and some women who can wield a 36-pounder.

As regards " sooping,"—the term used for sweeping the ice,— women are usually outclassed by men, but here again there are exceptions.   In the higher resorts where the ice is nearly always keen, women have a distinct advantage, but where ice is habitually " drug " or heavy and stones have to be swung far back, the more muscular man player need have no fear of being out-curled.

Having passed each individual snow and ice sport in review, we will conclude by making some general remarks on clothes, choice of resort and length of stay.

For the ordinary woman sportswoman who wants to try her

hand at each of the different sports in turn, the special type of skating and ski-ing dress previously mentioned is by no means necessary. Sensible country clothes, such as are usually worn at golf, will serve the purpose very well ; her outfit in such case will be a short tweed skirt cut fairly wide, some neat woollen jumpers, a short leather coat, and a couple of warm sport coats with possibly skirts to match. A leather coat is almost essential owing to the ice-cold wind that sometimes prevails at the higher resorts ; for the same reason it is well to bring at least one tweed or cloth skirt. Cloth knickers and warm wool stockings or gaiters are advisable. A cloth or knitted scarf is always useful. Of course a long fur coat or motor coat always comes in handy for sleigh drives or for sitting out to watch some sporting event, such as a skating competition or an ice-hockey match. A warm travelling-rug is likewise very welcome on occasions. Afternoon dresses, elaborate hats and coats are quite out of place ; on the other hand, several evening dresses, and at least one fancy dress, should be brought.

Those who only make a short stay are advised to hire ski, ski-ing boots and toboggans. Skates and skating boots should be brought or bought, as these can rarely be had for hire. Curling stones are supplied by the Club.

HOTELS

The question of " Where to stay ? " is a very important one for those who are planning a first visit to the Swiss Alps in winter. There are so many places to choose from, and so much to be said on behalf of the various resorts. A good deal should depend on the length of stay and the date selected. Most places are crowded during the Christmas holidays, which is naturally the gayest part of the winter. Unfortunately Christmas-time is not infrequently the date at which the unwelcome warm Föhn wind chooses to blow, with the result that the lower-lying resorts sometimes have no snow or ice at all, just at the very moment when it is most desired.

It is well to bear in mind that the higher up you go, the more reliable do winter sport conditions become. If possible, it is wise to choose a place at least 4,000 feet above sea-level ; better still 5,000 feet or over. Naturally the higher resorts demand higher prices, since they are more sought after. If money is no consideration, then without hesitation choose the Engadine

or one of the loftiest resorts of the Bernese Oberland. Book
your rooms well in advance, and, if you intend to travel just
about Christmas-time, reserve your sleeping berth or seat as
early as possible.

Those who are visiting Switzerland for the first time are
strongly advised to seek the advice of some well-known tourist
or travel agency. Such will supply all information and make
all arrangements. Some hotels are entirely reserved for British
clients ; others are more cosmopolitan in character. Decide
beforehand whether you wish to mix with foreigners or with
your own compatriots, and book your rooms accordingly.

Prices range approximately from 10s. to £1 a day for board
and lodging. Afternoon tea, baths and skating-rink subscrip-
tions are extras. At some hotels, however, an inclusive
arrangement can be made. The more fashionable the resort,
the higher the prices for everything, including rink subscrip-
tions.

February is a delightful month at some of the loftier places ;
hotels are less crowded than in late December and January,
so that cheaper rooms are more likely to be available then.
March is not too late for high mountain ski-ing ; skating
continues in the Engadine until the middle or end of that
month.

Winter visitors sometimes imagine that they can live more
cheaply by renting a private apartment or rooms, but generally
speaking, an attempt to cater for oneself turns out to be a
more costly business than staying at a moderate-priced hotel.
Fuel is extraordinarily dear, and foodstuffs bought in small
quantities anything but cheap. There is also the servant
question, which in some places is very acute. The inexperienced are, therefore, advised not to attempt to do their own
housekeeping.

Travelling expenses will probably cost from £10 to £16
second class, and nearly double that with a sleeper. Over-
weight of luggage can be avoided by taking only one small
trunk and carrying the rest of one's belongings in suitcases
small enough to fit on the carriage-racks. Those who wish
to economize by making their own afternoon tea should not
forget to provide themselves with a spirit lamp and pot ;
methylated spirit is very cheap in Switzerland. Milk can be
obtained at one of the dairies to be found everywhere, and

Swiss rolls and pâtisserie are as inexpensive as they are delicious.

One last word : don't rush things too much at first, especially at a high altitude.   If you ski most of the day and dance most of the night you will crock up, and your holiday instead of doing you good will send you home looking a wreck.   If you are really keen on sport you will be wise to get at least eight hours' sleep, and when you come in after a long day spent on the mountain slopes, lie down for an hour before dinner, and you will find that you are not a bit over-tired next day, but ready to set off again as fresh as the proverbial daisy !

INDEX

INDEX

Printed in Great Britain by Butler & Tanner Ltd., Frome and London